School
Leadership
and
Administration

Reference Books in International Education
Edward R. Beauchamp, Series Editor

School Leadership and Administration

ADOPTING A CULTURAL PERSPECTIVE

EDITED BY
ALLAN WALKER AND CLIVE DIMMOCK

RoutledgeFalmer
NEW YORK AND LONDON

Published in 2002 by
RoutledgeFalmer
29 West 35th Street
New York, NY 10001
www.routledge-ny.com

Published in Great Britain by
RoutledgeFalmer
11 New Fetter Lane
London EC4P 4EE
www.routledge.co.uk

RoutledgeFalmer is an imprint of the Taylor & Francis Group.
Printed in the United States of America on acid-free paper.
Design and typography: Jack Donner

10 9 8 7 6 5 4 3 2 1

Library of Congress Cataloging-in-Publication Data.

School leadership and administration : adopting a cultural perspective / edited by Allan Walker and Clive Dimmock.
    p. cm. — (References books in international education)
    Includes bibliographical references and index.
    ISBN 0-415-93293-9 — ISBN 0-415-93294-7 (pbk.)
    1. Educational leadership—Social aspects—Cross-cultural studies. 2. School management and organization—Social aspects—Cross-cultural studies. 3. Educational anthropology—Cross-cultural studies. I. Walker, Allan. II. Dimmock, Clive A. J. III. Series.

LB2806 .S3416 2002
371.2—dc21

                     2002017899

Contents

part II: The Influence of Societal Culture on Schools and School Leadership

Series Preface

This series of scholarly works in comparative and international education has grown well beyond the initial conception of a collection of reference books. Although retaining its original purpose of providing a resource to scholars, students, and a variety of other professionals who need to understand the role played by education in various societies or world regions, it also strives to provide accurate, relevant, and up-to-date information on a wide variety of selected educational issues, problems, and experiments within an international context.

Contributors to this series are well-known scholars who have devoted their professional lives to the study of their specializations. Without exception these men and women possess an intimate understanding of the subject of their research and writing. Without exception they have studied their subject not only in dusty archives, but have lived and traveled widely in their quest for knowledge. In short, they are "experts" in the best sense of that often overused word.

In our increasingly interdependent world, it is now widely understood that it is a matter of military, economic, and environmental survival that we understand better not only what makes other societies tick, but also how others, be they Japanese, Hungarian, South African, or Chilean, attempt to solve the same kinds of educational problems that we face in North America. As the late George Z. F. Bereday wrote more than three decades ago: "[E]ducation is a mirror held against the face of a people. Nations may put on blustering shows of strength to conceal public weakness, erect grand façades to conceal shabby backyards, and profess peace while secretly arming for conquest, but how they take care of their children tells unerringly who they are" (*Comparative Methods in Education*, New York: Holt, Rinehart and Winston, 1964, p. 5).

Perhaps equally important, however, is the valuable perspective that studying another education system (or its problems) provides us in understanding our own system (or its problems). When we step beyond our own limited experience and our commonly held assumptions about schools and learning in order to look back at our system in contrast to another, we see it in a very different light. To learn, for example, how China or Belgium handles the education of a multilingual society; how the French provide for the funding of public education; or how the Japanese control access to their universities enables us to better understand that there are reasonable alternatives to our own familiar way of doing things. Not that we can borrow directly from other societies. Indeed, educational arrangements are inevitably a reflection of deeply embedded political, economic, and cultural factors that are unique to a particular society. But a conscious recognition that there are other ways of doing things can serve to open our minds and provoke our imaginations in ways that can result in new experiments or approaches that we may not have otherwise considered.

Since this series is intended to be a useful research tool, the editor and contributors welcome suggestions for future volumes, as well as ways in which this series can be improved.

—Edward R. Beauchamp
University of Hawaii

Preface

More than three decades ago, Jacob Getzels, one of the leading theorists of his generation, stated:

> The objectives, curricula, methods, and administrative policies and procedures ... must be understood in the context of the culture and the component values to which they are inevitably related. (Getzels, Lipham, and Campbell, 1968, p. 102)

In the years that followed, a number of scholars in educational administration heeded Getzels' advice and focused their attention on school and organizational culture. Although this work extended our understanding of school operations, leadership, and attempts at educational reform, it failed to take into account how societal culture influences leader beliefs, actions, and effects. In this book, Walker and Dimmock, two leading figures in the cross-cultural study of educational administration, lay the foundation for investigating this important, but hitherto neglected, area of research.

They offer a persuasive argument for studying societal culture and the role it plays in school leadership and educational reform. Their argument links societal culture to globalization. Globalization, as the authors use the term, refers to the transfer of ideas, policies, and practices across national boundaries. This conception of globalization leads quite naturally to an examination of whether conclusions derived from research conducted in one cultural context are valid in another societal culture. It also raises interesting questions about the consequences of introducing educational reforms that were successful in a particular cultural context (usually Western) into quite different cultures. Readers intrigued by questions like these will discover some unexpected answers in this book.

Globalization can also be used in reference to the transfer of people from one culture to another. Having lived in California for 30 years, I have observed how a predominantly Anglo state has been transformed into a state where non-Whites have become the majority. Moreover, it has become a multicultural state consisting of the largest Afghan community in the United States and a substantial number of Mexican, Asian, Filipino, and Russian immigrants. Each of these groups brings its own culture, and this diversity presents major challenges to educational administrators and teachers. Some of these challenges stem from different styles of communication and varying beliefs about homework, bilingual education, teaching, learning, and the role of parents in their child's education. The same phenomenon is evident in other multicultural societies, and the book offers some valuable insights into the nature of these challenges for school leaders, and their effects on administrative attempts to institute reform in educational policy and practice.

In addition to advancing a compelling argument, the book presents a comprehensive conceptual framework for the cross-cultural study of educational leadership. This framework focuses on the school as the unit of analysis and connects management and leadership to the institutional core—curriculum, teaching, and learning—and societal culture. The book also contains a number of case studies that provide worthwhile insights into how societal culture influences educational leadership and what happens in schools.

Undoubtedly, this analytical framework and the various case studies will stimulate sorely needed research and debate about the role societal culture plays in educational leadership and reform. Cultural ignorance, blindness, and insensitivity are at the root of many of the world's problems, including those in education. The work of Walker and Dimmock points the way for remedying our past oversight and enables us to move beyond the more restrictive boundaries of school and organizational culture when studying educational leadership and school functioning.

—Edwin M. Bridges, Professor of Education
Stanford University, Stanford, CA, United States

Reference

Getzels, J. W., Lipham, J. M., & Campbell, R. F. (1968). *Educational administration as a social process.* New York: Harper & Row.

Acknowledgments

The idea for this volume stems from two special issues of journals that were edited by us, namely, *School Leadership and Management* and the *Asia Pacific Journal of Education.* We would like to thank the following publishers for their generous permission to reprint these articles either in their entirety or in reworked versions.

Tony Bush and Qiang Haiyan, *Asia Pacific Journal of Education, 20*(2), 58–67. Copyright 2000 by National Institute of Education. Published by Oxford University Press. Reprinted by permission of National Institute of Education, Nanyang Technological University, 1 Nanyang Walk, Singapore 637616.

Paul Begley, *Asia Pacific Journal of Education, 20*(2), 23–33. Copyright 2000 by National Institute of Education. Published by Oxford University Press. Reprinted by permission of National Institute of Education, Nanyang Technological University, 1 Nanyang Walk, Singapore 637616.

Leslie Sharp and Saravanan Gopinathan, *Asia Pacific Journal of Education, 20*(2), 87–98. Copyright 2000 by National Institute of Education. Published by Oxford University Press. Reprinted by permission of National Institute of Education, Nanyang Technological University, 1 Nanyang Walk, Singapore 637616.

Clive Dimmock, *COMPARE, 30*(3), *303*–312. Copyright 2000 by British Association for International and Comparative Education. Reprinted by permission of Taylor and Francis Ltd., P.O. Box 25, Abingdon OX14 3UE, United Kingdom.

David Watkins, *School Leadership and Management, 20*(2), 161–174. Copyright 2000 by Taylor and Francis Ltd. Reprinted by permission of Taylor and Francis Ltd., P.O. Box 25, Abingdon OX14 3UE, United Kingdom.

Allan Walker and Clive Dimmock, *School Leadership and Management, 20*(2), 143–160. Copyright 2000 by Taylor and Francis Ltd. Reprinted by permission of Taylor and Francis Ltd., P.O. Box 25, Abingdon OX14 3UE, United Kingdom.

Paul Morris and Lo Mun Ling, *School Leadership and Management, 20*(2), 175–188. Copyright 2000 by Taylor and Francis Ltd. Reprinted by permission of Taylor and Francis Ltd., P.O. Box 25, Abingdon OX14 3UE, United Kingdom.

Clive Dimmock and Allan Walker, *School Leadership and Management, 20*(2), 227–234. Copyright 2000 by Taylor and Francis Ltd. Reprinted by permission of Taylor and Francis Ltd., P.O. Box 25, Abingdon OX14 3UE, United Kingdom.

Philip Hallinger and Pornkasem Kantamara, *School Leadership and Management, 20*(2), 189–206. Copyright 2000 by Taylor and Francis Ltd. Reprinted by permission of Taylor and Francis Ltd., P.O. Box 25, Abingdon OX14 3UE, United Kingdom.

Allan Walker, *International Journal of Educational Reform, 8*(1), 15–24.

We are indebted to a number of people and agencies that helped make this book possible. Anthon Chu Yan-kit provided prompt and efficient technical support to the contributing authors and to the editors. The Hong Kong Institute of Educational Research at the Chinese University of Hong Kong also provided clerical and technical support to the project. We also acknowledge the funding support of the Research Grants Council (RGC) of Hong Kong for its support through an Earmarked Grant (CUHK 4237/98H). We would especially like to thank Professor Saravanan Gopinathan of the National Institute of Education, Singapore, and Professor Edward Beauchamp of the University of Hawaii. Without their encouragement and support, the book would not have materialized.

Allan Walker

Clive Dimmock

Notes on Contributors

Allan Walker is Professor in the Department of Educational Administration and Policy at the Chinese University of Hong Kong.

Clive Dimmock is Professor and Head of the Centre for Educational Leadership and Management at the University of Leicester, United Kingdom.

David Watkins is Professor in the Department of Education at University of Hong Kong.

Geoff Southworth is Professor in the School of Education at the University of Reading, United Kingdom, and Director of Research at the National College for School Leadership, Nottingham, United Kingdom.

John MacBeath is Professor of Educational Leadership at the University of Cambridge, United Kingdom.

Leslie Sharp is Associate Professor in the Department of Policy and Management Studies at the National Institute of Education, Nanyang Technological University, Singapore.

Lo Mun Ling is Principal Lecturer and Head of the Centre for the Development of School Partnership and Field Experience at the Hong Kong Institute of Education, Hong Kong.

Paul Begley is Professor at the Ontario Institute of Educational Studies, University of Toronto, Canada.

Paul Morris is Deputy Director (Academic) at the Hong Kong Institute of Education, Hong Kong.

Phillip Hallinger is Professor and Executive Director at the College of Management, Mahidol University, Thailand.

Pornkasem Kantamara is a doctoral student in the Department of Leadership and Organizations, University of Vanderbilt, Tennessee.

Qiang Haiyan is Professor of South China National University, Guangzhan, PRC.

Ron Heck is Chair Professor in the Department of Educational Administration at the University of Hawaii, Manoa, United States.

Saravanan Gopinathan is Professor and Dean of the School of Education at the National Institute of Education, Nanyang Technological University, Singapore.

Tony Bush is Professor of Educational Management at the University of Reading, United Kingdom.

Introduction

The Societal Cultural Context of Educational Administration and Leadership

ALLAN WALKER AND CLIVE DIMMOCK

Our interest in the complex and often confusing area of societal culture stems predominantly from our personal experience as academics working in Universities and with school leaders in different parts of the world. While attempting to make our work meaningful to our students within, what to us, were often unfamiliar contexts, we stumbled repeatedly as our theories and underlying assumptions failed to address the problems and specificities that comprised the different societal contexts and cultures in which we worked. Moreover, resorting to the literature for answers only revealed how contextualized the field is in English-speaking Western countries. Yet, in the absence of alternatives, we, along with many of our colleagues, base much of our teaching and research on these decontextualized paradigms without considering how the culture and context within which school leaders operate may influence their beliefs and actions.

This is not to defame previous work in what is becoming an increasingly sophisticated field; indeed, much of the research and literature in educational administration has broad application. The fact remains, however, that it has a fairly narrowly-conceived cultural basis. If we are to gain a better understanding of school leaders in societies outside the "Anglo-American world," research must be contextualized and take account of culture. With this firmly guiding our agenda, we explore ways in which societal culture influences school leadership, administration, and organization. Our aim is to build greater understanding of how and why leaders in different cultures do what they do, or as Hallinger and Leithwood (1996) put it, to "find out what we don't know we don't know."

This volume takes as its major theme the influence of societal culture on school administration and leadership through the development of a cross-cultural comparative approach to the field. Closely interwoven with this theme are two interconnected sub-themes. The first concerns the utility and appropriateness of using a cultural and cross-cultural approach as the basis of developing a comparative dimension to the field; and the second focuses on the school as the unit for comparison, and connects management and leadership to the curriculum, teaching, and learning.

In justifying the major theme we appeal to three interrelated arguments. First, it is acknowledged that the field of educational leadership and management has developed along ethnocentric lines, being heavily dominated by Anglo-American paradigms and theories (Walker & Dimmock, 2000).

It occurs to us that theory and policy in educational administration and leadership are possibly more strongly contextually bound than many researchers and policy makers in the Anglo-American world are prepared to acknowledge. Frequently, either a narrow ethnicity pervades research and policy, or an implicit assumption is made that findings in one part of the world will necessarily apply in others. It is clear that a key factor missing from many debates in educational administration and leadership is context. In this book, "context" is represented by societal culture and its mediating influence on theory, policy, and practice. Although societal culture is not the only mediating influence—culture at the organizational level, politics, economics and religion are other important forces in this respect—it appears to be a significant factor, and one duly recognized in other fields. International business management and cross-cultural psychology, for example, have both acknowledged the importance of societal culture for more than 20 years. Meanwhile, societal culture as an influence in the study of educational administration has been conspicuous by its absence. As Cheng (1995) argued, "the inclusion of the (societal) cultural element is not only necessary, but also essential in the study of educational administration" (p. 99).

The second reason prompting this volume also relates to culture. We see the significance of culture, especially at the societal level, stretching beyond its importance as a mediating influence on theory, policy, and practice. Both conceptually and empirically, we believe that societal culture holds the potential to be a powerful analytical tool with which to lay the foundation for developing a new branch of educational administration, leadership, and policy. We refer to the new branch as comparative educational administration and leadership. And our approach is predicated on cross-cultural analysis. This argument is expounded in chapter 1 of this volume and in more detail in Dimmock and Walker 1998 (also see Walker & Dimmock, in press). This claim is not meant to detract from efforts in the 1970s and 1980s to develop comparative educational administration. These early attempts, however, achieved fairly modest results in evoking models, theories, and concepts to underpin a systematic, empirical, and robust approach to comparative studies in educational administration and policy. Our current work, along with others, is attempting to develop comparative educational leadership and administration using culture as a foundation concept (see Dimmock & Walker 1998; Walker & Dimmock 1999).

Finally, the third reason for this book is that for some years, we have argued—along with others—that schools are the most important part of education systems (Dimmock, 2000). It may be trite to say, but they are the point at which schooling is delivered and where the quality of the service is best judged. Arguably, government policies espousing school-based management generally reflect recognition of this fact. Appropriately, a significant part of educational administration focuses on the school. However, we also believe that it is a mistake for school-based studies to approach administration and leadership in a vacuum, as though they were disconnected from the core business of teaching, learning, and curriculum. After all, *something* has to be led, managed, and organized. Undeniably, the main purpose of schools is the fostering of student learning, and this together with the curriculum and teaching form the core work of schools. In relation to this core, leadership, administration, and organization play supportive, facilitative, and promotive roles. They are no less important for that, but it is remarkable how we need to be reminded of it. It is difficult to imagine that an approach to good practice in educational administration could be advocated while at the same time ignoring the strong connections with curriculum, teaching, and learning. Equally important, of course, are linkages to the external and policy environment.

It is this direction of thinking that has prompted this book. We believe it important to anchor our approach to educational administration and leadership in the curriculum, teaching, and learning because that is the "core business" for which schools exist and for which leaders assume prime responsibility. Additionally, in developing a comparative approach to the field, we see the need for key constructs—centered on societal culture—as well as useful frameworks and data collection instruments to facilitate rigorous comparative analysis in the field. Accordingly, the contributing authors to this volume have each addressed the concept of culture and cross-cultural analysis in their own ways, and have either gone on to suggest useful models, approaches or perspectives to develop cultural analysis, or illustrated the connectivity between leadership and administration on the one hand and change, school improvement, or curriculum teaching and learning on the other.

Our intention as editors is to break new ground and to provoke among readers many questions concerning the future directions of the field. In looking at school administration and leadership in its cultural setting at the micro (organizational) level and macro (societal) level, our aim is to contextualize the field and signal some exciting directions for this new millennium.

The book is divided into two parts. Part I presents a set of five chapters that together, but in quite different ways, highlight the importance of context and culture in the study and understanding of school administration and leadership. The second part explores the potential contribution that the concept of societal culture can make to the study of school leadership, educational change, school improvement, curriculum, and school democracy in a number of specific contexts—namely, Thailand, the People's Republic of China, England, the United States, the United Kingdom, Singapore, and Hong Kong SAR. Although approached differently, each of the articles in this section provides unique insights into how societal culture influences school administration and leadership.

In the opening chapter, we claim that while the field of educational administration has experienced impressive development over the last three decades, the fact that a robust comparative branch of the field has failed to emerge, is equally noteworthy. We summarize a case for comparative educational administration and leadership, arguing that the development of conceptual frameworks and instrumentation are imperative if the field is to keep abreast of globalization of policy and practice. Accordingly, a conceptual framework is described and justified based on a cultural and cross-cultural approach focusing on the school level as the baseline unit for analysis. Specifically, the proposed framework is architectured around the interrelationship between two levels of culture—societal and organizational—and four elements comprising schooling and school-based management—organizational structures, leadership and management processes, curriculum, and teaching and learning. Finally, some limitations and implications of the model are discussed, including the need for the framework to be empirically validated.

Chapter 2 highlights the importance of societal culture to developing theory, policy and practice within an increasingly globalizing educational context. It argues that tensions exist between globalization and societal culture and that globalization makes the recognition of societal culture and cross-cultural similarities and differences more, not less, important. Consequently, the inclusion of societal culture as a factor in investigations covering such themes as the curriculum, teaching and learning, leadership, and school-based management is seen as an imperative for the future development of comparative education. Accordingly, the first part of the chapter clarifies the concept of "globalization." In the second part, globalization and societal culture are juxtaposed, and the interface between them is explored. Finally, Dimmock illustrates the argument for greater cultural sensitivity by raising some key issues concerning school reform and improvement.

Chapter 3, Begley uses what he labels "cultural isomorphs" to illustrate how quite distinctive social conditions may be obscured, veiled, or blurred by the perspectives adopted to describe social processes in schools. He suggests that although this is a natural outcome of generalizing the specifics of one context to a generalized set of abstract principles, it is accentuated by the ethnocentric nature of theory development in the field. He claims that one of the consequences of this is that the generalized experiences of one country may be inappropriately assumed to be instructive to the practices in radically different contexts, and that increased globalization makes the implications of this phenomenon more profound and more urgent. Turning specifically to school leaders working in increasingly pluralistic organizations and societies, Begley suggests that school leaders need to become more sophisticated in their leadership and management of education, and more sensitive to the value orientations of others. He presents several robust and empirically verified theory perspectives on values derived from the work of Hodgkinson as supports to the achievement of sophisticated and sensitive educational leadership practice. Although grounded in theory, these perspectives are presented in a practical and easily understood fashion that is relevant to school leaders.

The focus of Chapter 4 shifts attention to the core purpose of schooling— teaching and learning—and is based on the premise that a solid understanding of how students learn and teachers teach is essential in order to exercise effective school leadership. Until recently, little was known about cross-cultural differences in learning and teaching. Watkins provides a fascinating review of research on teaching and learning, but from a cross-cultural perspective, comparing Western and Chinese teachers and students. A meta-analysis undertaken indicates that across a number of very different cultures, higher quality learning strategies, at both school and university level, are associated with higher student self-esteem and an internal locus of control. Such strategies tend to be encouraged in classrooms where students feel involved, where the teachers are supportive, and where the workload is fair, even if all too frequently the students are not rewarded in higher examination marks. In-depth research on Chinese students questions the validity of a number of basic Western notions of educational psychology regarding the nature of motivation and the role of memorization. Other research suggests that the emphasis in Western teacher education on getting students on-task and coping with behavioral problems may not be as relevant in the Chinese context. Chinese educators tend to see both creativity and understanding as slow processes requiring much effort, repetition, and attention rather than relatively rapid, insightful processes. Such views are grounded in hundreds of years of Chinese philosophical thought. Any attempts to reform education by importing ideas from one culture to another must consider the overall contexts of the societies involved. This review of important cultural differences in teaching and learning raises the fascinating issue of the implications for school leadership, management, and organization.

Chapter 5, the final chapter of part I, describes several important conceptual and methodological issues for researchers to consider in advancing the study of school leadership processes across different cultural settings. Heck acknowledges calls for increasing attention to the study of educational administration across differing contexts (such as urban and rural communities, elementary and secondary school levels) and cultural (such as country) settings. He explains that this growing interest stems from three interrelated factors—namely, a recognition of the diversity in schooling practices within and across different societies, remarkable progress in global communication, and increased possibilities for collaboration with colleagues holding similar interests in varied global settings. While applauding the increasing number of studies on school leadership conducted in different cultural and national settings over the past 15 years, Heck laments the fact that few of those studies were designed to investigate school leadership comparatively. While discussing the various methodological and conceptual issues involved in advancing this area of study, Heck suggests that a new orientation to comparative research on school leadership will expose a host of issues that will need to be addressed. Despite this, however, he is optimistic about the state of the field and its future development.

The chapters comprising Part II focus attention on the influence of societal culture on different aspects of school administration—including leading change, curriculum change, school democracy, school improvement, and school-level leadership—in a number of diverse societies. Each author takes a different approach to the topic and provides valuable insights into how societal culture influences all aspects of schools and schooling.

In Chapter 6, MacBeath suggests that school leadership should involve the freedom and capacity to create an educational vision and direction based firmly upon what is important to students growing up in a twenty-first-century global economy. He then explains that, ironically, the global economy is placing considerable constraints on the latitude of schools to be creative, thinking, learning, democratic communities. MacBeath continues to suggest that concepts important to leadership, such as quality, standards, effectiveness, and accountability, have been coopted, narrowed, and starved of meaning by short-term political imperatives, or by what Berliner describes as the "manufactured crisis." This "crisis" requires schools to "deliver" short-term gains that are often antithetical to genuine improvement, are anti-democratic and fail to meet their own aims of preparing young people for a twenty-first-century society. MacBeath claims that reforms have led to an intensification of teaching and a disempowering of teachers and school leaders, but that these effects are different in different contexts. MacBeath considers the challenge to leadership in the diverse cultural contexts of Hong Kong, the United Kingdom, and the United States. In doing so he draws on school effectiveness and leadership studies in these three countries to illustrate some ways in which schools have been able to retain democratic learning as their central focus.

In Chapter 7, Hallinger and Kantamara explore the influence of culture on change leadership in Thailand. The authors analyze and reflect on the crucial nexus between school leadership and curriculum reform while adopting a cultural perspective. Their context is a case study of change leadership in a Thai school that serves their purpose of illustrating the need for multicultural perspectives on school leadership. The case study explores the role of leadership in implementing "modern" systemic reforms in a traditional Thai school. A cultural analysis of the change process is offered, using Hofstede's cultural dimensions that contrast the nature of the "empowering" reforms with the underlying cultural norms of Thai society. The results suggest important differences and tensions between the nature of the change process and its underpinning values and assumptions, and traditional Thai norms and behaviors rooted in the social culture of the country. In the concluding section Hallinger and Kantamara discuss a number of implications for leading school change in the East and West.

In Chapter 8, Morris and Lo describe and analyse first, the policy background to a major shift in the curriculum in Hong Kong (called the Target-Oriented Curriculum), and second, a case study of a school that attempted to introduce some of the reforms embodied in the TOC. In line with similar curriculum developments in the United States, United Kingdom, and Australia, the TOC represents a more student-centred, outcome-oriented curriculum, involving system-wide testing at key stages, regular assessment, more individualized teaching and learning approaches, and greater emphasis on student creativity and problem solving. Morris and Lo explore the interaction of cultures and curriculum reforms. They argue that the reform emerged from, and was adapted and enacted in, contexts or arenas that exhibited very different cultures. Their analysis focuses on three distinct arenas in Hong Kong that influenced the reform, and examines within each the key interest groups and their shared understandings. In their account of the efforts of a Hong Kong primary school to implement the TOC, some stark and vivid cultural conflicts are exemplified. Their paper thus provides an analysis that stresses the fragmented, pluralistic, and changing nature of culture within Hong Kong society, but particularly, the clashes and tensions between new curriculum policies and practices and traditional values underlying school leadership and management.

In Chapter 9, Sharp and Gopinathan examine the influence of societal culture on school leadership in Singapore. The authors present a sociocultural perspective on leadership and schooling in Singapore. They weave a strong case promoting a sociopolitical perspective as offering a rich detailing of culture in interaction within schooling. The first section of the chapter examines the explicit use of the school system in contributing to the development of a socially cohesive and economically productive society. Sharp and Gopinathan hold that "societal culture" in Singapore is an evolving mix of traditional and modernizing cultures, and that this mix is inseparably linked to social integration and economic development. They then present two case studies of two Singapore government schools that have shown quite remarkable and sustained improvement. The success of the schools transpired within the generally supportive "societal culture," but what made their performance outstanding were the initiatives taken by the school principals.

In Chapter 10, Bush and Qiang discuss the evolution of culture in the People's Republic of China through recognizing a number of evolutionary stages and their respective influences on education and school leadership. Among the stages recognized are traditional culture, socialist culture, enterprise culture, and patriarchal culture. To some extent these have developed sequentially, although all are claimed to be of relevance today. "Traditional culture" is reflected in continued respect for authority, collectivism, and harmony in schools. "Socialist culture" has, in many ways, reinforced aspects of traditional culture while, at the same time, further politicizing the principal's role, and "enterprise culture" has served to integrate market values into the education system. The influence of "patriarchal culture" continues to determine the role of men and women in schools, and particularly in school leadership. The chapter concludes by briefly discussing both the cumulative and enduring influence of the hybrid Chinese culture on education.

Chapter 11 analyzes the headship in English schools and traces their cultural and historical antecedents of leadership. Southworth describes how English education has been the subject of considerable reform over the last decade, with successive governments introducing waves of initiatives. He identifies a number of themes emerging from recent reforms that have helped to reshape the role of head teachers, and discusses their connection to cultural and historical roots. In other words, cultural norms and occupational traditions continue to underlie and anchor contemporary role shifts and emphases of headteachers. Southworth adopts the metaphor of a palimpsest to describe this coexistence and to explain the persistence of power relations in schools, which he sees as restricting notions of democracy to an environment that is largely non-participatory.

Chapter 12 returns again to Hong Kong and explores the dilemmas faced by a group of principals. After explaining that research into dilemmas has been largely restricted to Anglo-American contexts, Walker investigates principalship dilemmas in Hong Kong as a way of increasing understanding of school leadership in different cultural contexts. The first section of the chapter summarizes a case for studying dilemmas and discusses the absence of studies into leadership in non-Western contexts. Following sections provide a snapshot of the education reform environment in Hong Kong and a brief description of the methodology employed. The author then presents the types of dilemmas experienced by the group of principals and discusses the basis of these dilemmas, how they were managed by the principals and, finally, the consequences of this management. Interestingly, the author also points out that some principals did not conceive their lives in terms of dilemmas. When discussing the outcomes of the research, Walker suggests that although the dilemmas faced by principals may be generic across cultures, the way in which they are formed and managed appear intimately related to culture. Similarly, reasons for why some principals do not identify dilemma situations in their work appear grounded in cultural explanation.

In Chapter 13, we attempt to spotlight salient implications and issues emanating from the chapters in this volume by forming a number of propositions. These propositions, we suggest, provide promising avenues for the future development of comparative school administration and management and deeper understanding of the influence of societal culture on the field.

Our hope is that the chapters in this book will provide a worthwhile stimulus for further thought, discussion, and research into the influence of societal culture on the conception and practice of educational administration and leadership in all parts of the world. We acknowledge that the area remains in its infancy; our intention is to encourage discussion and debate in the area by recognizing the place societal culture plays in the lives of school leaders and school communities. Given the complexities involved in defining culture and operationalizing it for research purposes, we and the contributing authors do not claim to have definitive answers on the extent to which culture does or does not influence school leadership. Nor do we suggest that societal culture is the only, or even the most important, mediating influence on how leaders lead. For example, it would be foolhardy to discount the part played by personality, gender, organizational culture, or religion in determining what leaders do. The evolutionary confluence of factors that coalesce to form the context within which school principals operate is obviously multifaceted, and understanding can only be enhanced through viewing their work, perhaps simultaneously, using multiple lenses. We argue that societal culture is one of these lenses—one that has generally been neglected—and that it deserves far more attention in our field than it is presently accorded.

References

Cheng, K. M. (1995). The neglected dimension: Cultural comparison in educational administration. In K. C. Wong & K. M. Cheng (Eds.), *Educational leadership and change: An International Perspective* (87–102). Hong Kong: Hong Kong University Press.

Dimmock, C. (2000). *Designing the learning-centred school: A cross-cultural perspective,* London: Falmer Press.

Dimmock, C., & Walker, A. (1998). Comparative educational administration: Developing a cross-cultural conceptual framework. *Educational Administration Quarterly, 34*(4), 558–595.

Hallinger, P., & Leithwood, K. (1996). Culture and educational administration: A case of finding out what you don't know you don't know. *Journal of Educational Administration, 34*(5), 98–116.

Walker, A., & Dimmock, C. (1999). A cross-cultural approach to the study of educational leadership: An emerging framework. *Journal of School Leadership, 9*(4), 321–348.

Walker, A., & Dimmock, C. (2000). Developing educational administration: The impact of societal culture on theory and practice. In C. Dimmock & A. Walker (Eds.), *Future school administration: Western and Asian perspectives* (pp. 3–24). Hong Kong: Chinese University Press.

Walker, A., & Dimmock, C. (in press). Moving school leadership beyond its narrow boundaries: Developing a cross-cultural approach. In K. Leithwood & P. Hallinger (Eds.), *Second international handbook of educational leadership and administration.* Netherlands: Kluwer Press.

part I:
Conceptualizing
and Researching the Influence
of Societal Culture

1.

Cross-Cultural and Comparative Insights into Educational Administration and Leadership

An Initial Framework

ALLAN WALKER AND CLIVE DIMMOCK

Educators and politicians in Taiwan, Hong Kong, Japan and Korea expound the necessity for their East Asian school systems to become more like those in the West. They complain that there is too much rote learning, uniformity, and standardization and too little emphasis on creativity, diversity, and problem solving. In addition, competition is fierce for scarce places in elite schools and universities, leading to unfulfilled ambitions and wastage of talent among the high proportions of young people failing to gain entry. Meanwhile, their counterparts in North America, Australia, and Great Britain look in the reverse direction to these same East Asian countries and wonder what they can learn from the superior academic results of East Asian students on International Achievement Tests in mathematics and science (Atkin & Black, 1997).

This relatively new phenomenon—a reciprocal interest of East and West in each other's school systems—characterized much of the 1990s. Other factors, besides those mentioned, fuelled the tendency to look beyond national boundaries for answers to educational problems. While many developing countries have for some time looked to Europe and North America for their policy models, what was particularly new about the 1990s was the interest taken by the developed countries, such as the United States and United Kingdom, in the school systems of East and Southeast Asia (Dimmock, 2000).

In this chapter, we affirm that internationalism as an educational phenomenon is desirable, especially in the new millennium of global trade, multicultural societies, and the Internet. However, equally, in an era when many are prone to draw superficial comparisons between policies and practices adopted in different countries, we argue the need for caution (Walker & Dimmock, 2000a). In particular, such comparisons, we claim, can be fatuous and misleading without thorough understanding of the contexts, histories, and cultures within which they have developed. Our main purposes in this chapter are thus twofold. First, to argue the need to develop a comparative and international branch of educational leadership and management. Second, to propose a comparative model of educational leadership and management based on cultural and cross-cultural analysis. The chapter begins with the justification for developing a comparative branch of the field. It then goes on to explain the appropriateness of culture as a core concept in developing comparative educational management. A model is then proposed as a useful conceptual framework for drawing valid international comparisons in school leadership and management. Finally, we allude to some challenges and limitations of the approach.

Justification for Comparative and International Educational Leadership and Management

Growing awareness of and interest in the phenomenon of globalization of educational policy and practice is creating the need for the development of a comparative and international branch of educational leadership and management (Dimmock & Walker 1998a, 1998b). Interest in, if not willingness to adopt, imported policies and practices without due consideration of cultural and contextual appropriateness is justification for developing a more robust conceptual, methodological, and analytical approach to comparative and international educational management. Currently, educational management has failed to develop in this direction. Indeed, as we argue below, it shows every tendency to continue its narrow ethnocentric focus, despite the internationalizing of perspectives taken by policy makers and others to which we have already alluded. In this respect, it could be argued that our field is lagging behind conceptually and epistemologically trends and events already taking place in practice. In addition, it has already failed to keep pace with comparative and international developments in other fields, notably business management and cross-cultural psychology.

   Globalization of policy and practice in education is in part a response to common problems faced by many of the world's societies and education systems. Economic growth and development are increasingly seen within the context of a global market place. Economic competitiveness is seen to be dependent on education systems supplying sufficient flexible, skilled "knowledge workers." This phenomenon, however, emphasizes the need to understand the similarities and differences between societies and their education systems. No two societies are exactly alike demographically, economically, socially, or politically. Thus an attraction of an international and comparative branch to educational management is systematic and informed study leading to better understanding of one's own as well as others' education problems and their most appropriate solutions.

A strong argument for the need to develop an international and comparative branch to the field is the ethnocentricity underlying theory development, empirical research, and prescriptive argument. Anglo-American scholars continue to exert a disproportionate influence on theory, policy, and practice. Thus, a relatively small number of scholars and policy makers representing less than eight percent of the world's population purport to speak for the rest. Educational management has a vulnerable knowledge base. Theory is generally tentative and needs to be heavily qualified, and much that is written in the field is prescriptive, being reliant on personal judgement and subjective opinion. Empirical studies are rarely cumulative, making it difficult to build systematic bodies of knowledge. Yet despite these serious limitations, rarely do scholars explicitly bound their findings within geocultural limits. Claims to knowledge are made on the basis of limited samples as though they have universal application. A convincing case can be mounted for developing middle range theory applying to and differentiating between different geocultural areas or regions. During the next decade there is need to develop contextually bounded school leadership and management theories. This will allow us to distinguish, for example, how Chinese school leadership and management differs from, say, American or British.

A further concern leading to the need for a distinctive branch of comparative educational management is the need for more precise and discriminating use of language. Many writers, for example, glibly use terms such as "Western," "Eastern," or "Asian" in drawing comparisons. Little attempt is made, however, to define or distinguish these collective labels, a serious omission when there is likely to be as much variation within each of them as between them. For example, major contextual and cultural differences apply between English-speaking Western countries such as the United Kingdom and the United States, let alone between the United Kingdom, United States, France, and Germany, with their different languages and locations on two continents. Yet they are all examples of so-called 'Western' countries. Likewise, when referring to the 'East' or to 'Asia," major cultural differences are to be found between China, Japan, Korea, Malaysia and Singapore. Developing comparative educational management might introduce more rigor and precision in the terms used to define education systems geographically and culturally.

Why Cultural and Cross-Cultural Analysis as the Basis of Comparison?

In building a comparative and international branch of educational management, it is necessary to make a convincing case for an appropriate theoretical or conceptual foundation. For this we have turned to the notion of culture,

and societal culture in particular. An increasing recognition of the importance of societal culture and its role in understanding life in schools is very
recent. "Culture" is defined as the enduring sets of beliefs, values, and ideolo-
gies underpinning structures, processes, and practices that distinguishes one
group of people from another. The group of people may be at school level
(organizational culture) or at national level (societal culture).

Both Cheng (1995) and Hallinger and Leithwood (1996a) have argued for
greater cognizance to be taken of societal culture in studies of educational
leadership and educational administration. Our case for developing a cultural
and cross-cultural approach rests on at least three reasons: first, the suitability
of culture as a base concept for comparative study; second, the limitations
of existing models and concepts used in comparative study; and third, the
consequences of continuing to ignore culture as an influence on practice
and understanding in educational leadership and management (Walker &
Dimmock, 1999). Each of these reasons is examined in turn.

The Suitability of Culture

Culture at the organizational level is now a well-recognized and increasingly
studied concept in school leadership and management (Bolman & Deal, 1992;
Duke, 1996). Culture at the societal level, however, has not received similar
attention. Since culture is reflected in all aspects of school life, and people,
organizations, and societies share differences and similarities in terms of their
cultures, it appears a particularly useful concept with universal application,
one appropriate for comparing influences and practices endemic to educational leadership and management.

Since culture exists at multiple levels (school and sub-school, local, regional,
and societal), it provides researchers with rich opportunities for exploring their
interrelationships, such as between schools and their micro- and macro-
environments. It also helps identify characteristics across organizations that
have surface similarity but are quite different in modus operandi. For example,
schools across different societies look to have similar, formal leadership hierarchies, but these often disguise subtle differences in values, relationships, and
processes below the surface.

Most cross-national studies of educational leadership have ignored the
analytical properties of culture. Such neglect has been challenged recently
by researchers such as Cheng (1995), who assert that, "the cultural element
is not only necessary, but essential in the study of educational administration" (p. 99). Specifically, Cheng bemoans the fact that much research in
educational administration ignores culture and makes no reference to larger
macro-societal or national cultural configurations. The concept of national
culture has not been rigorously applied as a basis for comparison in educational leadership or as a means for comparing the organization of individual
schools. Neither has culture at the organizational level been developed as a

foundation for comparative analysis; rather, it has been applied to areas such as school effectiveness and organizational analysis.

Limitations of Existing Comparative Approaches

A second argument for a cross-cultural approach to comparative educational leadership and management is that existing comparative education frameworks tend to focus on single levels and to assume structural-functionalist approaches. Single-level frameworks ignore the relationships and interplay between different levels of culture, from school to societal, thereby failing to account sufficiently for context. For example, Bray and Thomas (1995) claim that national or macro-comparative studies tend to suffer from overgeneralization, and therefore neglect local differences and disparities. Likewise, within-school studies tend to neglect the external school context.

In unraveling the dynamic, informal processes of schools and the leadership practices embedded within them, theoretical tools that stretch beyond structural-functionalist perspectives should be considered. Although structural-functionalist models are useful for fracturing education systems into their constituent elements (structures), their explanatory potential is limited as to how processes, or why various elements, interact. As a result, their analytic power is diminished through adopting static rather than dynamic views of schools. Consequently, explanation remains at a surface level, and rigorous comparison remains rare. We suggest that multilevel cultural perspectives need to be taken in aiding analysis and understanding of schools and their leaders.

Cultural Borrowing of Educational Policies and Practices

Our third justification for adopting a cross-cultural approach to comparative educational management relates to the globalization of policy and practice (Dimmock, 1998; Hallinger & Leithwood, 1996b; Walker & Dimmock, 2000b). Policy makers and practitioners are increasingly adopting policy blueprints, management structures, leadership practices and professional development programs fashioned in different cultural settings while giving little consideration to their cultural fit. In seeking to understand why some leadership practices appear to be workable in some contexts but not others, and the nature of adaptation needed, there is a clear need to take the cultural and cross-cultural contexts into account.

The dominance of Anglo-American theory, policy, and practice denies or understates the influence that culture, and societal culture in particular, may have on the successful implementation of policy. There is serious risk at present that our understandings will remain too narrowly conceived. A comparative approach to educational leadership and management can expose the value of theory and practice from different cultural perspectives, which may then, in turn, inform and influence existing dominant Western paradigms.

A Model for Cross-Cultural Comparison in Educational Leadership and Management

An overview of our cross-cultural comparative model is provided in Figure 1.1. The model is comprised of two interrelated parts:

1. a description of the four elements constituting schooling and school-based management (see Figure 1.2 for a breakdown), and
2. a set of six cultural dimensions at each of the societal and organizational levels that provide common scales for comparison (see Figure 1.3).

Figure 1.1 illustrates the four elements of schools and the two sets of cultural dimensions—societal and organizational. Comparative analysis is aimed at the relationship between the two levels of culture and the four elements

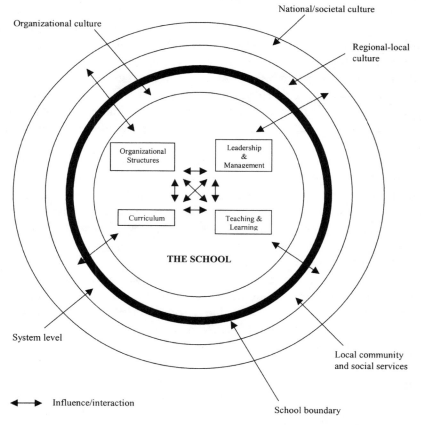

Figure 1.1 A cross-cultural school-focused model for comparative educational leadership and management.

constituting the school. In Figure 1.1, organizational culture is conceptualized as internal to the school but bounding the four elements, reflecting its capacity as both a dependent and independent variable with regard to the four elements of the school and schooling. National or societal culture, however, is depicted as circumscribing the school but at the same time, spanning the school boundary to interact with organizational culture and to affect the four elements of the school.

The school is taken as the unit of analysis for comparison in our framework and is assumed to comprise four elements: organizational structures; leadership and managerial processes; the curriculum, which is a school substructure; and teaching and learning, which is a sub-set of school processes (Figure 1.1). These four elements provide a convenient way of encapsulating the main structures and processes that constitute the schooling and school-based management. Two of the four comprise the managerial and organizational aspects of school life, while the remaining two elements form the core technology of the school concerned with curriculum, teaching, and learning. Elsewhere (Dimmock & Walker, 1998b), we have explained the four elements in full and the interrelationships between them. Relationships with other parts of the system, such as the district and central office, and with local community and social service agencies are also considered (see Figure 1.1). Below we provide a brief overview of all four.

The Four Elements of Schooling and School-Based Management

Organizational Structures

"Organizational structures" refer to the more or less enduring configurations by which human, physical and financial resources are established and deployed in schools. Structures represent the fabric or framework of the organization and are thus closely associated with resources and their embodiment in organizational forms. They also provide policy contexts within which schools have greater or lesser discretion. Thus, schools in strongly centralized systems experience more explicit and rigid policy "structures" imposed from system levels, with possibly less need for school decisional structures, whereas schools in more decentralized systems may have more school-based decision-making structures but fewer policy structures imposed from outside the school. A comparison between the structures of schools is based on the eight aspects outlined below.

First, schools have a physical fabric consisting of buildings of various sizes and layouts. For convenience, technology might also be included in the school's physical resources. Second, schools possess financial resources that structure possibilities and set constraints as to what schools can and cannot do. The extent to which schools can raise revenue themselves and control the distribution of financial resources provides a rich point of comparison. Third, government schools and many private schools are parts of larger school systems and as such are subject to system-imposed curricular frameworks. Schools in different systems vary according to the extent of curriculum prescription and over which parts of the curriculum they may have some control. Fourth, time is a key resource that, by virtue of the way it is organized, imposes a tight structure on schools. The organization of the school year, term, week, and day imposes nested layers of time structures on most schools. The timetable is a means of structuring the delivery of the curriculum and indicates the relative importance attached to each subject by virtue of the time afforded it.

Human resources and their configuration constitute a fifth aspect. In this respect, students may be selected for entry to schools on the basis of their ability, gender, or parents' wealth. Once they become school members, they are grouped into classes for learning. Classes are structures formed on the basis of age, ability, gender, or a combination thereof. Sixth, teachers likewise are subject to organizational structures, especially in their teaching. Seventh, schools vary according to whether and how their structures reflect guidance and counseling functions, and the extent to which these are separated from, or integrated with, the academic structures. Finally, schools are characterized by decision-making structures that normally include senior management teams, consisting of the principal and deputies, a host of other school committees or task groups, and a school council or governing body comprising professional and lay members and is responsible for overseeing school policy.

Leadership and Mangerial Processes
At the core of school administration lie a number of human resource management processes (Figure 1.2). As with structures, the manifestation and importance of these processes in schools reflect cultural characteristics and the relationship with other levels of the system, particularly the degree of centralization decentralization. Consequently, where school-based management has been extended, schools perform more of these processes. However, the processes vary even in schools in the same system. This is clearly evidenced by the nature of principalship, and the position, role, and power of the principal, which all differ between schools and between systems. In some countries, the principal is all-powerful and is seen as a chief executive of an autonomous unit, while in others, the role carries little more authority than the classroom teacher, and the principal is no more than a line manager or agent acting on behalf of the system. A second and related point of comparison concerns the principal's leadership, especially pertaining to style and orientation, reflected, for example, in the degree of authoritarianism/democracy displayed by the principal and the relative emphasis placed on instruc-

tion and/or administration. A third group of processes concerns the extent to which there is collaboration and participation of school personnel in the management of the school and the operation of the curriculum. Comparisons between schools are likely to reveal substantial differences in the extent to which staff collaborate and participate in their running. A fourth set of equally important management processes relates to motivation. In this regard, it is instructive to make comparisons between schools in terms of the extent to which staffs are motivated and how such motivation is achieved.

A fifth group of processes concerns planning, an aspect of school management of heightened importance of late. Both planning procedures and resultant plans appear to vary considerably between schools. A sixth set of management processes is concerned with decision making. Schools may be compared according to the criteria and the methods by which decisions are made. A seventh set of processes generic to school management relates to

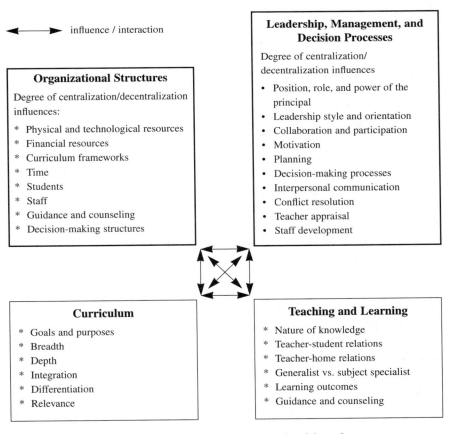

◄──────► influence / interaction

Organizational Structures

Degree of centralization/decentralization influences:

* Physical and technological resources
* Financial resources
* Curriculum frameworks
* Time
* Students
* Staff
* Guidance and counseling
* Decision-making structures

Leadership, Management, and Decision Processes

Degree of centralization/ decentralization influences

• Position, role, and power of the principal
• Leadership style and orientation
• Collaboration and participation
• Motivation
• Planning
• Decision-making processes
• Interpersonal communication
• Conflict resolution
• Teacher appraisal
• Staff development

Curriculum

* Goals and purposes
* Breadth
* Depth
* Integration
* Differentiation
* Relevance

Teaching and Learning

* Nature of knowledge
* Teacher-student relations
* Teacher-home relations
* Generalist vs. subject specialist
* Learning outcomes
* Guidance and counseling

Figure 1.2 The four elements of schooling and school-based management.

interpersonal communication. Schools vary, for instance, in their use of written and oral modes of communication and in the extent to which they rely on computer technology for communication inside and outside the school. An eighth group of management processes concerns conflict resolution. Comparisons between the ways in which disputes between school members are handled and resolved are instructive in highlighting similarities and differences in their managerial processes. The increasing expectation that schools conduct evaluation, performance management, and appraisal activities has added a ninth set of processes. School comparisons are instructive in terms of the extent to which each of these activities exists and the characteristic forms they take. Finally, a tenth group of processes relates to staff development. Comparisons between schools in this regard would illustrate the importance attached to staff development and its characteristics.

Curriculum

At the heart of schools is the core technology of curriculum, teaching, and learning. The curriculum is an organizational structure, since it represents the form in which knowledge, skills, and attitudes are configured for delivery to the students. However, as a structure concerned with core technology, it deserves separate recognition as an organizational structure in its own right. As previously stated, the culture and configuration of the relationship between system and school (degree of centralization/decentralization) will expectedly determine the discretion and responsibility afforded the school for the curriculum. With that in mind, the curricula of schools can be compared according to the following characteristics outlined below (see Figure 1.2).

The first characteristic concerns the goals and purposes of school curricula. Curriculum goals may vary in line with differences in how curriculum developers conceive the nature of knowledge and with how the purpose of the curriculum is defined. The curriculum may be seen, for example, as having primarily instrumental functions related to future employment, or it may be seen as having more intrinsic cognitive priorities. The relative emphasis placed on knowledge, skill, and attitude goals and on cognitive, affective-expressive-aesthetic, and psychomotor goals, may differ, as might the balance between academic and pastoral development. A second characteristic on which comparisons can be made is curriculum breadth, or the range or spread of subjects and disciplines offered to students. A third characteristic relates to curriculum depth, or the levels, standards, or grades at which the curriculum is offered. A fourth concept for curricular comparison is integration. Levels of curriculum integration vary vertically—that is, the extent to which the content and teaching methods for individual subjects are coordinated and coherent from one grade level to another—and horizontally— that is, the extent to which coordination and coherence is achieved between different subject areas at the same grade level. A fifth criterion is curriculum differentiation, which is the degree to which the curriculum caters for students of different abilities. Finally, a sixth aspect by which curricula may be compared, is relevance. Although elusive, this concept can apply to present and future education, employment, adult citizenship, social stability, and social change.

Teaching and Learning

Teaching and learning activities, as part of the core technology of schools, are processes that warrant separate identification from, even though they are related to, managerial processes. Differences in the ways in which schools conduct teaching and learning activities can be compared according to the following characteristics outlined below (see Figure 1.2).

An important characteristic concerns the ways in which teachers and students bring definition to teaching and learning. Asian and Western societies, for example, tend to adopt different understandings of what it is to teach and learn. This stems from a fundamentally different conception of the nature of knowledge and important differences in the relationship between the teacher and the student. In Asian countries, for example, teachers' knowledge and teachers per se are accorded more respect than in Western societies. A third concept for comparison is the teacher–parent relationship. In some cultures, parental involvement in their children's education is encouraged and seen as essential in promoting learning; in others, parents view teaching and learning as exclusively school activities and thus the responsibility of teachers.

A fourth criterion for comparison relates to teaching methods and approaches. While an array of different teaching methods and approaches exists, there are stark contrasts to be made between schools where teaching is predominantly teacher-centered, expository, and didactic and those where it is student-centered. A further characteristic is the role expectation placed on the teacher. In some schools, the teacher is expected to be a subject specialist, while in others, the teacher is more of a generalist, expected to teach a broader range of subjects. A sixth criterion relates to the importance placed on, and the nature of, specific learning outcomes as goals to guide, and benchmarks for assessing, student learning. Finally, comparisons may be made according to the emphasis placed in teaching on the guidance and counseling of students.

Recognition of common characteristics inherent in all cultures is necessary to facilitate cross-cultural comparison. This approach obviates the need to choose a particular culture as a baseline for comparison. Hence the first component of our model is the definition of a set of cultural dimensions commonly present in all cultures but to different degrees.

Six Dimensions of Societal Culture

Culture is a difficult phenomenon to measure, gauge, or even describe. The identification of cultural dimensions, which we define as core axes around which significant sets of values, beliefs and practices cluster, not only facilitates their description and measurement, but promotes comparison between cultures. Dimensions provide common benchmarks against which cultural characteristics at the societal level can be described, gauged, and compared (Dimmock & Walker, 1998b). It is important to note that the dimensions are continua that intend to provide considerable scope to make comparisons. The dimension labels offer extreme polarities that are intended for broad classification only. It is highly improbable that a school or group of schools would be located at such extremes; they would more likely fall somewhere along the different continua. Despite the usefulness of dimensions for measurement and comparison, however, we agree with Hofstede's (1994) cautionary remarks that, "They are also constructs that should not be reified. They do not 'exist'; they are tools for analysis which may or may not clarify a situation" (p. 40).

Our research—involving the review of existing frameworks—for the comparative study of educational leadership and management led to our fashioning the following six-dimensional model (Walker & Dimmock, 1999). Figure 1.3 lists both the national/societal cultural dimensions and organizational cultural dimensions.

Figure 1.3 Dimensions of national/societal and organizational culture.

National/Societal Cultures	Organizational Culture
Power-concentrated/Power-dispersed	Process/Outcome-Oriented
Group-oriented/Self-oriented	Person/Task-Oriented
Aggression/Consideration	Professional/Parochial
Fatalistic/Proactive	Open/Closed
Generative/Replicative	Control/Linkage
Limited relationship/Holistic relationship	formal—informal
	tight/loose
	direct/indirect
	Pragmatic/Normative

Note. *Adapted from Cultures and organizations: Software of the mind* by G. H. Hofstede, 1991.

Power-Distributed / Power-Concentrated

The first dimension is modeled on Hofstede's (1991) power/distance construct. We relabeled the dimension as power-distributed/power-concentrated because this more accurately captures the essence of power relationships in various cultures. Power is either distributed more equally among the various levels of a culture or is concentrated among relatively few. In societies where power is widely *distributed*, for example, through decentralization and institutionalized democracy, inequity is treated as undesirable and every effort is made to reduce it where possible. In societies where power is commonly concentrated in the hands of the few, inequities are often accepted and legitimized. People in high *power-concentrated* societies tend to accept unequal distributions of power.

Group-Oriented / Self-Oriented

The second dimension embraces Trompenaars' and Hampden-Turner's (1997) individualism/communitarianism category and Hofstede's (1991) individualism/collectivism dimension. Both of these schemata describe whether people within a given culture tend to focus on *self* or on their place within a *group*, hence our preference for the label "group-oriented/self-oriented." In *self-oriented* cultures, relations are fairly loose and relational ties tend to be based on self-interest. People in such societies primarily regard themselves as individuals first and members of a group second. In *group-oriented* cultures, ties between people are tight, relationships are firmly structured, and individual needs are subservient to collective needs. Important collectivist values include harmony, face-saving, filial piety, and equality of reward distribution among peers. In *group-oriented* cultures, status is traditionally defined by factors such as age, sex, kinship, educational standing, or formal organizational position. In *self-oriented* cultures, people are judged and status ascribed according to individual performance or what has been accomplished individually.

Consideration / Aggression

This dimension is built on Hofstede's masculinity/femininity dimension. We reconceptualized it because of the confusion surrounding Hofstede's label and its discriminatory nature. In what we have called *aggression* cultures, achievement is stressed, competition dominates, and conflicts are resolved through the exercise of power and assertiveness. In such cultures, school norms are set by the best students, the system rewards academic achievement, and failure at school is seen as serious; in an organizational context, assertiveness is taken as a virtue; selling oneself, decisiveness, and emphasis on career are all valued. By contrast, in *consideration* societies, emphasis is on relationship, solidarity, and resolution of conflicts by compromise and negotiation. At school, norms tend to be set by the average students, system rewards reflect students' social adaptation, and failure at school is taken as unfortunate.

Proactivism / Fatalism

Our fourth dimension draws on Trompenaars and Hampden-Turner's "attitudes to the environment" category, Hofstede's uncertainty/avoidance dimension, and our own thinking in respect of the concepts of opportunistic and pragmatic/idealistic. This dimension was relabeled to reflect the proactive or "we can change things around here" attitude in some cultures, and the willingness to accept things as they are—a fatalistic perspective, in others. The dimension addresses how different societies and cultures react to and manage uncertainty and change in social situations. In *proactive* societies, people tend to believe that they have at least some control over situations and over change. They are tolerant of different opinions and are not excessively threatened by unpredictability. In *fatalistic* cultures, on the other hand, people believe "what is meant to be, will be." Uncertainty is often viewed as psychologically uncomfortable and disruptive, and people seek to reduce uncertainty and limit risks by hanging on to tradition. This often involves the inflexible retention of rules and dogmas that breed orthodoxy.

Generative / Replicative

This dimension, original to our schema, was so labeled to reflect the fact that some cultures appear more predisposed toward innovation or the generation of new ideas and methods (generative), whereas other cultures appear more inclined to replicate or to adopt ideas and approaches from elsewhere (replicative). In *generative* cultures people tend to value the generation of knowledge, new ideas, and ways of working, and they seek to create solutions to problems, to develop policies and ways of operating that are original. In *replicative* cultures, people are more likely to adopt innovations, ideas, and inventions developed elsewhere. Whereas these sometimes undergo partial adaptation, they are often replicated in toto, with little consideration of alignment to the indigenous cultural context.

Limited Relationship / Holistic Relationship

This dimension builds on Trompenaars and Hampden-Turner's specific/diffuse and performance/connection categories and on our own work on the importance of relationships in cultures. The dimension reflects an assumption that in some cultures, interpersonal relationships are limited by fixed rules applied to given situations, whereas in other cultures, relationships are more holistic, or underpinned by association and personal considerations. In limited relationship cultures, interactions and relationships tend to be determined by rules that are applied equally to everyone. For example, in deciding a promotion, objective criteria are applied regardless of who are the possible candidates. In *holistic* cultures, on the other hand, greater attention is given to relationship obligations (for example, kinship, patronage, and friendship) than to impartially applied rules (Dimmock, 2000). Dealings in formal and structured situations in *holistic* cultures are driven more by complex, personal considerations than by the specific situation or by formal rules and regulations.

Six Dimensions of Organizational Culture

Qualitative differences between organizational and societal culture stem from the fact that national cultures differ mostly at the level of basic values, while organizational cultures differ mostly at the level of more superficial practices, as reflected in the recognition of particular symbols, heroes, and rituals (Hofstede, 1991). This allows organizational cultures to be managed and changed, whereas national cultures are more enduring and change only gradually over long time periods, if at all.

Research studies on the organizational cultures of companies found large differences in their practices (symbols, heroes, rituals), but only minor differences in their values (Hofstede, 1995). Most of the variation in practices could be accounted for by six dimensions, although further validation of these is required. These six provide a useful baseline for organizational culture in our framework. We have, however, adapted the six, in line with our own research (Dimmock & Wildy, 1995). In addition, while Hofstede presents the dimensions as either/or choices along six axes, we regard them, as with the societal cultural dimensions, as multidimensional rather than unidimensional. The six dimensions are as follows.

Process-Oriented and/or Outcomes-Oriented

Some cultures are predisposed toward technical and bureaucratic routines, while others emphasize outcomes. Evidence suggests that in *outcomes-oriented* cultures people perceive greater homogeneity in practices, whereas people in *process-oriented* cultures perceive greater differences in their practices. In education, some schools are process orientated, emphasizing the processes and the skills of decision making, teaching, and learning, while others are results-oriented, stressing learning achievements such as exam results. Many schools and school systems are currently reforming their curricula to reflect specific student learning targets or outcomes expressed in terms of knowledge, skills and attitudes, indicating a trend toward designing curricula on the basis of, and measuring student and school performance by, a learning outcomes approach. Strong cultures tend to be more homogeneous and therefore results- or outcomes-oriented.

Task-Oriented and/or Person-Oriented

In *task-oriented* organizational cultures, emphasis is placed on job performance and maximizing productivity, while human considerations, such as staff welfare, take second place and may even be neglected. Conversely, *person-oriented* cultures accentuate the care, consideration and welfare of employees. Blake and Mouton (1964) recognized these leadership orientations in the 1960s. Applied to schools, a task-oriented culture exacts maximum work effort and performance out of its teachers in a relatively uncaring work environment. A person-oriented culture, on the other hand, values, promotes, and shows consideration for the welfare of its teachers. It is conceivable that some schools might score high (or low) on both task and person orientations.

Professional and/or Parochial

In *professional* cultures, qualified personnel identify primarily with their profession, whose standards are usually defined at the national or international level. In *parochial* cultures, members identify most readily with the organization for which they work. Sociologists, such as Gouldner (1957) have long recognized this phenomenon in their distinction between locals and cosmopolitans. In the school context, some teachers, especially those with an external frame of reference, are primarily committed to the teaching profession as a whole, while others with a strong internal frame of reference are more committed to the particular school in which they work.

Open and/or Closed

This dimension refers to the ease with which resources, such as, people, money, and ideas are exchanged between the organization and its environment. The greater the transfer and exchange of resources between the environment and the organization, the more open the culture. Schools vary between those that champion outside involvement in their affairs and maximum interchange with their environment, and those that eschew such interaction and communication, preferring a more closed, exclusive approach. Trends in education over the last decade have favored the opening of school cultures, particularly to parental influence and involvement.

Control and/or Linkage

An important part of organizational culture concerns the way in which authority and control are exerted and communicated between members. In this respect, Hofstede's dimension identifies only one aspect—tightly loosely controlled cultures. We have added two more aspects—formal/informal and direct/indirect which. Taken together, the three aspects provide a more detailed account of this dimension in schools.

   Formal/Informal. Organizations vary in the extent to which their practices are guided by rules, regulations, and "correct procedures" on the one hand, and the extent to which they reflect a more relaxed, spontaneous and intuitive approach on the other. Highly formalized organizations conform to the classic bureaucracies; they emphasize definition of rules and roles, tend toward inflexibility and are often characterized by austere interpersonal relationships. By contrast, informal organizations have fewer rules dictating procedures, roles are often ill-defined, they display flexibility in their modes of work, and interpersonal relationships tend to be more relaxed.

Tight/Loose. This sub-dimension gauges the degree to which members feel there is strong commitment to the shared beliefs, values, and practices of an organization. Such strong commitment might come through hierarchical supervision and control, or through members' own self-motivation. An organization that has strong homogeneity and commitment in respect of its members' values and practices is tightly controlled (whether control is externally imposed by superordinates or self imposed by employees). Conversely, a loosely controlled culture is one with only weak commitment to, or acceptance of, shared beliefs, values, and practices, and little or no control is exerted to achieve homogeneity either by superordinates or by members themselves.

Direct/Indirect. This aspect captures the linkages and patterns of communication through which power, authority, and decisions are communicated. In some organizations, managers assume direct personal responsibility to perform certain tasks and to communicate directly with their staff, often leapfrogging intermediate levels in the vertical hierarchy or chain of command. In other organizations, managers exert control indirectly by delegating to staff the tasks they would otherwise do themselves.

Pragmatic and/or Normative

This dimension defines the way an organization serves its clients, customers, or patrons. Some display a flexible, pragmatic policy aimed at meeting the diversity of customer needs. Others, however, exhibit more rigid or normative approaches in responding bureaucratically, failing to meet individual needs. This dimension measures the degree of client orientation. In the educational context, some schools consciously try to meet individual student needs by offering a more diversified curriculum with flexible timetables and alternative teaching strategies. They mold their educational services to meet student needs. Others, particularly the more traditional schools, may be less student focused, expecting them to fit into the agenda determined for them by the school. These schools offer more standardized, normative programs.

Operationalizing the Model

Having identified key elements of schooling, school-based management, and cultural dimensions, the model needs operationalizing. This is achieved by applying the cultural dimensions to the elements of schooling and school-based management. For example, if the researcher is interested in comparing leadership styles and positions in two or more schools in different *societal* cultures, data would need to be gathered through applying our power-concentrated/power-distributed cultural dimension to leadership (see Figure 1.2). Other dimensions, such as consideration/aggression, might also be relevant. If the same interest in leadership style and position were examined at the *organizational* culture level, data would need to be generated by applying relevant organizational culture dimensions to leadership; in this case, person/task and control/linkage (see Figure 1.3).

In facilitating the data collection process, a number of instruments—both quantitative (survey questionnaires) and/or qualitative (interviews and case studies)—are needed to apply the cultural dimensions to the various elements of the school and school-based management. Depending on the research purpose, a selection of the relevant elements and dimensions may be sufficient. It may not be necessary to apply all of the dimensions to all of the elements—that is a demanding task. Which elements and dimensions are selected will depend on the research question and purpose.

Conclusion—Challenges and Limitations of the Approach

In pioneering new approaches there are bound to be imperfections, unresolved issues, and challenges. We are aware of many pitfalls and difficulties. The concept of culture itself has generated multiple definitions and ambiguities. Alone, it does not have the explanatory power to account for all the differences between schools in different societies. Economic, political, and demographic factors, for example, may play a key role. Cultures may not equate with national boundaries. Moreover, there are difficulties in operationalizing models such as the one espoused in this chapter (Walker, in press).

Nonetheless, we argue that educational leadership and management as a field of study and research has failed to keep pace with current events leading to the internationalizing and globalizing of policy and practice. We are concerned that unlike other fields, such as international business management and cross-cultural psychology, our field has generally failed to develop models, frameworks, and analytical tools by which to understand these dramatic changes and their effects in different societies. Equally, we are conscious of the limitations of existing models and theories that tend to be ethnocentric, and by generally failing to distinguish cultural boundaries, to assume a false universalism. We contend that a focus on culture as an analytical concept promises robust comparisons between school administration and policy across different geocultural areas. Such cross-cultural comparisons can embrace a wider rather than narrower perspective, incorporating school leadership, organizational structures, management, curriculum and teaching and learning, in order to present holistic and contextualized accounts. An international and comparative approach to educational leadership and management would bring greater refinement to the field. Few would dispute the need for such a development in the new millennium.

References

Atkin, J. M., & Black, P. (1997). Policy perils of international comparisons: The TIMMS case. *Phi Delta Kappan, 79*(1), 22–28.

Blake, R. R., & Mouton, J. S. (1964). *The managerial grid.* Houston, TX: Gulf Publishing.

Blunt, P., & Jones, M. (1997). Exploring the limits of Western leadership theory in East Asia and Africa. *Personnel Review, 26*(1/2), 6–23.

Bolman, L., & Deal, T. (1992). Leading and managing: Effects of context, culture, and gender. *Educational Administration Quarterly, 28*(3), 314–329.

Bray, M., & Thomas, R. M. (1995). Levels of comparison in educational studies: Different insights from different literatures and the value of multilevel analysis. *Harvard Educational Review, 65 (3),* 472–489.

Cheng, K. M. (1995). The neglected dimension: Cultural comparison in educational administration. In K. C. Wong & K. M. Cheng (Eds.), *Educational leadership and change: An international perspective* (pp. 87–102). Hong Kong: Hong Kong University Press.

Dimmock, C. (1998). School restructuring and the principalship: The applicability of Western theories, policies and practices to East and South-East Asian cultures. *Educational Management and Administration, 26*(4), 363–378.

Dimmock, C. (2000). *Designing the learning-centered school: A cross-cultural perspective,* London: Falmer Press.

Dimmock, C., & Walker, A. (1998a). Towards comparative educational administration: The case for a cross-cultural, school-based approach. *Journal of Educational Administration, 36*(4), 379–401.

Dimmock, C., & Walker, A. (1998b). Comparative educational administration: Developing a cross-cultural conceptual framework. *Educational Administration Quarterly, 34*(4), 558–595.

Dimmock, C., & Wildy, H. (1995). Conceptualizing curriculum management in an effective secondary school. *The Curriculum Journal, 6*(3), 297–323.

Duke, D. (1996, October). *A normative perspective on organizational leadership.* Paper presented at the Toronto Conference on Values and Educational Leadership, Toronto, Canada.

Gouldner, A. (1957). Cosmopolitans and locals: Toward an analysis of latent social roles-1. *Administrative Science Quarterly, 2,* 291–306.

Hallinger, P., & Leithwood, K. (1996a). Culture and educational administration: A case of finding out what you don't know you don't know. *Journal of Educational Administration, 34*(5), 98–116.

Hallinger, P., & Leithwood, K. (1996b). Editorial. *Journal of Educational Administration, 34*(5), 4–11.

Hofstede, G. H. (1991). *Cultures and organizations: Software of the mind.* London: McGraw Hill.

Hofstede, G. H. (1994). Cultural constraints in management theories. *International Review of Strategic Management, 5,* 27–48.

Hofstede, G. H. (1995). Managerial values: The business of international business is culture. In T. Jackson (Ed.), *Cross-cultural management* (pp. 150–165). Oxford, England: Butterworth-Heinemann.

Trompenaars, F., & Hampden-Turner, C. (1997). *Riding the waves of culture* (2nd ed.). London: Nicholas Brealey.

Walker, A. (in press). Developing cross-cultural perspectives on education and community. In P. Begley (Ed.), *The ethical dimensions of school leadership.* Netherlands: Kluwer Press.

Walker, A., & Dimmock, C. (1999). A cross-cultural approach to the study of educational leadership: An emerging framework. *Journal of School Leadership, 9*(4), 321–348.

Walker, A., & Dimmock, C. (2000a). Developing educational administration: The impact of societal culture on theory and practice. In C. Dimmock & A. Walker (Eds.), *Future school administration: Western and Asian perspectives* (pp. 3–24). Hong Kong: Chinese University Hong Kong Press.

Walker, A., & Dimmock, C. (2000b). One size fits all? Teacher appraisal in a Chinese culture. *Journal of Personnel Evaluation in Education, 14*(2), 155–178.

2

Educational Leadership

Taking Account of Complex Global and Cultural Contexts

Clive Dimmock

It is all the more surprising that educational policy, leadership, and management as a field of study has tended to neglect the importance of societal culture in an era of globalization. This chapter makes a plea to redress this situation. Its central argument pivots on the need for educational management, leadership, and educational policy at a time of globalization to incorporate societal culture—conceptually, theoretically, and practically—in redefining and refining the field. The following terms are used at various points throughout the discussion—"school leadership," "educational management" and "educational administration." Reference is made to all three since they are applied in different countries and universities to refer broadly to the same area of study and practice. Distinctions between policy', leadership' and management' are also difficult to make since the three are not entirely exclusive. For example, leadership may involve policy making and vice versa. In addition, commentators even within the Anglo-American world use the terms differently. In this chapter, leadership is taken to mean a higher order set of abilities such as goal setting, visioning, and motivating, while management is viewed as a lower order group of activities concerned with maintenance of performance through supervision, coordination, and control. Policy refers to macro- or system-level policy.

Specifically, the chapter highlights the importance of societal culture to developing theory, policy and practice within an increasingly globalizing educational context. By globalization is meant the tendency for similar policies and practices to spread across political, cultural and geographical boundaries. Societal culture refers to those enduring sets of values, beliefs and practices that distinguish one group of people from another. It appears that the avid focus on globalization has tended to ignore or diminish the importance of societal culture, the latter tending to act as a mediator or filter to the spread of ideas and practices across the globe, resulting in their adoption, adaptation, or even rejection. Thus in a globalizing world, the recognition of societal culture and cross-cultural similarities and differences becomes more, not less, important. Consequently, the inclusion of societal culture as a factor in investigations covering such themes as the curriculum, teaching, and learning, leadership and school-based management is seen as an imperative for the future development of the field.

The first part of the chapter clarifies the concept of globalization. In the second part, globalization and societal culture are juxtaposed, and the interface between them is explored. Finally, the argument for greater cultural sensitivity is illustrated by raising some key issues concerning school reform and improvement.

In evaluating the state of educational management and administration to date, there would be considerable agreement about the overreliance placed on prescription and opinion on the one hand, and the underdevelopment of theory, especially empirically supported theory, on the other. Theory that is acknowledged is largely Anglo-American in origin. Given the resources available to, and stage of development reached by, educators in North America, the United Kingdom, and Australia, this is understandable. It is of concern, however, that much of the theory generated is ethnocentric and consequently tailored to those contexts. Moreover, those generating the theory make little attempt to bound or limit their work geographically or culturally, an aspect that is particularly disconcerting for those who work outside Anglo-American societies. For example, while a global educational lexicon has emerged— "school-based management," "collaborative decision making," "parent participation" are familiar concepts across the globe—the meanings attributed to the terms differ appreciably between societies. On another level, tenets of policy reform are assumed to be universally applicable. But why should the principle of subsidiarity, for example, or the tenets of decentralization and school-based management be as apposite for Asian settings as they are deemed to be for Anglo-American contexts, taking into account important cultural differences of power and authority relations?

Furthermore, a substantial part of theory in educational management derives from business management. There are at least three justifiable reasons for this: first, organizations have generic functions, such as mission stating, goal setting, recruiting, monitoring, and evaluating; second, comparisons between types of organizations and their management may be instructive; and third, governments are keen to make school management more business like. There are, however, dangers in simply transferring and applying business management to diverse educational contexts in a less than critical fashion. While schools may share increasingly common characteristics with businesses, in shaping and educating young people they go beyond the rudiments of business. Unlike businesses, schools are not primarily in existence to make profit. They need to be equally concerned with processes and outcomes, many of which defy easy measurement or quantification. For these and other reasons, the appropriateness of leadership procedures and styles transferred from business are at least questionable for schools.

Indisputably, schools provide education, which is seen as constituting a social service. It is a matter of controversy as to whether market models and concepts from the business world should be imported into this social service as principles for organization and leadership. Markets, choice, performance league tables, competition between schools and public relations—all tend to threaten traditional notions of leadership and policy. Moreover, there is evidence of loss in transposing business leadership and management to education. For example, school principals become more isolated from teachers and students and from the core curriculum functions of the school as they become office managers focusing on administrative issues and meeting accountability expectations of central bureaucracies. An administrative rather than educational or instructional emphasis to the principal's leadership role is also more likely from the policy of school-based management. Self-implementing policies shift major responsibilities from the central bureaucracy to the individual school without necessarily providing a commensurate increase in resources.

The development of educational policy and practice is also dominated by Anglo-American initiatives. This, too, is understandable in that Anglo-American societies have a preeminent position in terms of global economic development, communications, and technology. As developed societies, they possess the resources and ideas to innovate and to lead change. Moreover, Anglo-American societies are advantaged by having English—increasingly accepted as the global language—as their mother tongue.

For much of the twentieth century, but particularly the second half, it became apparent that the developing world was taking its cues mostly from Anglo-American societies. The continuation of this phenomenon—otherwise known as globalization—seems assured as other developing countries follow suit. Generations of comparativists, from Sadler onwards (Jones, 1971), have pointed to the reasons for cultural borrowing. These include colonialism, cultural imperialism, the overseas education of leaders, the desire of less developed societies to emulate the more developed, a belief in education as a vehicle for economic and social advancement, international legitimacy for policy formulation, and closer links forged by international agencies, jet travel, and the electronic media. Comparativists have also acknowledged the benefits of studying foreign systems of education, including the resultant improved understanding of one's own system. There are exceptions, however, to the phenomenon of policy borrowing associated with globalization, even among close neighbors. For example, the Scots and Irish have developed their own education systems that are appreciably different from the English.

While globalization has been emerging, relatively little credence has been given to the concept of societal culture. Yet, as theory, policy, and practice are transported globally, they interface with the cultures of different host societies. The interaction between the two merits consideration for a number of reasons. First, as policies such as decentralization and school-based management spread from Anglo-American systems to become more globalized, what are the implications for leadership and management in the host societies? Leadership and management, as previously acknowledged, may not mean the same things in different societal cultures. In Western societies, for example, leadership is seen to rest on a set of technical skills, while in Chinese societies it is viewed more as a process of influencing relationships and modeling what are deemed to be desirable behaviors. Will meanings and styles of leadership converge in the future, or will they remain culture specific? And if Anglo-American influences over globalization increase in the future, what are the benefits and drawbacks to such developments? Can we assume that there are some organizational procedures and policies that are generically beneficial regardless of the cultural origins of such ideas? Responses to these questions will shape how school leadership and management are shaped in the future.

It follows that a key direction for school leadership and educational management in the twenty-first century is to embrace an international, cultural and cross-cultural comparative perspective. Elsewhere, we have provided a more detailed justification for such an approach (Dimmock & Walker, 1998a) and have developed a framework for its application (Dimmock & Walker, 1998b).

Globalization

A complex set of forces and trends is shaping the contemporary world. The nation state as we have come to know it is under threat—politically and economically. At the macro level, multinational corporations transcend nation states, affecting organizations and the lives of individuals. Plants can be closed down overnight and jobs relocated to other countries. Ohmae (1995) convincingly argues that the world economy is increasingly run by economic regions, such as Silicon Valley, and Hong Kong and adjacent parts of southern China, rather than by countries. Some also argue that globalization is reinforced by the growing influence of international agencies, such as The World Bank, the IMF, and the United Nations. In addition, regional conglomerations of nations, many of them trade blocs, such as the European Community and

North Atlantic Free Trade Association, have further undermined the autonomy of the nation state. American ascendancy in the political and economic arenas has also given a boost to globalization. The fortunes of organizations and individuals are just as much directly influenced by these global forces as they are by nation states.

At the same time, globalization has resulted in a proliferation of units smaller than the nation state. In other words, the demise of the nation state is accompanied in some parts of the world by a rise in nationalism, as indicated in the Balkans and the setting up of a Scottish Parliament. As Bottery (1999) asserted, whether the nation state is superfluous or not, "there is little doubt that the phenomenon of globalization has an impact upon organizations, individuals and values, which is both greater and smaller than the nation-state. . . ." (p. 300). He goes on to conclude that prudent organizations and individuals will take cognizance of global forces in their decision making. It is also worth noting that societal cultures do not necessarily equate with national boundaries or nation states as recent turmoil in the Balkans illustrates.

There is little doubt that increased opportunity for travel and communications, including the electronic media, have provided a big impetus to globalization. Bottery (1999), citing Waters (1995), suggested that to use the term "globalization" does not necessarily imply planetary-wide acceptance. Rather, the term connotes "a broad spectrum idea, suggesting that there are issues and trends which transcend any particular nation-state, which have significant potentiality for full global effects, but which may not yet have attained this" (Bottery, 1999, p. 301).

Furthermore, globalization takes a number of forms. Waters (1995), for example, recognizes the political, economic and cultural. To these, Bottery (1999) added the managerial and environmental. It is not the purpose here to expound on each of these, but it is worth noting some points of relevance for educational management. Forms of political organization beyond the nationstate threaten concepts of national citizenship—often an important consideration in schooling and curriculum—and national sovereignty over economic affairs. The economic form of globalization, as manifested in trade blocs and international agreements, has the capacity to influence national economic policy and expenditure on education and social welfare provision, thereby ultimately affecting school budgets.

Managerial and cultural forms of globalization are particularly relevant. While management concepts seem global in nature, the "actual practice of management is context-bound, mediated by the beliefs, values and aspirations of the managers and the managed" (Bottery, 1999, p. 303). Educational managers in the developed world have over the past two or three decades been exhorted to read management "gurus" associated with the private sector—

such as Handy, Drucker and Peters and Waterman—the consequence of which has been the introduction of a business terminology into educational management. They have also been urged to look at practice overseas—especially the United States, but also latterly Japan, Singapore, Taiwan, and other Asian systems—in order to identify "best practice" on a global scale. Insidious dangers, however, lurk in both directions. The first concerns the different agendas and purposes of business and educational management, and the second, the failure to respect the grounding of practices in their own cultural settings. It is to this latter issue that the next section turns.

Globalization and Societal Culture

Globalization in educational management implies the export of theory, policy and practice from some systems—chiefly the Anglo-American world—and their import into others, particularly non-Western and developing countries. More recently, signs of a reciprocal movement are apparent as the Anglo-American systems look with interest at, and try to explain, the enviable performance of East and Southeast Asian school students in mathematics and science (Dimmock, 2000; Reynolds & Farrell, 1996).

Importing policy reforms formulated elsewhere under different economic, political, and cultural conditions presents challenges for the new host cultures. Many observers not only question the suitability of the policy reforms for those systems importing them, but often question their appropriateness for the exporting systems. Theories, ideas, and practices derived in one social setting should not be assumed valid in other social-political-cultural contexts. Societal cultures, along with local economic, political, and religious conditions, act as mediators and filters to policies and practices imported from overseas. Consequently, policies may be accepted, adapted, or rejected.

For policy makers in some countries or states, globalized policy making has attractions. Imported policy gives it international legitimacy and allows the focus to switch readily and often too hastily to implementation. Contextual conditions in the host society are given scant attention. The policy formulation and adoption stages fail to act as effective filters and mediators, and problems are pushed down to the implementation stage.

The argument is not that globalization is a negative phenomenon, or that societal culture is unnecessarily obstructive. Rather, it is that the transfer and mobility of theory, policy, and practice between systems needs to be more "culture-sensitive." Neither should the argument for cultural sensitivity assume that cultures are static or passive entities always requiring the adaptation of imported policy and practice. Cultures themselves are dynamic and changing, and schools as centers of knowledge organization and transmission play a vital part in that process. For example, cultural transformation may focus on lessening an authoritarian and male-centered orientation to leadership and management.

Nonetheless, the argument for greater cultural sensitivity in a globalizing educational context is robust. If policy, theory, and practice are to be made more culture sensitive, then the process needs to begin at the formulation rather than at the implementation stage. International advisers and consultants as well as policy makers, especially those in the host societies, bear responsibility for making this happen. A more culture-sensitive approach requires a better understanding of culture and cross-cultural similarity and difference.

Leadership and Cultural Sensitivity

When policy, theory, and practice are transported between education systems, there is need to consider how societal culture may intervene to help or hinder the process. Hence the concept of cultural sensitivity. In concluding, the argument is illustrated by reference to some generic reforms presently adopted in diverse cultures.

In the global push for school-based management and decentralization, a reconfiguration in the pattern of decision making, responsibility, and power in favor of principals, teachers, and parents, is foreshadowed. Predictably, societal cultures in which power is traditionally distributed more equally—for example, Anglo-American societies—would be more receptive to school-based management than societal cultures in which power is concentrated—such as Chinese communities like Hong Kong and Singapore. The initiative to decentralize power and responsibility to schools has mostly come from the Anglo-American systems. However, the distribution and exercise of power in school systems is bound to an extent to reflect and mirror that in the wider society. Non-Western societies with very different traditions of power distribution not surprisingly run into difficulty when adopting such a policy. This may partly explain the different forms in which school-based management manifests itself—in some societies, simply reinforcing the power of the principal, while in others leading to more genuine participation of teachers and parents. Examples of problems encountered by Asian school principals transitioning between traditional and more contemporary styles of leadership—the latter expected by recent reforms—are beginning to filter through into the literature (see chapters by Hallinger & Kantamara, and Morris & Lo in this volume).

Different cultures deal with conflict and participation in different ways. According to Bond (1991), the disturbance of interpersonal relations and group harmony through conflict can cause lasting animosity in Chinese cultures. As a result, the Chinese tend to avoid open confrontation and assertiveness. In the school or group context, this is manifested by teachers and principals tending to avoid open disagreement, with the leader's view invariably and apparently being accepted (Walker, Bridges, & Chan, 1996). Principals in such cultures tend to avoid situations that risk conflict and instead to rely on authoritarian decision-making modes. A possible side effect of conflict avoidance, maintenance of harmonious relationships, and respect for seniority is that top-down decisions and policies are seldom challenged or modified by those lower in the hierarchy. In such cultures, principals may dutifully obey the central bureaucracy and teachers may readily accept the decisions and edicts of principals, thus preserving the status quo.

In many education systems, a trend toward individualizing curricula, teaching, and learning is discernible. While such an approach may be harmonious with, and acceptable to, cultures emphasizing individualism, its suitability for collectivist cultures may be legitimately questioned. Broadly, Hofstede (1991) identified Anglo-American cultures as individualist and most Asian cultures as collectivist. Conversely, some currently favored reform measures do appear to harmonize with collectivist characteristics. For instance, collaborative learning—generally acknowledged as an effective teaching-learning method—may actually be more suited to students in collectivist cultures than students in individualist cultures. Walker et al. (1996), using a small case study of mature-age Hong Kong Chinese students, reported the high propensity for collaborative group work, while upholding many familiar Chinese customs with respect to their way of communicating. For example, particular respect was shown to older and more senior members of the group, and a strong desire for consensus and harmony was shown throughout. Contrast this with the group dynamics that often pervade Anglo-American groups where consensus and decision making often fail to materialize due to confrontation or an unwillingness to bend to the views of others.

Cultural issues relating to individualism/collectivism also surface with regard to the implementation of appraisal schemes, especially when English-speaking Western models of appraisal are introduced into schools in host cultures where many of the key tenets and assumptions appear untenable (for a full discussion, see Walker & Dimmock, 2000). Problems tend to emerge in implementation details, such as whether the focus is on individuals or groups of teachers, who should be the appraisers, the relationships necessary for appraisal to be successful, the skills required by appraisers, and the need for open communication and "impersonality" (Chow, 1995).

Most Western appraisal models are predicated on assessing the performance of the individual. When such systems are uncritically imported into collectivist or group-oriented societies, their efficacy can be questioned on at least two fronts. First, a system based on the judgment of individuals appears incongruent with a strong group-orientation. If teachers are predominantly concerned with "fitting into" and supporting the group, individual performance becomes secondary, and any individual judgment or advice is of lesser significance than a person's role in, and contribution to, the wider group. Since group-oriented cultures tend to be characterized by the avoidance of conflict and competition, two-person, face-to-face appraisal discussions tend to remain at a surface level, with both parties extremely reluctant to risk saying or doing anything that might lead to confrontation. Second, since relationships are valued over tasks in many collectivist cultures (such as in Chinese organizations), Western notions of impersonality, objective measures, and personal achievement become troublesome when deciding upon the form appraisal should take. The Chinese are said to have a higher tolerance of subjectivity, and as long as they feel they can trust the leaders who conduct the appraisal, they will accept subjective evaluations of their performance.

The Western notion of appraisal based mainly on achievement is also a difficult concept to implement in Chinese organizations for two reasons. First, the Chinese tend to value effort over achievement (Lee, 1996). This makes it difficult to rate teachers performance outcomes on objective instruments, such as those suggested by central bodies. It also makes it difficult to challenge teachers' performances, even if they are weak, if they have committed the required effort to their work. Second, achievement in collectivist cultures holds different meanings from those held in individualistic cultures. According to Yu (1996, p. 29), achievement motivation in Western cultures reflects middle class Western values that are "self-oriented, person-oriented, or individual oriented." In other words, achievement is seen in relation to the individual. In group-oriented cultures, on the other hand, achievement motivation has wider connotations in terms of the family or the group, not so much for the individual (Westwood, 1992). If achievement is conceptualized in terms of the group rather than the individual, individualized forms of performance appraisal may be ineffective in schools in such societies. At the very least, an inappropriate picture of performance may be portrayed.

Given the group-orientation of the many Chinese societies, it is likely that a group form of appraisal process would be more efficacious. Interestingly, team- or group-oriented teacher evaluations have attracted attention in the United States over the last decade. The Chinese are generally uncomfortable with disclosing their inner self and criticizing or praising their own performance even in a group context. As a result, they are reluctant to be observed by peers and will attempt to cover up any inadequacies. Given these factors, it may be that a suitable form of appraisal for Chinese schools would combine a group emphasis with the stronger presence of the principal to judge progress (Walker & Dimmock, 2000).

A central tenet of the restructuring of curriculum and pedagogy in many school systems is that students accept more personal responsibility for their learning. Accompanying this phenomenon is the espousal of goal setting at the individual level and school development planning at the organizational level. Each of these tenets assumes the acceptance of responsibility for shaping the future—a capacity associated with proactivism found in Anglo-American cultures. In cultures displaying strong elements of "fatalism," where control is seen to be in the hands of others or outside human realms altogether, it is less likely that these tenets and behaviors are as appropriate.

A further characteristic of curricular restructuring is the emphasis placed on creativity, problem solving, and higher-order thinking skills. Recent school curricular reforms in Anglo-American societies have given prominence to these aspects, linking them with skills needed by future workers in an information society. The Asian economic crisis, beginning in October, 1997 stopped the phenomenal rate of economic growth achieved by the so-called Asian "tiger" economies in its tracks. It became apparent that economies such as Hong Kong needed a technologically skilled workforce capable of sustaining a qualitatively different economic structure in the future. While societies such as the United States have cultures (and to an extent school curricula) conducive to creativity—they are what we call "generative"—some in East Asia are more renowned for their replication and rote learning. Although these school systems are successful in producing high achieving students in mathematics and science, they are less likely to cultivate creativity in their young people.

Lastly, in the pursuit of quality schools and schooling, the part played by competent and effective teachers is generally acknowledged. In pursuit of this goal, it is an accepted principle in Anglo-American cultures that the appointment and promotion of staff be on the basis of merit, as gauged by performance against some measurable criteria. Anglo-American societies conform to what might be called "limited relationship" cultures—that is, decisions taken specifically on the issues at stake. By contrast, in Chinese cultures, where more holistic considerations of relationship hold sway, personnel decisions may be made as much on the basis of connections as on merit. For example, a teacher may be appointed because a trusted friend of the school may speak highly of her loyalty, and loyalty is seen as a desirable quality leading to commitment and eventually performance. This more holistic perspective may make the attainment of openness with respect to transparency of selection or promotion criteria more difficult than in Anglo-American "limited relationship" cultures.

In conclusion, the claim is not that societal culture is the only mediating influence on globalized trends in education policy, theory, and practice. Nor is it without conceptual and empirical difficulties. Indeed, culture itself is being affected by globalization. Thus it is misleading to see culture as simply a reactive and mediating phenomenon when it, too, is subject to change from globalization. How the tension between the two—globalization and societal culture—is resolved will predictably vary according to their relative strengths in particular societies. Projecting into the future, perhaps the best scenario would be that each society demonstrate capability of transforming globalized policies and practices in culturally sensitive ways that respect the integrity of their indigenous culture while allowing room for change and development. In these ways and for these reasons societal culture is an important and overlooked factor in the study of schooling and school leadership and management. Importantly, the incorporation of societal culture into educational policy, research, and practice will significantly enrich, contextualize, and refine our field. A key objective is the development of theories of school leadership and organization that are culture-sensitive or even culture specific. Research could then engage in debates about the similarities and differences of, say, Chinese and American theories of educational leadership and about Japanese and British theories of school organization, teaching, or learning.

References

Bond, M. (1991). *Beyond the Chinese face: Insights from psychology.* New York: Oxford University Press

Bottery, M. (1999). Global forces, national mediations and the management of educational institutions. *Educational Management and Administration, 27*(3), 299–312.

Chow, I. (1995). An opinion survey of performance appraisal practices in Hong Kong and the People's Republic of China. *Asia Pacific Journal of Human Resources, 32*(3), 67–79.

Dimmock, C. (2000). *Designing the learning-centred school: A cross-cultural perspective.* London: Falmer Press.

Dimmock, C., & Walker, A. (1998a). Towards comparative education: The case for a cross-cultural, school-based approach. *Journal of Educational Administration, 36*(4), 379–401.

Dimmock, C., & Walker, A. (1998b). Comparative educational administration: Developing a cross-cultural conceptual framework. *Educational Administration Quarterly, 34*(4), 558–595.

Hofstede, G. H. (1991). *Cultures and organizations: Software of the mind.* London: McGraw Hill.

Jones, P. (1971). *Comparative education: Purpose and method.* St Lucia: University of Queensland Press.

Lee, W. O. (1996). The cultural context for Chinese learners: Conceptions of learning in the Confucian tradition. In D. Watkins & J. Biggs (Eds.), *The Chinese learner: Cultural psychology and contextual influences* (pp. 25–42). Hong Kong: The Comparative Education Research Centre.

Ohmae, K. (1995). *The end of the nation state: The rise of regional economies.* New York: Free Press.

Reynolds, D., & Farrell, S. (1996). *Worlds apart: A review of international surveys of educational achievement involving England.* London: Her Majesty's Stationery Office, OFSTED (Office for Standards in Education).

Walker, A., Bridges, E., & Chan, B. (1996). Wisdom gained, wisdom given: Instituting PBL in a Chinese culture. *Journal of Educational Administration, 34*(5), 98–119.

Walker, A., & Dimmock, C. (2000). One size fits all? teacher appraisal in a Chinese culture. *Journal of Personnel Evaluation in Education, 14*(2), 155–178.

Waters, M. (1995). *Globalization.* London: Routledge.

Westwood, R. (Ed.). (1992). *Organizational behavior: Southeast Asian perspectives.* Hong Kong: Longmont.

Yu, A-B. (1996). Ultimate life concerns, self, and Chinese achievement motivation. In M. Bond (Ed.), *The handbook of Chinese psychology* (pp. 227–246). New York: Oxford University Press.

3.

Western-Centric Perspectives on Values and Leadership

Cultural Isomorphs of Educational Administration

PAUL BEGLEY

One of the more attractive perquisites associated with a career as a professor of educational administration is the opportunity to work with school administrators from many countries. Such experiences reveal cultural isomorphs that occur within and among specific cultures. By isomorph is meant social conditions or value postures appearing to share the same shape or meaning from country to country but actually structured of quite different elements. For example, school administrators in countries such as the United States, Sweden, Canada, and Hong Kong are much inclined to profess a belief and commitment to democratic processes and democracy in general. Yet the nature of democracy in each country is clearly based on sharply contrasting notions of what constitutes free speech, social consensus, and appropriate political participation by the citizenry. A comparison of the acceptable standards of free speech in the United States and China is an obvious example. However, isomorphs can occur even within a single nation or culture, not just among nations. Consider how in the United States citizens are currently debating the nature of personal freedom in terms of the proper relationship between the right to bear arms and democracy. Some Americans view the private ownership of firearms as anathema to democracy, others as a prerequisite. Yet, both groups definitely consider themselves patriots of democracy. Isomorphs aside, such is the nature of ethics when they are adopted as guides to action. Transrational values of any sort are rather vulnerable to multiple interpretation in application from one context to another.

In a more educational context, consider the isomorphs that can be detected within school improvement processes. When one examines the nature of school improvement processes as they occur in various countries, one discovers that the syntax and procedures seem very similar—at least on the surface.

Practitioners in Hong Kong tend to cite the same literature as those in Sweden or Canada, usually American in origin. In particular, educators tend to use the same syntax of terms and procedural phases. For example, they may speak of "goal-setting," establishing "consensus" on shared objectives, and "implementation strategies." However, Russian school administrators mean something very different from their Canadian or Asian counterparts when they speak of establishing consensus as part of the process of establishing a collective school improvement objective. For the Russians the consensus has traditionally been something handed down in fully approved form from a centralized authority, whereas in Canada consensus is usually something established by a group of professionals working together locally. Same term and concept, but the assigned meaning is composed of different elements. The Russian meaning reflects their more collective cultural norms. The Canadian meaning reflects their social emphasis on norms of personal and professional autonomy.

These examples of cultural isomorphs illustrate how quite distinctive social conditions may be obscured, veiled, or blurred by the perspectives adopted to describe social processes. In many respects this is a natural outcome, and it illustrates the limitations of language as a means of assigning meaning to concepts and events. It is also a natural outcome of generalizing the specifics of one context to a generalized set of abstract principles. However, the implications can be quite profound. For example, the field of educational administration can be thought of as having developed along ethnocentric lines, dominated by Western perspectives emanating mostly from the United States and United Kingdom (Dimmock & Walker, 1998a; Walker & Dimmock, 1999). The consequences are a risk that the generalized experiences of one country may be inappropriately assumed to be instructive to the practices in radically different contexts. As our world becomes more globalized and the exchange of information among educators more widespread, the implications of this phenomenon become more profound as well as more urgent (Dimmock & Walker, 1998b). As many administrators are discovering in our increasingly pluralistic organizations and societies, even some of the most cherished ethical foundations, especially those derived from a Western Judeo-Christian tradition, sometimes must be carefully reexamined in terms of their appropriateness to changing social circumstances. As our communities and societies become more diversified, school administrators must become more sophisticated in their leadership and management of education, and more sensitive to the value orientations of others. Hodgkinson (1991) advised that administrators engage in praxis—that is, the linkage of theory and practice through reflection and values analysis. Applying a values perspective to administration is one way of achieving such a degree of praxis. In particular, a sensitive and sophisticated administrator must be able to distinguish between the holding, articulating, or manifesting of a value as opposed to an actual commitment to that value. For their part, researchers must move beyond their traditional orientation toward generalization and description to consider the deeper matters of intent and motivational base.

This chapter proposes that the achievement of conditions approximating reflective practice in educational administration in an increasingly globalized society is a function of three particular leadership qualities: the pursuit of administrative *sophistication* by individual educational administrators, the development of *sensitivity* to the value orientations and needs of self and others, and the *synergy* of good leadership that results when the first two qualities are consciously cultivated. A case for the achievement of these conditions is presented within this chapter using the following sequence of argument. First, a context is established for the promotion of reflective administrative practice by looking at the prevailing or dominant social isomorphs associated with school administration in the English-speaking world. Then several robust and empirically verified theory perspectives on values derived from the work of Hodgkinson (1991, 1996), a Canadian philosopher of administration, are presented as supports to the achievement of sophisticated and sensitive educational leadership practice. Although grounded in theory, these perspectives can be presented in a practical and easily understood fashion that is relevant to practitioners. The application and use of these perspectives in the setting of educational leadership practices is then demonstrated. Within this discussion, examples of recent research findings that stand as empirical verification of these theoretical frameworks are presented.

Cultural Isomorphs of School Leadership

In 1984, Clark, Lotto, and Astuto published a most useful comparison and analysis of the Effective Schools and School Improvement modes of inquiry. In rereading that chapter today, one is struck by the extent to which the vocabulary and ideas associated with this body of research have become comfortably familiar to the thinking, if not the practices, of most school administrators in English-speaking countries. They now constitute the vernacular of the practitioner—reinforced over time through the content of formal preparation courses, debated at conferences focussed on administrative practice, and very much evident in professional literature on school leadership. In many respects these notions now form the foundation of professional knowledge for aspiring school administrators. However, virtually all these images of effective practice, share one persistent limitation. They are founded on research findings that are basically descriptive or correlational in nature. They represent cultural isomorphs; that is, they describe conditions in schools that appear to share the same shape or meaning from district to district or country to country, but actually are often structured of quite different elements. As a result, practices may be espoused even when they may not have a good fit in a particular community or leadership context. Often schools and principals are described in the literature as effective without saying much about how they become effective. The focus has been on the empirical and the technical, and the bulk of the literature has been blind to what Barnard (1938) proposed as the moral dimension of leadership.

In response to these limitations of traditional scientific research method-ologies, a number of researchers (e.g., Begley, 1996; Begley & Johansson, 1998; Leithwood & Hallinger, 1993; Prestine & LeGrand, 1991) have shifted their attention to theories of human cognition as a better way of explaining the nature of expert leadership, justifying particular organizational configu-rations, and deriving insights into the interests and motivations of individual administrators. This trend represents a renewed academic interest in the moral aspects of educational leadership, especially the notion of administrator values as an influence on practices (Begley 1999; Begley & Leonard, 1999) and the more strategic notions of moral leadership (see Quong, Walker, & Stott, 1998). A more contextualized view of the thinking and learning process has gained prominence, and greater emphasis is accorded to the internal and external influences on school leadership practices. The limitations of gener-alized descriptive research findings now seem more apparent, and greater support has accrued for more qualitative research methodologies. When these notions are extended to the design and development of administrator preparation programs, important changes are implied for the content and process associated with the development of expert school leaders. Furthermore, solutions are suddenly available for several persistent problems that have regu-larly confounded the efforts of those committed to the development of expert school leadership practices—for example, situated learning and cognitive apprenticeship strategies (see Begley, 1995).

New Expectations for School Leadership in a Global Community

The quest for sophistication by educational leaders is not a new phenomenon. It has always been a desirable trait. However, the need for this quality has inten-sified in recent years. Not so long ago school communities in most countries tended to reflect the relatively stable cultural homogeneity of the communi-ties they served. Administrators carried out their role in schools through a fairly limited repertoire of managerial processes. There was seldom a need to reflect on the suitability of these established practices as guides to action, although such reflection has always been the mark of a wise leader. Management was largely a function of comfortable and proven procedures. In the North American context at least, the school was an arena for professional activity, the community stayed at a comfortable distance, and professional expertise was sufficient warrant for the trust of the community.

However, circumstances have changed radically in the past decade. Societies have become more pluralistic, and the demands and needs of interest groups in communities more diversified and insistent. The nature of school administration has altered dramatically. One very obvious outcome is the increase in value conflicts that occur in school environments. Always present to some extent, if only as a consequence of the generation gap between adult faculty and younger students, value conflicts have now become a defining characteristic of the school leadership role. The work of educational leaders has become much less predictable, less structured, and more conflict-laden. For example, in Canada there is considerable social pressure for greater stakeholder involvement in significant decision making within school organizations. However, the achievement of consensus on educational issues among even the traditional educational stakeholders has become more difficult. School administrators increasingly encounter value conflict situations where consensus cannot be achieved, rendering obsolete the traditional rational notions of problem *solving*. Administrators must now often be satisfied with merely responding to a situation since there may be no solution possible that will satisfy all. Such value dilemmas can occur within the mind of the individual—for example, the relatively unnegotiable personal core values of the individual competing with each other or running counter to professional or organizational expectations. Value conflicts may also be the outcomes of interactions among two or more individuals. Finally, value conflicts may be outcomes of an incongruence or incompatibility among one or more of several values arenas—that is, conflicts occurring among the domains of personal values, professional values, and/or organizational values. More than ever before administrators recognize that the values manifested by individuals, groups, and organizations have an impact on what happens in schools, chiefly by influencing the screening of information or definition of alternatives. The more reflective among administrators have also become more conscious of how their own personal values may blind or illuminate the assessment of situations.

To summarize current social circumstances, the traditional parameters of managerial and procedural responses to administrative situations must now be augmented with more enlightened and sensitive approaches to leadership. Traditional isomorphic notions of administrative knowledge, grounded in the experience of many instances, must be superseded by a superior class of knowledge based on the form, essence, or idea underlying each instance. One way of developing such knowledge is through reflection, cognitive flexibility, and sophistication. Acquiring this administrative sophistication is a function of understanding the influence of personal values and collective valuation processes as they occur in schools. As proposed earlier, it is values that link theory and practice and generate praxis. Aspects of this proposition are explored in more detail in the remainder of this chapter.

Making the Case for a Values Perspective on Administration

Some respected scholars still dismiss values as a concept too abstract and resistant to inquiry to be of any practical use to school administrators. Indeed, the need to clarify values only becomes important when one needs to know about intents and purposes, or when difficulty is encountered attempting to establish consensus within a given population. As previously argued, school leaders in many sectors of the world are clearly encountering such situations these days. This is definitely the current situation in Ontario, Canada where teachers and administrators have endured several years of unrelenting educational chaos at the hands of a government with a ruthless economic agenda. Similarly, a group of principals from Karelia in the former USSR report similar conditions associated with the collapse of their political union. Hong Kong is experiencing much the same circumstances since the reunification with China in 1997 (Walker & Dimmock, 1998). School administrators there are still struggling to identify and understand the implications of reunification with China. The school administrators from all these countries have intuitively developed an increased appreciation for the relevance of values to administrative practice. As the traditional managerial strategies of school leadership increasingly fail to accommodate the specifics of particular social cultures, educational administrators confront a challenge to respond creatively with new forms of leadership. One approach to which they intuitively resort is relying on the clues provided by the actions and attitudes of people around them to obtain predictive insights into the nature of values held by these individuals. In effect there is a readiness among administrators for adopting a values perspective as a guide to administrative practice. Unfortunately, universities and scholars to date have largely failed to provide good support to achieving this degree of administrative sophistication. This is the case for several reasons that bear further examination.

Practitioners can be rather insistent about the need for relevance. Scholars, on the other hand, tend to focus on a need for rigor. Accordingly, practitioners often manifest a low tolerance for abstract models and theoretical debate that stray any distance from the practical problems of the day. Unfortunately, the literature on values and ethics has tended to remain relatively indigestible for most practitioners. Most of it has remained too heavy, some too light. In the former category are the discussions of philosophical dualisms and epistemological wrangling characteristic of much theoretical and philosophical literature. On the other end of the continuum is the literature that lacks sufficient substance to be relevant as guides to practice. The "feel-good," expert-opinion writing on "moral leadership" generated by some authors illustrates this. As Greenfield asserted in his recent review of the values literature (1999), it is essential that we move beyond just the rhetoric of "moral leadership."

Fortunately, research on administrator values conducted in several countries provides some justification for optimism. Often conducted as action research or through case analysis (e.g. Begley & Johansson, 1998), these studies highlight the value orientations of skillful principals—illustrating how values can influence practice and which value types predominate in principals' problem-solving processes. The strongest finding by far across multiple studies is that rational values reflecting a concern for consequences and consensus appear to be the primary currency of the administrators from countries as widely separated as Canada, Russia, Sweden, Barbados, and Australia. Personal preferences grounded in self-interest are also evident as influences on decisions and administrative action, but are infrequently articulated by administrators. Transrational principles or ethics tend to be avoided when possible as a guide to action, but quickly adopted under the particular circumstances that require them.

Tempting as it may be to use such findings as a basis for developing a prescriptive guide to value-added leadership, a catalog of correct values that principals ought to adopt without question, the processes of valuation in school leadership situations are much too context-bound to permit this quick fix. Confronted once again is the risk of developing misleading cultural isomorphs. Furthermore, although we may know something about the problems currently confronting schools, none of us can predict with any degree of certainty the nature of future school leadership beyond the certainty that there will be more problems to solve and new dilemmas to confront. As a result, school leaders cannot merely emulate the values of other principals currently viewed as experts. Leaders of future schools must become reflective practitioners in the sense that many scholars have advocated for some time. The first step toward achieving this state is, predictably enough, to engage in personal reflection—familiar advice to anyone who has kept up with the leadership literature. However, the adoption of a values perspective on school leadership can transform this perhaps-vague advice into something specific enough for school administrators to act upon. Once a degree of improved self-knowledge has been achieved through personal reflection, administrators must then strive to develop a sensitivity to the values orientations of others in order to give meaning to the actions of the students, teachers, parents, and community members with whom they interact. The payoff occurs when understanding the value orientations of others provides leaders with information on how they might best influence the practices of others toward socially defensible educational outcomes.

Sophisticated and Authentic Leadership through Self-Knowledge

Two figures, presented below and derived from the work of Hodgkinson (1991), constitute a conceptual framework for developing an understanding of the personal motivations of self as well as those of others. The multiple layers of the figures suggest an onion. The first onion figure represents a syntax of values terminology; the other illustrates the arenas where valuation occurs. Although theoretically derived, these simple graphics have proven to be very useful metaphors for supporting the analysis of social situations in schools as well as the general promotion of reflective practice by school administrators.

When considering Figure 3.1 it is important to keep in mind the perspective of one person, one individual, and not a collective or social context. Also this graphic portrays the interface of the psychological and empirical world in a linear fashion, and suggests a layering and sequence of influence that is not necessarily consistent with what real people perceive in their world. It is a conceptual organizer intended to promote reflection and dialogue on values and valuation processes.

The outer ring in Figure 3.1 represents the observable actions and speech of the individual, the only way of making empirical attributions of the value orientations of the individual. Most people intuitively know to rely on the

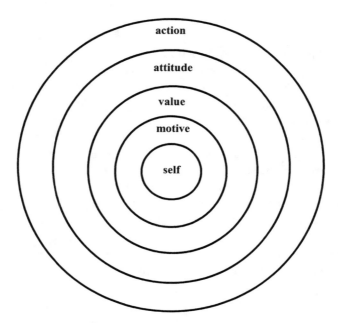

Figure 3.1 Onion 1—Schema of value terms.

clues provided by the actions and attitudes of people around them to obtain predictive insights into the nature of the values and intentions of these individuals. This is a generally sound strategy, but there are some limits to its reliability. For example, observable actions may or may not be accurate indicators of underlying values, particularly when individuals articulate or posture certain values while actually being committed to quite different values. Political leaders are usually a rich source for examples of such behavior.

The next layer into the onion represents attitudes. This is the thin membrane between the values and actions or speech of the individual. To appreciate the nature of attitudes, consider how a father might say to an adolescent son, after witnessing callous behavior or speech at the dinner table, that the son needs an attitude adjustment. The son might predictably protest that he hasn't done anything, to which the father might then reply, "Yes, but I can tell you are about to." The point being, attitudes often reflect our values and predict actions. Attitudes are the residual and often quite persistent influence of values acquired in a context separate from the one in which the individual currently finds himself/herself. The next layer of the onion represents the locus for the specific values a person holds or manifests. It is important to understand that any one value can be held in response to a wide range of motivations. For example, a person might subscribe to honesty as a value to avoid the pain of sanction for dishonesty, or because this is a shared community orientation, or because the consequence of widespread dishonesty is social chaos, or because it is the *right* thing to do at an ethical level.

The next layer of the onion provides the key to understanding the nature and function of values. It represents the motivating force dimension behind the adoption of a particular value. Hodgkinson argued (1991) that motivational bases are at the core of the being of individuals, and values held by an individual reflect these motivational bases. However, care must be exercised before attributing a motivational base to a particular manifested value. Once again, a given value may be held at any of several levels of motivation ranging from preferences, the rational values of consequence and consensus, to the level of transrational principles.

Finally, at the center of the onion is situated the self, the essence of the individual—the biological self as well as the existential or transcendent self.

Existing research evidence (e.g. Begley & Johansson, 1998) suggests that the nonrational motivational bases of *personal preference* (self-interest) and *transrational principles* (social ethics) occur much less frequently in administrative situations than do the rational value types. Principles or ethics become relevant to a given administrative situation when particular circumstances require an ethical posture (e.g., role of the arts in school), where consensus is perceived as difficult to achieve (e.g., an incident of racism in the school), or when urgency requires quick action (e.g., student safety). Furthermore, it may be that the weak influence of personal preferences on administrative practice could be viewed as a good thing. After all, principals are in the end "agents of society" and accountable to society for their actions. While values of personal preference are definitely evident as influences on some administrative processes, existing research suggests that such values were *articulated* infrequently by administrators, probably because of a prevailing social bias toward the rational value types. This rational bias is perhaps an outcome of organizational socialization and cultural expectations, particularly in North America and Europe.

The Arenas of Valuation in School Administration

The second onion (Figure 3.2) illustrates the arenas where valuation processes occur and the dynamics among these arenas. Once again, the graphic conveys a linear sequence that is better considered a conceptual organizer than an accurate predictor of relationship among the various sources of values for real people. With this second onion the individual is represented within the center ring as *self.* This central positioning of the self is appealing to many North Americans who like to emphasize the existential nature of the individual. Those who prefer to highlight the social formation of values in the European and Asian tradition would likely prefer the center core to extend through each of the other rings to reflect the formation of the individual within the multiple contexts of his/her society. The second ring out from the center is termed the arena of the *group.* This ring encompasses the notions of family, peers, friends, and professional colleagues. The third ring is the arena traditionally of most concern to academics in the field of educational administration, the *organization.* Organizational values and the organizational perspectives represented by this arena have traditionally tended to dominate the literature of educational administration. Indeed, much of the author's scholarly career has been devoted to promoting a more balanced view of the administrative process—one that accords at least as much attention to personal perspectives as to organizational perspectives. Nevertheless, a proper appreciation of and sensitivity to the meta-values of organizations is also an essential quality of the sophisticated and sensitive administrator. The fifth arena of the onion figure is devoted to the greater community or society, and *culture.* Finally, an outer ring titled *transcendental* could easily be added to this graphic to convey a category of influence that many individuals sense. This outer ring would accommodate notions of the transcendental—God or the Holy Spirit.

This second onion portrays the various *sources of values,* the arenas where values are encountered, learned, or adopted. However, the onion also illustrates the *sources of value conflicts.* For example, personal values may conflict

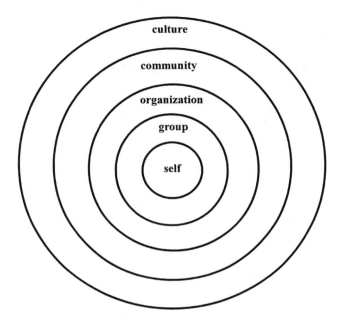

Figure 3.2 Onion 2—Arena of value action.

with those of a community, or professional values may conflict with those of the organizations with which people associate. As a final thought and extension of the onion metaphor, consider what happens when an onion stays in the pantry too long and begins to sprout. When sliced in half, as well as bringing tears to one's eyes, the onion will also show that germination started at the center and worked out through the layers. With an onion, germination does not start in the middle layers! That imagery highlights the central importance of the individual as the catalyst for growth and development within our groups, organizations, communities, and culture. This is especially important when one considers the burgeoning literature that would personify organizations and organized groups (e.g., "learning organizations"). Of course, the flow could equally be construed as going from the outside rings inward if one considers how values are shaped and acquired.

Obstacles to Authentic Leadership in a Global Community

This final section of the chapter examines some obstacles to the achievement of sophistication and sensitivity in the practice of educational administration. A synergy can occur when sophisticated leadership is carried out in a sensitive, reflective manner. Such synergy is a function of authenticity—that is, clearly articulated and socially justifiable intents pursued in a consistent manner by a skillful leader who enjoys the trust and respect of the followership. This type of leadership is far removed from the procedures-oriented managerial orientations of the past. It is a function of sophisticated reflective practice that includes knowledge of oneself, appreciation of the needs and orientations of others, combined with the skills required to establish a shared vision of worthwhile attainable goals among a team of professionals. Although this is an attainable goal, several common personal, social, and/or organizational circumstances confound or complicate the achievement of enlightened administration by managers and leaders of our educational organizations. Some of these obstacles to administrative sensitivity can be best understood as persistent myths that obstruct practices; others are more like social or organizational pathologies. In either case, they are barriers to sensitive and sophisticated leadership practices and common enough that all administrators should be aware of them.

Is Values Consistency Within Individuals, Organizations, and Society a Myth?

Pauline Leonard (1999) of the University of Saskatchewan has conducted research that illustrates the myth of value consistency within individuals and organizations in Canadian schools. She conducted a case study of one school staff in Canada that involved an analysis of the value orientations of individual teachers, teams of teachers, the administrative team, and the formally stated school and district mission statements—all within the same school. She was able to illustrate some quite remarkable variations in value orientations among individual teachers, teams of teachers, and the administration staff. In several situations teachers did not perceive value conflicts despite significant variations in manifested values regarding purposes of education, pedagogical style, and school/community values. Yet there were also other situations where variations in values, often of a relatively minor nature, caused the same teachers to identify significant personal value conflicts. The key to predicting whether or not a variation in value orientations would generate an actual perceived value conflict seems to be the extent to which a value held by a person is a personally defining or core values orientation. Otherwise teachers, at least in this school setting, seem to have a high tolerance for variations in value orientations within their teaching practices, those of their peers, and the articulated values orientations of the school as an organization. Value consistency within these organizations would indeed appear to be a myth. However, once again, further research, particularly in Asian countries such as Hong Kong or Russia with more collective notions of social norms and less emphasis on individual rights, might provide contrasting findings.

Ritual rationality. One of the most familiar theoretical bases for administrative decisionmaking in the Western philosophical tradition is objectivity and rationality. In fact this image of correct or appropriate practice is so pervasive that decisions made by administrators can often be described as "ritual rationality"—a term used to describe the conditioned responses of administrators to the organizational situations they encounter. Ritual rationality occurs when the decisionmaker masks the real intention or likely effects of a decision process by highlighting values acceptable to the stakeholders. For example, in the Canadian province of Ontario the government has frequently demonstrated ritual rationality in relation to justifying educational decisions involving unpopular economic cutbacks. It is important for school leaders to be able to recognize such patterns. One way of doing this is through a values analysis of their own decision processes as well as those of others. Although North Americans have been socialized to worship rationality and taught to strive for it in all they do, especially in professional roles—to the extent that nonrational influences such as emotion and intuition are then suppressed—this is probably impossible and ultimately an undesirable situation. Consider, for example, how the logical outcome of mastering one's emotions, one of the more óbvious nonrational influences, implies an equally undesirable condition of becoming a slave to rationality.

Thick values create community, thin values promote inclusion. Strike (1999) presented compelling arguments about the nature of community and the pursuit of equity. He used the example of Catholic schools in the United States as an illustration of organizations with values "thick" enough to constitute and sustain community. However, there is a cost to adopting values that create community in that they are inevitably *exclusive* in some regard. In contrast, values "thin" enough to promote wide-based inclusion are not conducive to the establishment of community. Strike suggested the problem with many American schools is that in their quest to be inclusive they have ceased to be communities, going so far as to compare them to shopping malls with which one has an instrumental relationship but to which one does not belong in the community sense. This tension between constitutive values and inclusive values is instructive to present concerns for equity in the educational administration context. Strike's solution, to the extent that he offered one, is that schools should adopt "big tent" values, such as democracy, as a way of creating community without restricting inclusiveness. This may be a reasonable approach for the great melting pot of the United States or perhaps Sweden where a single language, robust economy, and homogeneous notion of liberal democracy prevail. However, the same strategy would not suffice in large cosmopolitan Canadian cities like Toronto and Montreal, or Asian cities like Hong Kong. As pointed out at the outset of this chapter, the ethic of democracy has many potential manifestations, not all of which are as inclusive as the American version and all of which are exclusive of some ideas, individuals, and groups. The mistake made by some Americans is assuming that their version of democracy is identical to that of other democracies. In fact these notions of democracy are often cultural isomorphs—similar configurations or shapes, but constructed from radically different elements.

Conclusion

Present social circumstances in many countries imply that more power and influence will accrue to school leaders, or at least there is the potential for this to occur. Depending on the nation being considered, this is as an outcome of deliberate decentralization or general social instability. School administrators could capitalize on these circumstances to do some good. Whenever a leadership vacuum develops, it presents an opportunity to alter the status quo, in this case for the betterment of educational administrative practice. However, this kind of reform will require more than the prevailing managerial orientations of the past and, regrettably, most school administrators remain comfortably mired in managerial tasks. To move beyond the managerial to the greater artistry of sophisticated, sensitive reflective practice implies "action at the margins" or "working the edges" of predominantly managerial work orientations. School administrators need to get out of, or expand, the boundaries of the box of their prevailing working environments. The new leadership literature of educational administration focussing on the values, intents, and motivations of administrators may be one source of inspiration for such enlightened practice. However, because of a prevailing North American bias in much of the literature, educators in other parts of the world, Asia in particular, need to be alert to the potential of misleading cultural isomorphs.

References

Barnard, C. I. (1938). *The functions of the executive.* Cambridge, MA: Harvard University Press.

Begley, P. T., & Johansson, O. (1998). The values of school administration: Preferences, ethics and conflicts. *The Journal of School Leadership. 8*(4), 399–422.

Begley, P. T., & Leonard, P. (1999). *The values of educational administration.* London: Falmer Press.

Begley, P. T. (1995). Using profiles of school leadership as supports to cognitive apprenticeship. *Educational Administration Quarterly, 31*(2),176–202.

Begley, P. T. (1996). Cognitive perspectives on values in administration: A quest for coherence and relevance. *Educational Administration Quarterly, 32*(3), 403–426.

Begley, P. T. (Ed.). (1999). *Values and educational leadership.* Albany, NY: SUNY.

Clark, D. L., Lotto, L. S., & Astuto, T. A. (1984). Effective schools and school improvement: A comparative analysis of two lines of inquiry. *Educational Administration Quarterly, 20*(3), 41–68.

Dimmock, C., & Walker, A. (1998a). Comparative educational administration: Developing a cross-cultural conceptual framework. *Educational Administration Quarterly, 34*(4), 558–595.

Dimmock, C., & Walker, A. (1998b). Toward comparative educational administration: The case for a cross-cultural, school based approach. *Journal of Educational Administration, 36*(4), 379–401.

Greenfield, W. (1999 April). *Moral leadership in schools: Fact or fancy?* Paper delivered at the annual meeting of the American Educational Research Association, Montreal, Quebec.

Hodgkinson, C. (1991). *Educational leadership: The moral art.* Albany: SUNY.

Hodgkinson, C. (1996). *Administrative philosophy.* Oxford, England: Elsevier-Pergamon.

Leithwood, K. A., & Hallinger, P. (1993). Cognitive perspectives on educational administration. *Educational Administration Quarterly, 29 (3),* 296–301.

Leonard, P. (1999). Examining educational purposes and underlying value orientations in schools. In P. T. Begley (Ed.), *Values and educational leadership* (pp. 217–236). Albany, NY: SUNY.

Prestine, N. A., & LeGrand, B. F. (1991). Cognitive learning theory and the preparation of educational administrators: Implications for practice and policy. *Educational Administration Quarterly, 27*(1), 61–89.

Quong, T., Walker, A., & Stott, K. (1998). *Values based strategic planning.* Singapore: Simon & Schuster.

Strike, K. (1999). Can schools be communities? The tension between shared values and inclusion. *Educational Administration Quarterly, 35*(1), 46–70.

Walker, A., & Dimmock, C. (1998). Hong Kong's return to Mainland China: Education policy in times of uncertainty. *Journal of Educational Policy, 13*(1), 3–25.

Walker, A., & Dimmock, C. (1999). A cross-cultural approach to the study of educational leadership: An emerging framework. *Journal of School Leadership, 9*(4), 321–348.

4.

Learning and Teaching

A Cross-Cultural Perspective

DAVID WATKINS

Introduction

Our understanding of the processes of teaching and learning has come a long way in recent years. By combining insights from different disciplines such as psychology, sociology, and linguistics we now have a much clearer picture of the factors that influence learning outcomes (Biggs, 1987; Fraser, Walberg, Welch, & Hattie, 1987; Ramsden, 1988, 1992; Wittrock, 1986). The problem is that we now appreciate that these processes are complex and operate at many different interrelated levels: from that of the individual learner and teacher, the class, the school, the school system, the particular society, the wider cultural level, and the global level (Biggs, 1996). This means that any educational practice must be understood from multiple perspectives, and changes brought about at any one level will probably interact with other factors at the same and other levels. The implication is that educational reform that involves changes to just one factor, teacher training or the mode of assessment say, is unlikely to succeed in improving the quality of education because it may not have taken into consideration the complex, systemic nature of the processes involved. It is the cultural and global levels of this system that are least understood at the moment. The purpose of this paper is to describe recent advances from the cultural perspective.

It is now recognized that many of the findings presented in psychology textbooks around the world are based on research with American psychology undergraduates, typically 20-year-old white males (Lonner, 1989). Moreover, most of the major theories being described and tested such as Kohlberg's theory of moral development, Piaget's theory of cognitive development, Maslow's theory of self-actualization, and Herzberg's theory of job satisfaction are based on the values of Western culture: in particular an individualistic, independent conception of the person. In one of the most influential papers to date in all the psychological literature, Markus and Kitayama (1991) argued that an interdependent conception of the self was more appropriate for most persons from non-Western cultures and that this has implications for basic psychological processes such as cognition, motivation, and emotion.

Much the same criticism could be leveled at our educational textbooks where much of the theorizing and research, such as those described in the first paragraph, have a strong Western influence (if not bias). This does not mean that we should assume that such literature is inappropriate for other cultures but rather that we should find out through research what is appropriate. This would place us in a much stronger position when we come to advise developing countries about how to improve their educational outcomes. Moreover, by understanding how other cultures go about the practice of education we may well find ways of improving Western education. At the very least this understanding may encourage us to reconsider some of the taken-for-granted bases of our educational system at its various levels. Thus, over the last 10 years or so, spurred on by at least superficially disappointing results in international comparisons of educational achievement, American educators have proposed reforms based on analyses of Japanese educational methods (see LeTendre, 1999, for a recent critique of this approach to educational reform).

This chapter describes two areas of cross-cultural research in which this writer and his colleagues have been involved that have distinctive aims and methodologies. The aim of the first is to provide evidence relevant to the issue of the cross-cultural validity of Western principles of student learning. An etic approach to research is adopted where learning process questionnaires developed in the West are used to compare, by means of a method of quantitative synthesis that I refer to as cross-cultural meta-analysis, correlates of approaches to learning and learning outcomes with characteristics of the individual and the learning context in a diverse range of countries. The second uses an in-depth, emic approach to study how Chinese students and teachers think and go about learning and teaching. The results question the cross-cultural relevance of some basic notions of Western theories related to the nature of teaching and learning.

Correlates of Approaches to Learning

In any etic type of research the first step is to demonstrate the equivalence of the measures of interest in the cultures involved. This is a complex task as there are various levels of equivalence that need to be established depending on the aims of the particular study (Hui & Triandis, 1985). In this case, as we wish to compare patterns of correlations across cultures, there is no need to demonstrate the highest and most difficult level of equivalence, metric, because raw scores have the same meaning across cultures, making valid a comparison of means. Rather, we need to establish the equivalence of the underlying concepts and the validity of the constructs measured (for a fuller description of the methodology and findings of this work see Watkins, 2001).

The concepts involved here stem from research into student learning from both qualitative and quantitative perspectives, which have merged into what has become known as the Student Approaches to Learning (SAL) position (Biggs, 1993). The initial thrust came from a paper by Marton and Säljö (1976) which reported a study of Swedish university students who were asked to read an academic article and then explain what and how they had learned. Analysis showed that there were two main ways of doing this task. Some tried to memorize details or key terms in order to be able to answer subsequent questions. They tended to focus on the reading at word or sentence level. Most of the other subjects tried to understand the message that the passage was trying to impart. They tended to focus on the themes and main ideas and generally tried to process the reading for meaning. These intentions and their associated reading strategies were called "surface" and "deep" approaches, respectively. The researchers reported qualitative differences in learning outcomes depending on the approach to reading that had been utilized. Those adopting a deep approach were able to provide a more sophisticated overview of the authors' intentions and frequently used extracts from the reading to support their reasoning. However, students who had adopted a surface approach typically could not explain the authors' message and could only recall isolated factual fragments of the passage.

Quantitative research from the SAL approach was founded by the work of Biggs in Australia and Entwistle in the United Kingdom. Both researchers developed, relatively independently, learning process inventories that owe a debt to the papers of Marton and Säljö (1976) and later literature in their tradition by adopting the "surface/deep" and "approaches to learning" terminology.

Biggs (1987), in developing his Learning Process Questionnaire (LPQ) and its tertiary counterpart, the Student Process Questionnaire (SPQ), and Entwistle and Ramsden (1983), in developing their Approaches to Studying Inventory (ASI), added a third approach, "achieving." Students adopting this approach tried to achieve the highest possible grades by such strategies as working hard and efficiently, and being cue-conscious. They would use any strategy, be it rote memorizing lots of facts or understanding basic principles, that they perceived would maximize their chances of academic success.

Conceptual Equivalence

To assess the conceptual equivalence of the constructs underlying the SAL measures requires qualitative analysis. To my knowledge such studies in non-Western cultures have been conducted to date with students in China, Hong Kong, Nepal, and Nigeria.

To illustrate, there are several studies that support the proposition that the concepts underlying the SAL position are relevant to Nigerian students. An ethnographic study based on 120 hours of observations in Lagos primary schools claimed that Nigerian pupils are trained to believe that getting the right answer by any means, even cheating, is the essence of learning (Omokhodion, 1989). Neither the teachers nor the pupils considered the processes of understanding the problem and of obtaining the solution of any importance. Thus it was concluded that a superficial, surface approach to learning was being encouraged. Further evidence comes from a study where 250 Nigerian university students responded to the question "What strategies do you use to study?" (Ehindero, 1990). Content analysis indicated three main themes in the students' responses: diligence, building up understanding, and memorizing content material without understanding. These themes seem to correspond to the constructs of achieving, deep, and surface approaches to learning, respectively. Further support for the cross-cultural relevance of these constructs came from a study by Watkins and Akande (1994) who content-analyzed the answers of 150 typical Nigerian fourteen to sixteen-year-old secondary school pupils to the question, "What do you mean by learning?"

Construct Validity

A basic condition for the validity of measuring instruments is the adequate reliability of responses to its items. Watkins (1998) reported that the median internal consistency reliability coefficients for responses to the 6 scales of the SPQ by 14 independent samples of 6,500 university students from 10 countries ranged from .55 to .72. In this research only questionnaires with scale alphas for the particular sample exceeding .50 in magnitude were utilized: this is considered to represent an adequate level of reliability for research purposes at the group level (Nunnally, 1978).

Considerable research has shown that the basic constructs of approaches to learning are supported by factor analyses of responses to different learning process instruments in a range of cultures. Thus exploratory factor analysis of responses to the SPQ by university students from eight countries (Watkins, 1998) and confirmatory factor analysis of responses to the LPQ by 10 samples of school students from six countries (Wong, Lin & Watkins,

1996) reported underlying dimensions of deep and surface approaches to learning. A recent review of factor analytic studies of the Appriaches of Studying Inventory (ASI) reached similar conclusions (Richardson, 1994).

While the above evidence of within-construct validity is considerable, there is much less evidence of between-construct validity across cultures. However, evidence that scales of instruments such as the SPQ and ASI are measuring similar constructs comes from between-scale correlations reported by Wilson, Smart, and Watson (1996) and Watkins (2001).

Hypotheses

The purpose of this cross-cultural meta-analysis was to test the generalizability of propositions derived from SAL theory. In particular it is hypothesized that across different cultures deeper, more achievement-focused approaches to learning will be associated with higher academic achievement and greater student self-esteem and an internal locus of control. The basis for these latter two predictions is the proposition that adopting such approaches requires a sufficiently high level of self-confidence and self-responsibility on behalf of students that they can rely on their own understanding and not be overly dependent on the teacher (Biggs, 1987; Schmeck, 1988). We also examined the relationship between the learning environment and the approach to learning students adopt in different cultures. These relationships were all reported for the sample as a whole and for subsamples of Western and non-Western school and university students.

Results

The data for this research was gathered after a search of the literature data bases and personal requests for relevant published and unpublished data from a number of well-known researchers in this area (and included over 20 studies conducted by the writer and his students and collaborators). Table 4.1 reports the average correlations between approaches to learning and self-esteem, locus of control, and academic achievement for school and university students from Western and non-Western countries.

The average correlations between self-esteem and surface, deep, and achieving approaches to learning scales were found to be -.05, .30, and .28, respectively. These figures were based on data from 8,710 respondents from 15 countries and 28 independent samples. The average correlations between deep and achieving approaches and self-esteem exceeded .20 for Western and non-Western school and university subsamples but was particularly strong (.39) for Western university students with the deep approach.

The average correlations between an internal locus of control and surface, deep, and achieving approaches to learning were -.20, .09, and .12.

These figures were based on 28 correlations involving 13,012 respondents from 11 countries and 27 independent samples. Further, it appears that the negative correlation with the surface approach may be higher at school level in both non-Western and Western samples, particularly the latter.

The average correlations between academic achievement and surface, deep, and achieving approaches to learning were found to be −.11, .16, and .18, respectively. These figures were based on data from 28,053 respondents from 15 countries and 28 independent samples; the average correlations appeared to be somewhat higher at school level for Western samples.

It is more difficult to conceptualize learning environments, but based on data from about 4,000 school students from seven studies in four countries it was found in all samples that a deep approach to learning is encouraged by a classroom where the students feel involved and believe their teachers to be supportive. The university data base was from a like-sized sample from three countries and once again good, supportive teaching was typically associated with a deep approach to learning. A surface approach tended to be associated with student perceptions that the workload was too heavy and the assessment inappropriate.

Table 4.1 Average Correlations between Approach to Learning Scales and Self–Esteem, Internal Locus of Control, and Academic Achievement.

Group	Sample Size	Surface Approach	Deep Approach	Achieving Approach
Self–Esteem				
Total	8,710	−.05	.30	.28
School (Western)	2,951	−.04	.25	.31
University (Western)	2,527	−.02	.39	.30
School (non-Western)	1,681	−.05	.27	.28
University (non-Western)	1,551	−.11	.27	.21
Locus of Control				
Total	13,012	−.20	.09	.12
School (Western)	3,248	−.25	.04	.07
University (Western)	1,091	−.03	.18	.25
School (non-Western)	7,534	−.24	.08	.10
University (non-Western)	1,139	−.18	.11	.15
Academic Achievement				
Total	28,053	−.11	.16	.18
School (Western)	3,814	−.21	.18	.28
University (Western)	7,209	−.12	.18	.20
School (non-Western)	14,248	−.13	.12	.18
University (non-Western)	2,782	−.06	.16	.13

The Chinese Learner

Chinese students, particularly those in Hong Kong and more recently the People's Republic itself, have been the focus of much recent research. Much of this work has centered around what has been referred to as "the paradox of the Chinese learner" (see Watkins & Biggs, 1996, for a fuller account of this apparent paradox and related research). This is based on the following premises: rote learning is known to lead to poor learning outcomes; most Chinese students are rote learners; therefore Chinese students should perform badly academically. But the evidence is that students from Hong Kong, Singapore, Taiwan, and at least some areas of China tend to outperform Western students in international comparisons of educational progress and as international students at Western universities (Stevenson & Lee, 1996). An additional aspect of this paradox is why Chinese students typically appear to Western teachers to be "rote learners" when they report not to be when responding to learning strategy questionnaires.

In our discussion of the resolution of this paradox John Biggs and I have pointed to a number of misperceptions of Western educators based on their invalid application of some basic tenets of the Western educational literature to Chinese students.

Memorizing and Understanding

There is no doubt that Western education earlier this century depended too much on rote learning (memorizing without understanding). However, over the last 20 years, educators in countries such as the United Kingdom have tended to reject such learning, and memorizing has fallen into disrepute. (This writer remembers well a phone call from his 14-year-old daughter just starting boarding school in Australia who was dismayed at being asked to memorize something by a teacher—something she had never been asked to do in 9 years in the UK system). There is no doubt that memorizing without understanding can lead at best to very limited learning outcomes. However, the mistake that many Western teachers make when they see a Chinese student memorizing is to assume that he/she is rote learning. Our research, using both learning process questionnaires and in particular in-depth interviews with teachers and students in Hong Kong and China, indicates that many of the teachers and better students do not see memorizing and understanding as separate but rather interlocking processes (Kember, 1996; Marton, Watkins, & Tang, 1997; Watkins & Biggs, 1996) and believe that high quality learning outcomes usually require both processes, which can complement each other. This then was the solution to the "paradox": Chinese students were observed correctly by their Western teachers as making great use of memorization. Indeed if they felt it appropriate they were often able to reproduce model answers many pages long in the exam situation. But many of them were in fact not rote learning at all as their Western teachers supposed but developing their understanding through the process of memorization.

The Role of Repetition

In subsequent research, Dahlin and Watkins (in press) pinpointed the role of repetition in building such an understanding. Through in-depth interviews with Western international school and Chinese system secondary school students in Hong Kong, we were able to show that Chinese students, unlike their Western counterparts, used repetition for two different purposes. On the one hand, it was associated with creating a deep impression and thence with memorization, but on the other, repetition was used to deepen or develop understanding by discovering new meaning. The Western students tended to use repetition to check that they had really remembered something. This finding was consistent with another cross-cultural difference identified by Dahlin and Watkins (in press), namely, that whereas the Western students saw understanding as usually a process of sudden insight, the Chinese students typically thought of understanding as a long process that required considerable mental effort.

Effort versus Ability Attributions

Viewed in the above light, the frequent finding (Biggs, 1996; Hau & Salili, 1991; Salili, 1996) that Chinese students were much more likely to attribute academic success primarily to effort rather than to both effort and ability, like Western students, makes more sense. After all, if you believe that understanding is a sudden, insightful process, then what is the use of a lot of effort? If, however, like the Chinese students, you believe that understanding is a slow process requiring much hard work, then effort attribution for academic success seems logical. To many Chinese students, teachers, and parents, intelligence itself is not something inate and relatively fixed but rather something that can be improved by hard work (Watkins & Biggs, 1996). The wide use of ability grouping of students both between and within secondary schools in Hong Kong and China is difficult to explain, given this belief.

Intrinsic versus Extrinsic Motivation

Other Western dichotomies that do not seem to travel to the Orient are related to the construct of motivation. Western psychology books treat intrinsic and extrinsic motivation as a bipolar construct. The intrinsic end is considered the more desirable by Western educators: "To offer a prize for doing a deed is tantamount to saying that the deed is not worth doing for its own sake" (Neill, 1960, p.162). Contrast this with the Confucian saying that "there are golden houses and beautiful girls in books" (see Lee, 1996). Whereas for

Western students intrinsic motivation is a precursor of the desired deep learning strategies (Biggs, 1987), Watkins and Biggs (1996) argued that for Chinese students the adoption of deep strategies "may be activated by a head of mixed motivational steam: personal ambition, family face, peer support, material reward, and, yes, possibly even interest" (p. 273). At an even more fundamental level, in a Confucian heritage culture are "internal dispositions (that) create a sense of diligence and receptiveness" (Hess & Azuma 1991, p. 7). Such dispositions help make academic tasks "meaningful and worthwhile" at a much more basic level than the Western notion of intrinsic motivation: "in short, the familiar extrinsic/intrinsic polarity collapses" (Watkins & Biggs, 1996, p. 273).

Achievement Motivation: Ego versus Social
Another mainstay of Western educational psychology—achievement motivation—also seems to take a different form in Confucian heritage cultures. In Western societies, achievement motivation is treated as a highly individualistic, ego-enhancing concept. It is characterized by individual competition where the need for success tries to overcome the fear of failure, where winning is its own reward (Atkinson, 1964). But in East Asian societies the notion of success needs to be reinterpreted in a collectivist framework that may involve significant others, the family, peers, or even society as a whole (Holloway, 1988; Salili, 1996). The pressure to succeed academically is there for all children irrespective of the parents' educational level and is very much a matter of "family face" (Ho, 1993).

Collective versus Individual Orientation
The above discussion is linked to the dimension of individualism-collectivism, which has been widely used in cross-cultural psychology to explain differences between cultural groups (Hofstede, 1980; Kim, Triandis, Kagitcibasi, Choi, & Yoon, 1994), though not without criticism (Bond, 1994). Countries of the non-Western world are usually characterized as being collectivist in nature, placing more emphasis on group rather than individual good. The relationships between student and teacher and student and student do seem to take on a somewhat different character in collectivist East Asia. The latter has been less studied, but it has been found that peer tutoring works well in Hong Kong schools (Winter, 1996); Hong Kong students spontaneously collaborate to study outside the tertiary classroom more than do Western students (Tang, 1996); classrooms in Japan and China are characterized by high levels of support and lack of teasing for weaker students (Jin & Cortazzi, 1998); and Hong Kong students prefer a more collaborative learning environment which they see as promoting deeper learning strategies (Chan & Watkins, 1994).

The Chinese Teacher

It is the relationship between teacher and student that is fundamental to understanding the role of the teacher in Chinese classrooms. According to Chinese tradition, the relationship between a teacher and his students is akin to that of a parent and his sons. This is another area where Western observers often see only part of the picture. Thus the comment by Ginsberg (1992, p. 6) that a lecturer in China is an authority figure, "a respected elder transmitting to a subordinate junior," certainly has a ring of truth. However, the typical method of teaching is not simple transmission of superior knowledge but utilizes considerable interaction in a mutually accepting social context.

The Good Teacher

The cultural differences here were brought out in a study of British and Chinese secondary school students by Jin and Cortazzi (1998). The British students characterized a good teacher as one who is able to arouse the students' interest, explain clearly, use effective instructional methods, and organize a range of activities: these are very much the "teaching skills" taught in typical Western teacher education method courses. The Chinese students, however, preferred the teacher to have deep knowledge, be able to answer questions, and be a good moral model. In terms of teacher–student relationships, the British students liked their teachers to be patient and sympathetic regarding students who had difficulty following the lesson, whereas the Chinese students considered their relationship with a good teacher would be a friendly, warm one well beyond the classroom. This perception of Chinese teachers as friendly and warm-hearted has been noted by a number of researchers and linked to the Confucian concept of "ren" (Gao, 1998; Jin & Cortazzi, 1998), which translates to something like human-heartedness or love. Indeed, according to Jin and Cortazzi (1998), all education in Mainland China is based on Confucian principles even though the teachers and students are often unaware of their source. These principles include the high value placed on education by society; that learning involves reflection and application; that hard work can compensate for lack of ability (see above); that the teacher is a model both of knowledge and morality; and the value that learning is a moral duty and studying hard is a responsibility to the family (see also Lee, 1996).

The Good Student

The latter value seems to be accepted by students throughout much of East Asia and has a major impact on the classroom climate. Whereas in Britain it is the good students who obey and pay attention to what the teacher is saying, in China that is something both the students and teachers take for granted of all students (Jin & Cortazzi 1998). Thus the teacher in China spends little time and effort on disciplinary matters and can focus on other aspects of education.

Chinese Conceptions of Teaching

The view that the Chinese teacher should not only be of good character but should also be concerned with the moral development of his/her students is a strong theme of a study by Gao (1998). A major aim of that study was to develop a model of conceptions of teaching appropriate for secondary school physics teachers in the Guangdong province of China. After numerous in-depth interviews, classroom observations, and a pilot quantitative survey, Gao developed a model with five basic conceptions (knowledge delivery, exam preparation, ability development, attitude promotion, and conduct guidance). The first two of these were grouped into a higher order "moulding" orienta-tion that corresponds fairly well with the "transmission" dimension identified in Western research (see, for example, Kember & Gow 1994). The remaining three lower-level conceptions were grouped by Gao into a higher order "culti-vating" orientation. This not only involved a concern with developing student understanding and higher quality learning outcomes, as in the "facilitating" dimension of Kember and Gow, but broadened it to focus on affective outcomes such as developing the students' love of science and also moral (not ideological) aspects such as their responsibilities to their families and society as a whole.

Group Work, Chinese-Style

Another source of misperception of Western observers is the way Chinese teachers use group work. The usual Western approach is to split the class up into pairs or small groups, say of four to five, and then have members of each group discuss an issue or work on a problem together at the same time as other groups. As Jin and Cortazzi (1998) argued, many Western teachers try to involve students in the class activities through simultaneous pupil talk. Large class sizes are seen as a constraint on this teaching method. By way of contrast, Chinese teachers often use sequential talk for the purpose of involve-ment. A typical approach is for two pupils to stand in different parts of the classroom, then for one to ask the other a question or comment on the answer given by the other student to the teacher's question. On other occasions two pupils may come to the front of the class to perform a dialogue that has been prepared in advance to the teacher and the rest of the class. To many Western observers this seems a travesty of group work as only two pupils are involved at a time. What makes this approach work in the context of the Chinese classroom is that the rest of the class consider they learn through listening to the teacher or their peers. Jin and Cortazzi (1998) presented evidence from observation, videos, and photographs that during such group work the remainder of the class is indeed paying attention and thinking about what is being said for they may well be asked to comment next. They argued that this Chinese approach to group work is cognitive-centered in contrast with the Western approach which tends to be more skills-centered particularly in the language learning area. A fundamental reason such a group approach works well in China is due to the emphasis on moral training discussed earlier: to listen attentively is one's duty and shows respect for the teacher, other pupils, and indeed learning itself. The approach seems to work well—even in large classes—so that Chinese teachers are not dismayed by facing 50 to 60 pupils as their Western counterparts may well be.

Questioning in the Chinese Classroom
The group performances described above are "talking of the known rather than talking to know" (Jin & Cortazzi, 1998, p. 743). According to these authors, student questioning of the teacher in classrooms in China also takes on a similar function. Whereas Western teachers expect questions to be asked by students during the process of learning to fill in gaps in their knowledge or to aid understanding of the reasoning involved, Chinese students ask questions after they have learned independently of the teacher. They consider that questions should be based on knowledge. Jin and Cortazzi (1998) pointed out that this can cause problems for Chinese studying overseas who may consider Western classmates rude for asking questions based on their ignorance. Western teachers cannot understand why Chinese students do not ask questions earlier in the learning process.

Conclusions

Perhaps not surprisingly, to understand cultural influences on the teaching and learning process turns out to be rather complex. Indeed cultural, individual difference, and contextual influences may be so closely interwined that it may not be possible to separate these factors. What is clear though is while at a relatively basic level fundamental Western concepts such as surface and deep approaches to learning are relevant in a number of non-Western countries, at a deeper level cultural differences emerge that question some of the tenets of Western educational psychology and approaches to teacher training.

The meta-analysis described in this paper does indicate that across a number of very different cultures and at both school and university levels, higher quality learning strategies are associated with higher student self-esteem and internal locus of control. Of course we need to be careful from making causal inferences from correlational evidence. But these results are consistent with the theoretical propositions that deeper approaches to learning are more likely to be adopted by students who are confident in their own capacity to learn and accept responsibility for their own learning (Biggs, 1987; Schmeck, 1988). The writer has postulated that these are necessary but not sufficient conditions for higher quality learning processes in any culture (Watkins, 2001). Attempts to improve student learning outcomes in non-Western countries could try to adapt recently developed Western methods for improving self-esteem and locus of control (see, for instance, Hattie 1992) but more culturally relevant approaches may be needed.

Unfortunately, higher quality learning outcomes are not always reflected in higher academic grades in any culture. Thus the relatively low correlations reported here between approaches to learning and academic achievement in both Western and non-Western cultures are disappointing but not unexpected. Indeed, research has consistently shown that high achieving cue-conscious students, of whom the Chinese are prime examples, are likely to adopt superficial learning strategies if they believe that quantity rather than quality of learning will be rewarded by course assessment (Scouller, 1998; Thomas & Bain, 1984). As the assessment system is under the control of classroom teachers or other educators, it is up to them to convince students that higher quality learning outcomes will be rewarded by the assessment system: less use of multiple-choice questions is often a good place to start. It also seems that in both Western and non-Western classrooms deeper learning outcomes are associated with students feeling that they are involved in their classes, supportive teachers, and a fair workload. Again, these are factors often under the control of the classroom teacher.

Our in-depth research of Chinese students also indicates that a number of basic concepts of Western educational thought need to be reconsidered in the context of Chinese classrooms. Before reviewing these findings I would like to say a little about the degree to which our findings are due to Chinese cultural influences. In discussing this issue in our edited book (Watkins & Biggs, 1996), Biggs and I argued that Chinese students, whether in Singapore, Hong Kong, the People's Republic, or anywhere else in the world, shared a Confucian cultural heritage that influenced their attitudes to and methods of learning. We do not, of course, claim all Chinese students are the same, but we do believe from the research evidence that many Chinese students—because of their cultural heritage—approach education in a different way from most Western students. Biggs (1996) described the Chinese as "docile" students. He used that term in its original sense of "teachable": they enter the classroom believing that their teachers are their friends and moral guides who have valuable knowledge that it is their duty as students to learn. This attitude permeates so much that goes on in the Chinese classroom. Unlike the situation in the West, teachers in China do not have to spend much time and effort getting the students on-task in the classroom or to work hard at home.

One of the consequences of this is that some of the Western teacher education emphasis on getting students on-task and coping with classroom behavioral problems may not be so necessary in the Chinese context. However, my own postgraduate students, most of whom are full-time teachers, assure me the situation in Hong Kong is rather different, and indeed a common request from our student teachers is for more classes on classroom disciplinary and management techniques.

A common criticism of East Asian classrooms is that while they may be effective for transmitting reproductive knowledge and for skills learning, creativity is stifled. However, Jin and Cortazzi (1998) argued that in China teachers see creativity as a slow process that depends on solid basic knowledge. Consequently while for many British teachers "children learn through being creative" (Jin & Cortazzi, 1998, p. 756), Chinese teachers see the process as reversed. These views of creativity seem to have something in common with cross-cultural differences in conceiving of understanding as a rapid, insightful rather than a slow, developmental process reported by Dahlin and Watkins (in press).

Educators in Hong Kong, Singapore, and Japan are currently trying to propose reforms that will encourage more independent, creative learning outcomes. Perhaps, before rushing in to adopt Western methods, they should look more seriously at the validity of these views at least in their cultural context if not more broadly. Likewise when Western educators look to East Asia to improve their own countries' educational outcomes they need to seriously consider the cultural context of such reforms.

References

Atkinson, J. W. (1964). *An introduction to motivation.* New York: Van Nostrand.

Biggs, J. B. (1987). *Student approaches to learning and studying.* Melbourne: Australian Council for Educational Research.

Biggs, J. B. (1993). What do inventories of students' learning processes really measure? A theoretical review and clarification. *British Journal of Educational Psychology, 63,* 3–19.

Biggs, J. B. (1996). Western misperceptions of the Confucian-heritage learning culture. In D. Watkins & J. Biggs (Eds.), *The Chinese learner: Cultural, psychological, and cultural influences* (pp. 45–68). Hong Kong / Melbourne: Comparative Education Research Centre/Australian Council for Educational Research.

Bond, M. H. (1994). Into the heart of collectivism: A personal and scientific journey. In U. Kim, H. C. Triandis, C. Kagitcibasi, S. C. Choi, & G. Yoon (Eds.), *Individualism and collectivism: Theory, method, and applications* (pp. 66–76). Newbury Park, CA: Sage.

Chan, Y. Y. G., & Watkins, D. (1994). Classroom environment and approaches to learning: An investigation of the actual and preferred perceptions of Hong Kong secondary school students. *Instructional Science, 22,* 233–246.

Dahlin, B., & Watkins, D. (in press). The role of repetition in the processes of memorizing and understanding: A comparison of the views of Western and Chinese secondary school students in Hong Kong. *British Journal of Educational Psychology.*

Ehindero, O. J. (1990). A discriminant function analysis of study strategies, logical reasoning ability and achievement across major teaching undergraduate curricula. *Research in Education, 44,* 1–11.

Entwistle, N. J., & Ramsden, P. (1983). *Understanding student learning*. London: Croom Helm.

Fraser, B. J., Walberg, H. J., Welch, W. W., & Hattie, J. A. (1987). Synthesis of educational productivity research. *International Journal of Educational Research, 11*, 145–252.

Gao, L. B. (1998). *Conceptions of teaching held by school physics teachers in Guangdong, China and their relations to student learning*. Unpublished doctoral dissertation, University of Hong Kong.

Ginsberg, E. (1992). Not just a matter of English. *HERDSA News, 14*(1), 6–8.

Hattie, J. A. (1992). *The self-concept*. Hillsdale, NJ: Lawrence Erlbaum.

Hau, K. T., & Salili, F. (1991). Structure and semantic differential placement of specific causes: Academic causal attributions by Chinese students in Hong Kong. *International Journal of Psychology, 26*, 175–193.

Hess, R. D., & Azuma, M. (1991). Cultural support for schooling: Contrasts between Japan and the United States. *Educational Researcher, 20*(9), 2–8.

Ho, D. Y. F. (1993). Relational orientation in Asian social psychology. In U. Kim & J. W. Berry (Eds.), *Indigenous psychologies* (pp. 240–259). Newbury Park, CA: Sage.

Hofstede, G. (1980). *Culture's consequences: International differences in work-related values*. Beverly Hills, CA: Sage.

Holloway, S. D. (1988). Concepts of ability and effort in Japan and the US. *Review of Educational Research, 58*, 327–345.

Hui, C. H., & Triandis, H. C. (1985). Measurement in cross-cultural psychology: A review and comparison of strategies. *Journal of Cross-Cultural Psychology, 16*, 131–152.

Jin, L., & Cortazzi, M. (1998). Dimensions of dialogue, large classes in China. *International Journal of Educational Research, 29*, 739–761.

Kember, D. (1996). The intention to both memorize and understand: Another approach to learning? *Higher Education, 31*, 341–354.

Kember, D., & Gow, L. (1994). Orientations to teaching and their effect on the quality of student learning. *Journal of Higher Education, 65*, 58–74.

Kim, U., Triandis, H., Kagitcibasi, C., Choi, S. C., & Yoon, G. (Eds.). (1994). *Individualism and collectivism*. Newbury Park, CA: Sage.

Lee, W. O. (1996). The cultural context of Chinese learners: Conceptions of learning in the Confucian tradition. In D. Watkins & J. Biggs (Eds.), *The Chinese learner: Cultural, psychological, and cultural influences* (pp. 25–41). Melbourne: Australia Council for Educational Research.

LeTendre, G. K. (1999). The problem of Japan: Qualitative studies and international educational comparisons. *Educational Researcher, 28*(2), 38–45.

Lonner, W. (1989). The introductory psychology text and cross-cultural psychology. In D. Keats, D. Munro, & L. Mann (Eds.), *Heterogeneity in cross-cultural psychology* (pp. 4–22). Amsterdam: Swets & Zeitlinger.

Markus, H. R., & Kitayama, S. (1991). Culture and the self: Implications for cognition, emotion, and motivation. *Psychological Review, 98*, 224–253.

Marton, F., & Säljö, R. (1976). On qualitative differences in learning: Outcome and process. *British Journal of Educational Psychology, 46*, 4–11.

Marton, F., Watkins, D., & Tang, C. (1997). Discontinuities and continuities in the experience of learning: An interview study of high school students in Hong Kong. *Learning and Instruction, 7*, 21–48.

Neill, A. S. (1960). *Summerhill*. New York: Hart.

Nunnally, J. C. (1978). *Psychometric theory* (2nd ed.). New York: McGraw Hill.

Omokhodion, J. O. (1989). Classroom observed: The hidden curriculum in Lagos, Nigeria. *International Journal of Educational Development, 9*, 99–110.

Ramsden, P. (1988). *Improving learning: New perspectives*. London: Kogan Page.

Ramsden, P. (1992). *Learning to teach in higher education*. London: Routledge.

Richardson, J. T. E. (1994). Cultural specificity of approaches to studying in higher education: A literature survey. *Higher Education, 27*, 449–468.

Salili, F. (1996). Accepting personal responsibility for learning. In D. Watkins & J. Biggs (Eds.), *The Chinese learner: Cultural, psychological, and cultural influences* (pp. 85–106). Melbourne: Australia Council for Educational Research.

Schmeck, R. (Ed.). (1988). *Learning strategies and learning styles.* New York: Plenum.

Scouller, K. (1998). The effect of assessment method on students' learning approaches: Multiple choice question examination versus assignment essay. *Higher Education, 35,* 453–472.

Stevenson, H. W., & Lee, S. Y. (1996). The academic achievement of Chinese students. In M. H. Bond (Ed.), *The handbook of Chinese psychology* (pp. 124–142). Hong Kong: Oxford University Press.

Tang, K. C. C. (1996). Collaborative learning: The latent dimension in Chinese students' learning. In D. Watkins & J. Biggs (Eds.), *The Chinese learner: Cultural, psychological, and cultural influences* (pp. 183–204). Melbourne: Australia Council for Educational Research.

Thomas, P., & Bain, J. (1984). Contextual differences in learning approaches: The effects of assessment. *Human Learning, 3,* 227–240.

Watkins, D. (1998). Assessing approaches to learning: A cross-cultural perspective. In B. Dart &. G. Boulton-Lewis (Eds.), *Teaching and learning in higher education* (pp. 124–144). Melbourne: Australia Council for Educational Research.

Watkins, D. (2001). *Correlates of approaches to learning: A cross-cultural meta-analysis.* In R. Sternberg & L. F. Zhang (Eds.). *Perspectives on thinking, learning, and cognitive styles* (pp. 165–196). Mnwah, NJ: Lawrence Erlbaum.

Watkins, D., & Akande, A. (1994). Approaches to learning of Nigerian secondary school children: Emic and etic perspectives. *International Journal of Psychology, 29,* 165–182.

Watkins, D., & Biggs, J. (Eds.). (1996). *The Chinese learner: Cultural, psychological, and contextual influences.* Melbourne: Australia Council for Educational Research.

Wilson, K. L., Smart, R. M., & Watson, R. J. (1996). Gender differences in approaches to learning in first year psychology students. *British Journal of Educational Psychology, 66,* 59–72.

Winter, S. (1996). Peer tutoring and learning outcomes. In D. Watkins & J. Biggs (Eds.), *The Chinese learner: Cultural, psychological, and cultural influences* (pp. 221–242). Melbourne: Australia Council for Educational Research.

Wittrock, M. (Ed.). (1986). *Handbook of research on teaching* (3rd ed.). New York: Macmillan.

Wong, N. Y., Lin, W. Y., & Watkins, D. (1996). Cross-cultural validation of models of approaches to learning: An application of confirmatory factor analysis. *Educational Psychology, 16,* 317–327.

5

Issues in the Investigation of School Leadership across Cultures

Ron Heck

Over the past decade or so there have been calls for increasing attention to the study of educational administration across contexts and national settings (e.g., Chapman, Sackney, & Aspin, 1999; Dimmock & Walker, 1998; Greenfield, 1995; Hallinger, 1992, 1995; Hallinger & Leithwood, 1996; Hallinger & Murphy, 1986, Hughes, 1988; Paige & Mestenhauser, 1999; Teddlie & Reynolds, 2000). Researchers' interest in studying educational administration comparatively is because of the realization internationally that schooling practices are diverse and, with tremendous progress in world communication, there are increased possibilities for collaboration with colleagues holding similar interests in varied global settings. The cross-fertilization of approaches toward educational policy and practice across nations has produced increased awareness of other systems, exchange of ideas, international assessments of progress, and research aimed at understanding important global educational problems such as educational effectiveness, decentralization, school restructuring, and accountability (Baker Akiba, LeTendre, & Wiseman, 2001; Chapman et al., 1999; Dimmock & Walker, 1998; Hallinger & Leithwood, 1996; Schmidt & Prawat, 1999).

One area that has drawn attention internationally is how schooling processes affect student learning and, more specifically, how school leadership (i.e., as exhibited by principals or others in the school) contributes to the schooling effort. Since the emergence of research focusing on school effectiveness in the late 1970s (e.g., Brookover, Schweitzer, Schneider, Beady, Flood, & Wisenbacker, 1978; Edmonds 1979; Rutter M., Maugham, B., Mortimore, P., Ouston, J., & Smith, A., 1979), educators internationally have come to view school leadership as central to school effectiveness and academic improvement. School leaders play central roles in linking the internal and external environments of the school (Firestone & Louis, 1999). As Teddlie and Reynolds

(2000) concluded in an international review of school effectiveness studies, "We do not know of a study that has not shown that leadership is important within effective schools. . . . Indeed, 'leadership' is now centrally synonymous with school effectiveness for many, including many operating within the school improvement paradigm also" (p. 141). In fact, since 1980 school leadership has also become an influential domain within the field of educational administration, despite the fact that the empirical knowledge base on which this view is based has been described as ambiguous and disconnected (Hallinger & Heck, 1999; Ouston, 1999).

Despite the optimism of these claims across several empirical literatures, there are still considerable gaps in our knowledge about how school leadership influences schooling processes and improvement from a global and comparative perspective. Past research on school effects has more often focused on variables that explained differences in schools' effectiveness (e.g., such as strong principal leadership), rather than on identifying the processes through which schools can actually become more effective over time (Ouston, 1999; Teedlie & Reynolds, 2000). It has also been described as largely ethnocentric (Reynolds, 2000), as opposed to comparative. Moreover, the studies were not specifically designed to investigate how school leadership might impact on effectiveness. In school effectiveness studies, leadership (defined in a variety of different ways) was generally a part of a constellation of school processes that affect student learning. The school effectiveness movement, which often assumed that organizational change was a rational process, therefore, may have overemphasized the role of the school principal in actually making such improvements happen (Hallinger & Heck, 1999; Ouston, 1999).

In contrast to the school effectiveness literature, the school improvement literature (e.g., Berman & McLaughlin, 1978; Corbett, Firestone, & Rossman, 1988; Louis, Toole, & Hargreaves, 1999) has focused on identifying processes of site-level change (e.g., initiating change, implementing change) and, more recently, managing change (Fullan, 1996). Establishing whether change in fact leads to higher outcomes has been less studied from the school improvement perspective. While the school improvement research has documented the internal process of school change, including the contribution of leadership, most of this research in recent years has involved small-scale studies that employ qualitative methods (Reynolds, 2000). This approach produces results suggesting that change is school based and contextually dependent. This research, therefore, has not demonstrated much of a comparative focus, although there have been a few attempts to implement findings from one context into improvement attempts in another context (Reynolds, 2000). In fact, as Ouston (1999) and Reynolds concluded, for much of the international community, school effectiveness and school improvement represent two relatively unlinked literatures in terms of their core conceptualizations, beliefs, and proposed strategies for improving schools. Resulting blueprints that explain what school leaders and personnel can do to help schools improve, and are based on solid empirical evidence that documents the improvement over time (including changes in test scores), have been slow to appear.

Another research program that has drawn considerable international attention is the leadership role of school principals. This research also determined that leadership is central to school effectiveness and to efforts to improve the school academically (Hallinger & Heck, 1999). A review of these studies found that the principal's role has changed considerably in many nations over the past two decades, requiring a range of new responsibilities and, notably, the sharing of authority and leadership among others within the school community. The studies showed considerable diversity in terms of their purposes, research questions, methods, and findings. The accumulated research produced identifiable research strands of varying sophistication on the nature of the school leader's work, leadership effects, the micropolitics of the school, the social construction of leadership, and leadership's contribution to wider issues of social justice (Heck & Hallinger, 1999). Similar to the school effectiveness and improvement studies, however, few of the school leadership studies were specifically designed to investigate leadership comparatively.

The absence of an international and comparative perspective across many of the research programs that focus on school effects, school improvement, and school leadership hampers efforts to solve educational problems in many countries that are heavily engaged in research on schooling. A few examples of these current issues internationally include the implementation of educational standards, the comparison of educational progress, and the decentralization of educational decision making. Changes in the governance of schools and their relationship to other socializing agencies across nations make the comparative study of education important. As societies become more culturally diverse and globally interdependent, comparative studies can give insights into the assumptions, structures, processes, and outcomes of educational systems (Dimmock & Walker, 1998; Hallinger & Leithwood, 1996; Reynolds, 2000).

Currently, the field of educational administration lacks cross-cultural models, theoretical frameworks, and taxonomies for comparing schools and school systems internationally (Dimmock & Walker, 1998; Hallinger, 1995; Hallinger & Leithwood, 1996; Reynolds, 2000). While there are several well-defined conceptual frameworks for studying school leadership supported by empirical evidence, researchers know less about how the wider sociocultural context affects leadership and other school processes (Hallinger & Heck, 1996a; Hallinger & Leithwood, 1996). Proposing a new orientation toward international and comparative research on school leadership is likely to open up a host of issues that will need to be addressed (e.g., Dimmock & Walker, 1998; see Hallinger & Leithwood, 1996). The purpose of this chapter is to present a number of conceptual and methodological issues that may be relevant in investigating school leadership processes and their impact across cultural or national settings. More specifically, the aims are (1) to describe how the field has investigated school leadership in the past (e.g., its research purposes, epistemological frames, models, and methods); and(2) to comment on how some of these understandings might help us frame the study of school leadership comparatively.

Approaches to the Study of School Leadership

Twenty years ago, Bridges (1982) raised the concern that much of the research being done in educational administration was atheoretical and poorly conducted. In contrast to Bridges' earlier review, however, Hallinger and Heck (1999) noted a considerable trend toward the accumulation of knowledge in one specific subset of educational administration research. This subset was research conducted on school leadership during the two decades after Bridges' review. Hallinger and Heck also found increasing conceptual and methodological sophistication within the set of studies, which were conducted in quite a number of different national settings. At the same time, immersion in the set of studies revealed the need to foster the examination of school leadership through more diverse lenses and methods (Heck & Hallinger, 1999). Other orientations toward the study of school leadership have emerged in recent years that offer potential for increasing our understanding from a global perspective. These orientations derive from a broader range of epistemological views, raise different research questions, and employ a more diverse set of research methods.

Broadly speaking, several epistemological orientations toward the study of school leadership exist that have their roots in positivist, interpretive, and socially critical theories of knowledge. All three of these more general theories partition the domain of knowledge rather arbitrarily and when traced to their origins, they seem to be discipline-related expressions of ideological commitment, rather than universally reliable truths (Macpherson, 1996). Each has spawned various theoretical approaches toward the study of school leadership (e.g., structural-functionalism, political-conflict theory, constructivism, critical theory). The proliferation of approaches, however, makes it difficult to establish any "neat" system of categorizing previous research. Thus, the research categorization schemes proposed previously in educational administration (e.g., Evers & Lakomski, 1996; Goetz, LeCampte, & 1988; Heck & Hallinger, 1999; Hoy, 1994; Maxcy, 1995; Slater, 1995) do not easily fit with each other.

Heck and Hallinger's (1999) review of research on school leadership methods suggested that researchers often work on a particular problem from a relatively narrow focus (e.g., one or two specific research questions and their resultant method of investigation). This type of more focused approach to inquiry has been called filling in "blank spots" in the empirical knowledge base (Wagner, 1993). An example of one particular research focus was describing the work (e.g., tasks and behavior) of the principal. In the process of filling in the blanks, however, other researchers' orientations to the study of school leadership can be overlooked by a particular research program. These other orientations become "blind spots" in a particular program of research. An example of one of these blind spots mentioned previously is the relatively unrelated empirical literatures from the school effectiveness and the school improvement research programs.

Theorists suggest that researchers' thinking about these types of conceptual and methodological issues is embedded in their cultural conditions and circumstances (Gronn & Ribbins, 1996; Hallinger & Leithwood, 1996; Paige & Mestenhauser, 1999). Over time, there has been surprisingly little research on school leadership that is cross-cultural (Bajunid, 1996; Dimmock & Walker, 1998). Because researchers in the past have focused almost exclusively on their own national settings, the potential influence of cultural beliefs, values, and traditions on school leadership represents another of those blind spots in our understanding. In the next section, several of these different research orientations are presented as a way of summarizing how school leadership has been studied in the past and suggesting what possibilities and limitations might exist for studying it more internationally and comparatively in the future.

The Structural-Functional Approach
Historically within educational administration, research on school leadership has focused predominantly on the principal's role, as the notion of leadership has been most often associated with formal organizational roles (Boyan, 1988). The structural-functional (or rational) approach has been the dominant research lens (Ogawa & Bossert, 1995). From this perspective, organizations are viewed as relatively closed systems with their own cultures, values, and mechanisms (structures) that function toward the primary end of maintaining the equilibrium of the system. External environmental and cultural influences may be acknowledged but have been largely ignored in the empirical research. The structural-functional perspective emphasizes two features about organizations—formal structure and the pursuit of goals (Scott, 1992).

This perspective includes several assumptions about the nature of leadership and, hence, how it should be researched: (a) leaders are individuals who possess certain attributes or act in certain ways; (b) individuals in specific organizational roles (such as the principal) exercise leadership; and (c) leaders function to influence organizational performance (i.e., to maintain the organization). Leadership in the rational view of organizations, therefore, is generally defined as the influence that individuals in higher positions exert through their demographic traits (e.g., experience, education) and actions on the culture and performance of the organization. This orientation also produced a number of related leadership conceptualizations including situational theory and contingency theory; however, these latter conceptualizations have fallen out of favor with researchers over the past decade or so (Slater, 1995).

Empirical descriptions from a rational perspective about the functions of principals' roles (what they do and why) have appeared in the literature for nearly 45 years now (e.g., Crowson & Porter-Gehrie, 1980; Gronn, 1984; Inbar, 1977; Kmetz & Willower, 1982; Peterson, 1978; Salley, McPherson, & Baehr, 1979; Wolcott, 1973). These studies of the nature of principals' position and work were the norm during the 1960s to early 1980s (Bridges, 1982), resulting in lists of their personal "traits" and the time they spent on individual tasks (Boyan, 1988). One representative study (Salley et al., 1979) examined how personal traits of school administrators such as experience, gender, intelligence, training, locus of control, and leadership style correlated with the nature of their work or their behavior. Researchers did not attempt to link these descriptions to other processes and outcomes (Boyan, 1988; Bridges, 1982).

A small number of these descriptions included preliminary comparisons of principals' work between cultural settings (e.g., Chung & Miskel, 1989; Gali, 1988; Sara, 1981). For example, Chung and Miskel (1989) interviewed and observed five secondary principals in Korea and compared their findings to observational studies on principals conducted in the United States. They emphasized similarities in the nature of the work across the two settings (e.g., long hours, fast-paced work, involved in few instructional activities). From this, Chung and Miskel concluded that cultural differences were relatively insignificant. Gali (1988) also concluded that studies conducted on administrators' work across a variety of settings yielded little support for the influence of culture in defining principals' work. With these initial discouraging results, this early comparative work directed at describing the tasks and behavior of principal died out.

Over time, it appears that much of the knowledge accumulated from this specific orientation toward the study of school leadership has been of limited use for building theory. For example, administrative traits have never been shown to be valid indicators of important theoretical domains of leadership, nor consistent predictors of school outcomes (Hallinger & Heck, 1996a; Heck, 1991; Slater, 1995). As Boyan concluded in 1988, the cumulative set of studies on administrative work and determinants of administrator behavior over 30 years "appears to be an incomplete anthology of short stories connected by no particular story line or major themes" (p. 93). This would underscore its limited value in developing a comparative research perspective on school leadership for the future.

Administrative effects. By the early 1980s, descriptive studies of school administrators (especially in urban, elementary school settings) often had as their goal the creation of lists of "effective" school correlates and the traits of "effective" administrators (Hallinger & Heck, 1996a). This specific concern began a shift in thinking toward discovering how principals' attitudes, values, and actions impacted on school processes and outcomes (Pitner, 1988). This shift away from the description of the school principal's work to the impact of this work had two general sources. First, research on change implementation identified the important part principals played (e.g., support, gatekeeping) in planned efforts directed at improving the school academically (Berman & McLaughlin, 1978; Firestone & Corbett, 1988). Second, concurrent "effective schools" research conducted in both Great Britain and the United States concluded that strong principal leadership was among those factors within the school that contributed to student learning (Brookover & Lezotte, 1977; Brookover et al., 1978; Edmonds, 1979; Rutter et al., 1979).

Given policy makers' concerns with improving schools and research findings on the centrality of the principal's role to the school improvement during the 1970s and 1980s, the accumulated research on principal effects, undertaken largely from a structural-functional perspective, demonstrated the positive impact of principals on a variety of school processes, school achievement, and other measures of effectiveness (e.g., Firestone, 1990; Greenfield, Licata, & Johnson, 1992; Johnson & Holdaway, 1990; Leithwood, 1994; Silins, 1994; Pounder, Ogawa, & Adams, 1995; Tarter, Bliss, & Hoy, 1989). In one review of this accumulated research, Hallinger and Heck (1996a) found that some 40 principal effectiveness studies had been conducted in over 12 separate countries (e.g., Australia, Canada, Hong Kong, Israel, the Netherlands, Singapore, United Kingdom, United States). Because of the flexibility in theoretical models of leadership employed (e.g., instructional leadership, transformational leadership), diversity in research settings, sampling and instrumentation, and techniques used to analyze the data, the convergence of findings across the studies gave considerable credibility to conclusions about the principal's direct impact on school processes and indirect impact on outcomes.

At the same time, however, the preoccupation with documenting whether or not principals make a difference in school outcomes subtly reinforced the assumption that school leadership was synonymous with the principal's role, and that the focus of this role was directed toward achieving the goal of high outcomes (Heck & Hallinger, 1999). This limited perspective was largely driven by educational accountability (Glasman & Heck, 1992), at least in many international settings. Scholars during this period, therefore, largely ignored other sources of leadership within the school such as assistant principals, teachers, and parents, as well as other ways in which leadership was influential. Another limitation was that although geographic scope of the research was global and its findings influential, it was not specifically designed to be comparative in nature. Therefore, little was discovered about how various cultural settings might have impacted upon the specific expression and impact of school leadership within each setting. A third limitation was that the studies were typically based on Western models of leadership consistent with a more singular set of educational values and conditions emerging over the past two decades in those countries (e.g., accountability, decentralization of authority and power to the local level, a focus on school improvement, to name a few). For example, several of the countries where studies were published have close ties with, or educational systems modeled on, the United States or the United Kingdom.

New Orientations for the Study of School Leadership

Over the past couple of decades, an enormous amount of criticism in educational administration has been directed at traditional research conceptualizations (i.e., positivism, structural functionalism), methods of analysis (e.g., hypothesis testing, quantitative methods), and constructions of knowledge (Bates, 1980; Everhart, 1988; Evers & Lakomski, 1996; Foster, 1986; Greenfield, 1980). This criticism resulted in considerably more flexibility in studying the principal's role (e.g., Anderson, 1990, 1991; Blase, 1989, 1993; Dillard, 1995; Greenfield, 1991; Gronn & Ribbins, 1996; Hall & Rutherford, 1983; Hoy, 1994; Leithwood & Hallinger, 1993; Marshall, 1995; Mawhinney, 1999; Maxcy, 1995; Slater, 1995), as well as leadership that is exercised by others within the school setting (Hart, 1994; Ogawa & Bossert, 1995; Pounder et al., 1995). In many ways, these newer orientations represent reaction against dominant ways of thinking about and studying administrative roles in the past, for example, the educational administration field's preoccupation with more highly visible line administrators (e.g., superintendents, principals) who hold the most power and authority within the system (Marshall, Patterson, Rogers, & Steele, 1996).

Alternative conceptualizations present new strategies for understanding administrative problems not addressed in prior research orientations toward school administrators. These newer perspectives are less concerned with describing the work or the impact of principal leadership on school effectiveness. Instead, they capture different concerns about school leadership including the micropolitics of schools, how leadership roles are constructed through sense making, and school leaders' cognitive and problem-solving processes. They also critique how societal and cultural contexts affect the exercise of leadership, as well as how leadership is studied and written about (Evers & Lakomski, 1996; Maxcy, 1995). A substantial body of work from researchers in several different countries is beginning to accumulate from these various stances, but it is also generally not comparative in nature. Instead, it often focuses on a particular principal (e.g., Dillard, 1995) or a particular school context (Anderson, 1991, Blase, 1989, 1993; Greenfield, 1991; Gronn, 1984;

Keith, 1996; Robinson, 1996). Studying leadership more comparatively in the future will require a shift in thinking about the goals of some of these research programs.

Role or Political-Conflict Perspective

The role, or political-conflict, perspective toward school leadership focuses primarily on political relations within the school setting (Hoy, 1994). Studies from the political-conflict perspective begin to move away from the structural-functional approach to understanding school life from the perspective of the rational and bureaucratic organization (Ogawa & Bossert, 1995; Ouston, 1999). In contrast to more functionalist studies concerned with traits, position, and behavior, studies from this perspective are useful in understanding the political turmoil surrounding efforts to reform or restructure schools (e.g., Anderson, 1991; Bass & Avolio, 1989; Blase, 1989, 1993; Greenfield, 1991; Jantzi & Leithwood, 1996).

Researchers working from this perspective accept that schools are characterized by multiple goals, diverse instructional strategies, and relatively high degrees of teacher autonomy and proceed to understand how leaders function under such conditions (Hoy & Miskel, 1996). The political-conflict approach suggests the relations between teachers and administrators are complex and multidirectional. Moreover, it implies that at times administrators are subordinate to teachers in the sense that they serve teachers and facilitate teaching and learning processes at the school level (Hoy & Miskel, 1996). The focus on role relationships within the school has also been termed the "micropolitics" of the school (Anderson, 1990; Bacharach & Mundell, 1993; Blase, 1993; Greenfield, 1991). Anderson suggested that studies of the micropolitics of the school provide a new perspective on how control and legitimation of activities unfold at the school level (e.g., see Blase, 1993; Greenfield, 1991). Proponents of this approach argue that the dominant rational systems paradigm tends to ignore key political issues altogether. For example, this oversight is clearly evident in the effective schools studies. The political-conflict approach begins with the assumptions that order inside the school is politically negotiated and that such negotiation is at the heart of what we might term leadership. One type of comparative research on school leadership from this perspective might focus on how school politics differ across cultural settings.

Meaning and Sense Making

The sense-making, or constructivist, perspective highlights how leaders and others in the organization construct meaning surrounding schooling activities (Duke, 1986; Duke & Iwanicki, 1992; Everhart, 1988; Hoy, 1994). From a sense-making perspective, the study of leadership focuses on the meaning behind the actions and the way it is communicated in relationships (Slater,

1995). This view holds that leadership is best understood as perception or attribution (Duke & Iwanicki, 1992). One proposition about school leadership Duke and Iwanicki investigated was the principal's "fit" with the school. They suggested that how well the leader fits with the school surroundings derives from the interactions between the leader and the other members of the school community within the culture in which they exist. The data for this investigation consisted of perceptions of leadership expectations and whether these perceptions were congruent with the context of the schools in which they were manifested.

Other sense-making work on school leadership has focused on how school leaders and others make sense out of various aspects of school life, including change or reform processes. Such studies may draw our attention to norms and values related to teachers' efforts to resist change (Anderson, 1991; Corbett, Firestone, and Rossman, 1987; Ogawa, 1991), the manner in which school principals and teachers implement change (Lambert, 1995), how students construct metaphors of their principal's leadership (Lum, 1997), or differences in the ways that male and female principals may lead (Marshall, 1995; Ortiz, 1992). Several researchers are studying the relationship of social cognition and values to leaders' problem solving and decision making (Beck, 1993; Begley, 1996; Hodgkinson, 1983, 1991; Leithwood, Begley, & Cousins, 1992; Leithwood & Hallinger, 1993; Leithwood & Stager, 1989; Leithwood & Steinbach, 1991). As opposed to the rational perspective on decision making, a process described as relatively closed and goal oriented (e.g., administrators make decisions that affect teachers), in these newer studies, researchers' concern is less with the goals-effectiveness approach and more with the choice-making processes through which leadership is ultimately expressed. For example, Evers and Lakomski (e.g., 1991, 1996) have begun to synthesize how cognitive theories related to information processing form a basis for explaining how administrators act in decision making and problem solving. Begley (1996) has examined how values are critical in the process of administrators making choices. While a promising line of inquiry for comparative study, Begley concludes that the empirical literature on values and cognition in viewing school leaders still remains clouded by conceptual and epistemological difficulties.

Critical Constructivist, Feminist, Postmodern, and Related Approaches
Also rooted in a constructivist view of social life, the critical approach to social analysis involves the critique of existing social relationships and the advancement toward desired ones (Keith, 1996). The critical approach takes in a variety of perspectives such as feminist, neo-Marxist, gender and cultural studies, and participatory research. These approaches extend beyond the notion of sense-making within schools to understanding the surrounding societal reasons why various educational practices persist. This approach has been

largely ignored by both positivist and interpretive stances because of the different manner in which the research questions are posed and the more varied role the researcher can play in investigating the phenomenon under study and in presenting the research text.

Researchers adopting a critical stance examine the often legitimating role that school leaders play in endorsing existing social arrangements within society and the role of research in defining and changing those relationships (Anderson, 1991; Chase, 1992; Dillard, 1995; Gronn & Ribbins, 1996; Ortiz, 1992; Regan, 1990). Anderson (1990, 1991), for example, called our attention to how current constructions of social reality are created. He suggested that researchers in educational administration must find ways to study the invisible and unobtrusive forms of control exercised in schools in order to address the problems of the underprivileged clients who attend them. Other critics suggested that traditional theories of leadership are no longer valid in understanding the practical realities of schools (Dillard, 1995; Marshall, 1993; Marshall et al., 1996) because the notion of paradigm talk tends to suppress challenges to dominant ways of thinking (Donmoyer, 1999; Kuhn, 1962; Marshall, 1995). Marshall and colleagues argued that paradigms framing most theories concerning research and practice in school leadership have fallacies including the superiority of the bureaucratic organizational structure, a focus on visible administrators at the top of the structure, and White male domination.

One example of the power of paradigms to suppress is in the area of school leadership and its relationship to larger issues such as gender, race, and class. As Ortiz and Marshall (1988) noted, the need for an analysis of organizational theories and research perspectives for their representation of women's experiences has persisted. This stance appears more concerned with social justice, moral, and democratic processes, as opposed to specific actions and behavior of school leaders. A major role of school administrators has been to legitimate their respective functions as allocators of social values. In this manner, schools (and their leaders) can play a major role in institutionalizing inequity. Because the critical perspective centers on social change, it could be an important lens through which to view school improvement efforts (Slater, 1995). From this perspective, the study of leadership might focus on those examples that are more nontraditional, informal, and often, interim (Maxcy, 1995). It might also focus on how education might function over time to benefit (or marginalize) particular cultural groups. One case study is how members of the Native Hawaiian community (which had been left outside the educational decision-making process due to colonialism) over a period of years successfully pressured the Hawaii Department of Education to create immersion schools with instruction conducted in the Hawaiian language within the public school structure (Benham & Heck, 1998).

The Cultural Lens in Studying School Leadership

The investigation of culture and leadership represents another line of inquiry that emphasizes the social construction of meaning. The cultural lens, similar to other newer perspectives, may illuminate previously unnoticed aspects of school leadership, including the manner by which societal norms shape and support the practice of school leaders (Hallinger, 1995; Heck & Hallinger, 1999). Early ethnographic studies in anthropology sometimes mentioned the cultural transition of knowledge in primitive societies. Yet, these applications rarely consisted of focused empirical study in educational settings (Everhart, 1988).

From a review of previous studies on school leadership, it is difficult to determine the possible influence of cultural contexts on leadership (Hallinger & Heck, 1999). Beginning with the work of Getzels, Lipham, and Campbell (1968), theorists in educational administration attempted to develop comprehensive conceptualizations of school leadership. The Getzels and colleagues' model located the school administrator within a sociocultural context, suggesting that cultural values could impact the thinking and behavior of leaders and others in the school (Hallinger & Leithwood, 1996). Over time, researchers have investigated various aspects of the model, although the impact of the broader cultural context has been mostly ignored. More recently, researchers have begun to discuss the cultural foundations of leadership (e.g., see Bajunid, 1996; Cheng & Wong, 1996; Chung & Miskel, 1989; Hallinger & Leithwood, 1996; Heck, 1996; Walker, Bridges, & Chan, 1996). This research perspective may help illuminate a number of previously hidden aspects of leadership across nations and regions including differences in philosophy and values, school improvement practices, academic orientations, and conceptualizations of effectiveness. Yet, there are also considerable conceptual and methodological challenges in studying leadership more comparatively from a cultural perspective.

Broadly speaking, culture has been conceptualized as an adaptive system—that is, the ways that groups adapt to the challenges of their particular environment—or as a system of subjective, but socially shared, symbols and meanings (Lewellen, 1992). As Lewellen argued, most current researchers in the social sciences have focused on the latter definition; that is, conceptualizations suggest that societies are integrated systems of shared symbols and meanings. In reality, however, any cultural system is likely comprised of multiple and competing realities, rather than ordered systems that make intuitive sense to members (Tierney, 1996). It is generally accepted, however, that cultural contexts lend to individuals a set of attitudes, values, and norms of behavior that may be very different from those used in other contexts.

While anthropologists seek a holistic view of how participants construct values and norms of behavior, the complexity of the cultural systems they study often requires the isolation of smaller subsystems. Specific cultural or geographic settings may also not be synonymous with national boundaries. There may be a number of different ethnic groups present who have very different political, social, and educational goals. In many settings there may also be the presence of lengthy colonialism that has a profound impact on local traditions in politics, economics, social relations, and access to, and outcomes from, education. In such complex settings, understanding school leadership in a particular setting, therefore, may focus on the manner in which individuals, or groups, accept or reject a variety of different cultural cues. Thus, in making comparisons of school leadership across cultural settings, the researcher runs the risk of decontextualizing the leadership norms, values, or behaviors from their wider contextual setting. Yet, the notion of generalization (or transfer) of phenomena across settings is at the center of comparative work. Researchers are therefore faced with a conceptual and methodological dilemma in studying culture and school leadership comparatively—because culture is holistic and socially constructed by its members, it suggests the need for in-depth, field-based study. To give meaning to the experience observed, however, requires the ability to transfer it to other settings.

The nature of the educational systems themselves can make comparison of their school leadership processes difficult. In contrast to a number of Western countries where educational systems have experienced considerable decentralization in decision making to the local school level (e.g., Australia, United Kingdom, United States), in many developing countries in Asia and the Pacific the educational systems are more centralized (e.g., Thailand, Singapore, Indonesia). Descriptive studies in some of these settings lend the impression that educational bureaucracies rely heavily on principals for local program improvement, implementation, and administration. As Hallinger, Taraseina, and Miller (1994) suggested, however, centralized authority structures in these systems may actually result in decision paralysis, where school administrators become fearful of taking the initiative to make changes without explicit orders from above. Additional barriers to school action can include lack of effective communication from superiors, geographic barriers, and lack of community infrastructure. Moreover, the reward structures in such systems may further reduce their willingness to initiate school improvement (Hallinger et al., 1994). As Hallinger and colleagues observed in Thailand, principals' conceptualization of their instructional leadership was not directed toward school improvement in any discernible way, as it might be in the United States. Rather, Thai principals defined their role as meeting institutional mandates (e.g., curriculum) and fostering staff and community cohesion.

Besides differences in the educational systems and the expectations for school leaders within those systems, few previous studies on school leadership have employed indigenous conceptualizations of leadership in non-Western cultures (Bajunid, 1996). In one study that tried to compare Eastern and

Western educational practices, Cheng and Wong (1996) found that many practices noted in Western studies of school effectiveness were also observed in typical Chinese schools (e.g., clear school mission, safe environments, high expectations for achievement, rewards and recognition). In other ways, other traditional Chinese values were also present (value of effort in learning, a holistic approach to the education of students, a focus on moral education and discipline). Cheng and Wong also suggested that the concept of leader effectiveness in East Asia was different from Western conceptualizations, focusing more on moral dimensions rather than particular leadership skills. At times, these cultural traditions clashed, as modern trends influenced the traditional system. They concluded that social culture exerted a strong influence on how Chinese administrators conceived of and enacted their roles.

In another study that employed a more indigenous conceptualization of school leadership, Bajunid explored in-depth the derivation of Malaysian school leadership norms in Muslim religion and Malay culture. At the same time, he found, similar to Cheng and Wong (1996), that there was an important place in Malaysian school administration for borrowed Western methods of leadership. The infusion of Western values into more traditional settings may create new demands, expectations, and dilemmas. These methods, however, must be adapted to the existing norms of the particular society.

Contributing to the challenge for researchers in making comparisons of school leadership across cultural or national settings is that different actions may serve similar purposes within each context. For example, while overseeing the school's governance processes (e.g., making decisions, solving problems, implementing policies) may be a common concept to the school principal's role, whether or not parents (or teachers) are involved in decision making may be more culturally specific behavior. Conversely, the same actions regarding involving parents in governance may even have very different meanings across cultures, and, therefore, perhaps different motivations and effects (see Heck, 1996, for discussion of culturally specific versus culturally common indicators of school leadership). Nevertheless, both differences and similarities in how school leadership is conceptualized and expressed across cultural settings represent grist for the mill of scholars in years to come (Heck & Hallinger, 1999).

Conducting International Research on School Leadership

The investigation of school leadership across cultural settings is potentially a rich area for empirical exploration, in that it may both broaden and deepen our understanding of how cultural context may impact the theory and practice of school administration. There are still considerable gaps in our theories and understandings of how these processes work, and previous research in school leadership provides little guidance in terms of how to proceed. While more recent research on school leadership has focused on the interplay between the school's context and its processes (Hallinger & Heck, 1996a), it is obvious that these constellations of variables are also embedded in state or national contexts as well (Dimmock & Walker, 1998; Teedlie & Reynolds, 2000).

Perhaps one of the most basic questions in thinking more globally about leadership and culture is whether researchers should conceive of culture as a specific variable that influences school leadership (i.e., leadership as determined by culture), or whether they should view leadership as merely culturally situated. Adopting the latter perspective, for example, might suggest a preliminary research program focused on describing leadership practices in rich detail in a number of different cultural settings (e.g., using the case-study approach), paying particular attention to how culture may contribute to similarities or differences in specific school leadership practices observed in the individual cases. In contrast, a more ambitious goal focused on developing theory with culture at the center of the expression of school leadership (i.e., as determined by cultural norms, values, and traditions) may require a different type of research program and methods of investigation. For example, little is known about what aspects of school leadership may be more global and what aspects may be more idiosyncratic, or culturally specific. Another way to describe this particular research concern is to say there is a need to understand what aspects of school leadership "travel" across cultural settings and which do not (Reynolds, 2000). National cultures may provide codes that make up the way that organizations including schools operate; hence, what researchers observe and conclude within particular settings, therefore, may be reflective of national cultures and expectations (Mawhinney, 1999).

Although the changes that educational systems undergo in various cultural settings (e.g., decentralization, educational accountability) may look similar on the surface, they can have very different purposes, meanings, and outcomes. One challenge for developing this type of comparative research would be how to include several cultural settings within one study applying a particular leadership model (that may have different meanings across settings), defining a set of common variables (some of which may be common across contexts and others of which may be specific to a context), selecting multiple samples, and analyzing the data (Heck, 1996). Some of the concerns are outlined briefly in this final section of the chapter.

What Current Leadership Models?

Various types of models and organizing schemes have been proposed to map the school leadership research terrain (e.g., focusing on the purposes of inquiry and their research orientations and methods; e.g., see Donmoyer, 1999; Heck & Hallinger, 1999) or models of school leadership (e.g., Leithwood & Duke,

1999). Hoy and Miskel (1991), however, summarize the diversity in views and definitions of school leadership as being almost as many as the researchers engaged in its study. For example, these conceptualizations of the principal's role have changed considerably over the past several decades from manager, to street level bureaucrat, change agent, instructional leader, educational leader, and, most recently, to transformational leader (Hallinger & Heck, 1996b). More recently, Leithwood and Duke organized previous research on school leadership around six different models or approaches they found grounded in the current literature on school leadership (i.e., since 1988). These models included instructional leadership, transformational leadership, moral leadership, participative leadership, managerial leadership, and contingency or other "styles" of leadership.

A number of these models (e.g., instructional leadership, transformational leadership), however, are likely too limited to adequately explain the diversity of school leadership practices in a global setting. For example, while the notion of instructional leadership has been popular in many U.S. studies conducted on the principal in the past 20 years, Dutch researchers have been generally unable to validate its importance within their cultural setting (Reynolds, 2000). Moreover, most of these leadership conceptualizations are Western, which may not entirely transfer to non-Western settings. Similarly, the transformational approach may describe Western efforts to restructure schools more accurately than it captures traditional school leadership in villages in Asia or the Pacific Islands.

Because of the relationship of instrumentation to the construct validity of leadership models, preliminary studies suggest that instrumentation is a significant issue to consider across national contexts, beyond the surface problem of translating the text into different languages. For example, Hallinger and colleagues (1994) concluded that their American instrumentation on instructional leadership failed to capture facets of school leadership as constructed by Thai secondary school principals. Similarly, Heck (1996) found that while a set of school leadership constructs held across American and Pacific settings, about half of the items defining those leadership constructs were culturally common, while the rest were culturally specific. As this brief discussion suggests, it will be a considerable challenge to bring isolated studies of school leadership (using a variety of leadership models) together into a larger theory or framework about how school leadership processes work within various contextual conditions and across broader cultural or national settings (Hallinger & Leithwood, 1996).

Development of Theory

In previous work on school leadership, there is little theory that connects the nature of schooling across cultures to leadership practices and thus advances our thinking about how various environmental pressures including geography, increasing population, technology, and resources may affect the development of schooling and leadership processes. Comparisons across nations or cultures are likely to require the identification of new processes and variables that need to be considered in a comparative analysis. As opposed to previous studies of school leadership conducted in singular settings, studies defined as comparative will require researchers to redefine what it means to create empirical knowledge that is more global.

Needed theoretical work that situates leadership within a larger sociocultural context has only recently begun to be addressed (see Dimmock & Walker, 1998; Greenfield, 1995; Hallinger & Leithwood, 1996). Hallinger and Leithwood, for example, revisited Getzels and colleagues' (1968) work on developing a comprehensive conceptualization of educational leadership (including antecedents of leadership, mediating variables, and outcomes). This theoretical model located the leadership construct within a larger cultural context that at least partially shaped the thinking and behavior of those around the school. In the first chapter of this book, Walker and Dimmock also lay out a cross-cultural framework around the interrelationships among culture, organizational structures, leadership and management processes, curriculum, and teaching and learning (also see Dimmock & Walker, 1998). Empirical research will need to follow that can determine whether these methods are useful in understanding cross-cultural differences in school leadership.

In addition to needed theory about how cultural context and leadership are related, Paige and Mestenhauser (1999) identified several general dimensions that should be considered in making empirical work in educational administration more global in its implications. International research on school leadership should include an *integrative dimension* (i.e., how well the knowledge from diverse settings can be incorporated into a general and evolving perspective on school leadership), an *intercultural dimension* (i.e., identifying and examining how culture and cultural variables influence leadership and schooling), a *comparative dimension* (i.e., identifying similarities and differences in the various settings studied), and a *global dimension* (i.e., examining how world economic, political, and sociocultural trends may affect leadership globally).

Methodological Issues

Although the concept of culture can provide one unifying view for international comparative research on school leadership, in actual studies the concept is filled with potential contradictions. Each study, whether qualitative or quantitative, brings potential methodological challenges. For example, a sense-making approach is likely to be one useful means of investigating school leadership because of its dominant focus on the context of the setting and how leadership is constructed among participants in the school. As suggested, however, most previous studies using this approach have focused on a single school site or a small number of school sites. It is probably not enough to look at one case per cultural setting in comparative studies. Deciding the extent to which cases may be representative of a particular cultural setting and then comparing cases across cultural settings will likely be a more difficult undertaking. One way to proceed might be to look at several cases in a cultural context and then construct a narrative about school leadership in that context from the several cases. Next, the leadership narratives could be compared across the settings.

In quantitative comparative research, it is also important to highlight that researchers must guard against inappropriately comparing and generalizing findings, without taking into consideration likely differences between the members that comprise the schools within the settings that are being compared. Often such comparisons are inappropriately made between groups that really have not been shown to be similar in any way (e.g., subjects may come from different backgrounds within chosen samples or have different levels of training, experience, knowledge, or intelligence). The fact of the matter remains that nonprobability sampling makes it impossible to estimate sampling errors and make valid inferences to a particular population. In reality, however, it is not always possible to obtain ideal, random samples for comparison across populations (such as principals in two countries). Sampling problems, therefore, are compounded when one attempts to compare leadership across different settings. Samples drawn from different cultures may in fact be related to different populations.

Another example of the challenge in developing quantitative comparative studies is in determining what context variables are likely to affect leadership within and across cultural settings. In the past, researchers have attempted to include context variables in their studies of school effects and leadership processes, but it is evident that these variables are defined differently by researchers in different nations (Teedlie, Stringfield, & Reynolds, 2000). For example, a number of studies in the United States have shown that contextual indicators such as community socioeconomic context affect principal leadership and overall school effectiveness (e.g., Hallinger & Murphy, 1986). School leadership studies conducted in other countries have not necessarily found the same pattern of contextual relationships to hold (e.g., Heck, 1993). Hence, while there is general agreement that school and cultural contexts may interact with leadership processes, there is little consistency in empirical studies in terms of the types of contextual variables that may be important to consider in general models of leadership (Hallinger & Heck, 1996a, 1996b; Teedlie & Reynolds, 2000).

Conclusion

This discussion of challenges to developing a more international and comparative perspective on school leadership returns us to the notion that theory and method play a mutually reinforcing nature in the creation of new knowledge. This chapter represents an attempt to bring together previous research on school leadership conducted generally in relative isolation with preliminary thinking about how to expand our perspectives on school leadership to include more international and comparative components. While much theoretical and empirical work remains in extending our understanding of school leadership, especially in understanding how it is expressed differently in diverse settings, as a field we are making progress in the application of theory and methods of research in attacking this potentially important problem of practice. The comparative study of leadership should yield a broader appreciation of various ways in which schooling assumptions, structures, educational processes, and leadership practices differ across diverse cultural contexts. The preliminary discussion of the various philosophical lenses, models, and methods for investigating school leadership encourages even greater flexibility, experimentation, and eclecticism in terms of philosophical stances and methodologies used to study school leadership comparatively in the coming years.

To undertake this type of ambitious research program, attention must be given to the careful design of comparative studies, with respect to the overall purposes of the research, the leadership models used, and the corresponding methods of conducting the studies. It will likely take teamwork among researchers internationally. While there is much to learn about leadership by studying it across settings, there are also considerable problems that will need to be addressed in undertaking these studies. Alternative conceptualizations of school leadership and research methods that move away from strict positivist and structural-functional views have broadened our understandings of how school leadership is constructed. Developing a comparative perspective on school leadership is also likely to yield knowledge about how to resolve schooling problems of international concern. If in 15 years, methodological and conceptual advancements in comparative research on school leadership can be claimed similar to the past two decades in school leadership research, I am confident that the field will have made much more significant headway in addressing important educational problems of interest to practitioners, policy makers, and researchers internationally.

References

Anderson, G. (1990). Toward a critical constructivist approach to school administration: Invisibility, legitimation, and the study of non-events. *Educational Administration Quarterly, 26*(1) 38–59.

Anderson, G. (1991). Cognitive politics in principals and teachers: Ideological control in an elementary school. In J. Blase (Ed.), *The politics of life in schools: Power, conflict, and cooperation* (pp. 120–138). Newbury Park, CA: Sage.

Bacharach, S., & Mundell, B. (1993). Organizational politics in schools: Micro, macro, and logics of action. *Educational Administration Quarterly, 29*(4), 423–452.

Bajunid, I. (1996). Preliminary explorations of indigenous perspectives of educational management: The evolving Malaysian experience. *Journal of Educational Administration, 34*(5), 50–73.

Baker, D. P., Akiba, M., LeTendre, G. K., & Wiseman, A. W. (2001). Worldwide shadow education: Outside-school learning, institutional quality of schooling, and cross-national mathematics achievement. *Educational Evaluation and Policy Analysis, 23*(1), 1–17.

Bass, B., & Avolio, B. (1989). Potential biases in leadership measures: How prototypes, lenience, and general satisfaction relate to ratings and rankings of transformational and transactional leadership construct. *Educational and Psychological Measurement, 49*(3), 507–527.

Bates, R. (1980). Educational administration, the sociology of science, and the management of knowledge. *Educational Administration Quarterly, 16*(1), 1–20.

Beck, C. (1993). *Learning to live the good life.* Toronto: Ontario Institute for Studies in Education.

Begley, P. (1996). Cognitive perspectives on values in administration: A quest for coherence and relevance. *Educational Administration Quarterly, 32*(3), 403–426.

Benham, M., & Heck, R. (1998). *Culture and educational policy in Hawaii: The silencing of native voices.* Mahwah, NJ: Lawrence Erlbaum.

Berman, P., & McLaughlin, M. (1978). *Federal programs supporting educational change, vol. VIII: Implementing and sustaining innovations.* Santa Monica, CA: Rand.

Blase, J. (1989). The micropolitics of the school: The everyday political orientations of teachers toward open school principals. *Educational Administration Quarterly, 25,* 377–407.

Blase, J. (1993). The micropolitics of effective school-based leadership: Teachers' perspectives. *Educational Administration Quarterly, 29*(2), 142–163.

Boyan, N. (1988). Describing and explaining administrative behavior. In N. Boyan (Ed.), *Handbook of research in educational administration* (pp. 77–98). New York: Longman.

Bridges, E. (1982). Research on the school administrator: The state-of-the-art, 1967–1980. *Educational Administration Quarterly, 18*(3), 12–33.

Brookover, W., & Lezotte, L. (1977). *Changes in school characteristics coincident with changes in student achievement.* East Lansing, MI: Michigan State University Press.

Brookover, W., Schweitzer, J., Schneider, J., Beady, C. Flood, J., & Wisenbacker, J. (1978). Elementary school climate and school achievement. *American Educational Research Journal, 15,* 1–18.

Chapman, J., Sackney, L., & Aspin, D. (1999). Internationalization in educational administration: Policy and practice, theory and research. In J. Murphy & K. Seashore-Louis (Eds.), *The handbook of research on educational administration* (2nd ed., pp. 73–97). San Francisco: Jossey-Bass.

Chase, S. (1992, June). *Narrative practices: Understanding power and subjection and women's work narratives.* Paper presented at the Qualitative Analysis Conference, Carleton University, Ottawa.

Cheng, K., & Wong, K. (1996). School effectiveness in East Asia: Concepts, origins and implications. *Journal of Educational Administration, 34*(5), 32–49.

Chung, K., & Miskel, C. (1989). A comparative study of principals' administrative behavior. *Journal of Educational Administration, 27*(1), 45–57.

Corbett, H., Firestone, W., & Rossman, G. (1987). Resistance to planned change and the sacred in school cultures. *Educational Administration Quarterly, 23*(4), 36–59.

Crowson, R., & Porter-Gehrie, C. (1980). The discretionary behavior of principals in large-city schools. *Educational Administration Quarterly, 16*(1), 45–69.

Dillard, C. (1995). Leading with her life: An African American feminist (re)interpretation of leadership for an urban high school principal. *Educational Administration Quarterly, 31*(4), 539–563.

Dimmock, C., & Walker, A. (1998). Comparative educational administration: Developing a cross-cultural conceptual framework. *Educational Administration Quarterly, 34*(4), 558–595.

Donmoyer, R. (1996). Editorial: Educational research in an era of paradigm proliferation: What's a journal editor to do? *Educational Researcher, 25*(2), 19–25.

Donmoyer, R. (1999). Paradigm talk (and its absence) in the second edition of the *Handbook of research on educational administration. Educational Administration Quarterly, 35*(4), 614–641.

Duke, D. (1986). The aesthetics of leadership. *Educational Administration Quarterly, 22*(1), 7–27.

Duke, D., & Iwanicki, E. (1992). Principal assessment and the notion of fit. *Peabody Journal of Education, 68*(1), 25–36.

Edmonds, R. (1979). Effective schools for the urban poor. *Educational Leadership, 37*(6), 15-24.

Everhart, R. (1988). Fieldwork methodology in educational administration. In N. Boyan (Ed.), *The handbook of research on educational administration* (pp. 703–727). New York: Longman.

Evers, C., & Lakomski, G. (1991). *Knowing educational administration.* Oxford, England: Pergamon Press.

Evers, C., & Lakomski, G. (1996). Science in educational administration: A postpositivist conception. *Educational Administration Quarterly, 32*(3), 379–402.

Firestone, W. (1990). The commitments of teachers: Implications for policy, administration, and research. In S. Bacharach (Ed.), *Advances in research and theorems of school management* (pp. 154–171). Greenwich, CT; JAI Press,.

Firestone, W., & Corbett, H. D. (1988). Planned organizational change. In N. Boyan (Ed.), *The handbook of research on educational administration* (pp. 321–340). New York: Longman.

Firestone, W., & Louis, K. (1999). Schools as cultures. In J. Murphy & K. S. Louis (Eds.), *Handbook of research on educational administration* (2nd ed., pp. 297–322). San Francisco: Jossey-Bass.

Foster, W. (1986). *Paradigms and promises: New approaches to educational administration.* Buffalo, NY: Prometheus.

Fullan, M. (1996). Leadership for change. In K. Leithwood, J. Chapman, D. Corson, P. Hallinger, & A. Hart (Eds.), *International handbook of educational leadership and administration* (pp. 701–722). Boston: Academic Publishers.

Gali, J. (1988). The structure of managerial behavior: An international aspect in educational administration. *Studies in Educational Administration and Organization, 15*, 41–56.

Getzels, J., Lipham, J., & Campbell, R. (1968). *Educational administration as a social process.* New York: Harper & Row.

Glasman, N., & Heck, R. (1992). The changing leadership role of the principal: Implications for assessment. *Peabody Journal of Education, 68*(1), 5–24.

Goetz, J., LeCompte, M., & Ausherman, M. (1988, September). *Toward an ethnology of student life in classrooms.* Paper presented at the American Anthropological Association meeting, Phoenix, AZ.

Greenfield, T. (1980). The man who comes back through the door in the wall: Discovering truth, discovering self, discovering organizations. *Educational Administration Quarterly, 16*(3), 25–59.

Greenfield, W. (1991). The micropolitics of leadership in an urban elementary school. In J. Blase (Ed.), *The politics of life in schools: Power conflict, and cooperation* (pp. 161–184). Newbury Park, CA: Sage.

Greenfield, W. (1995). Toward a theory of school administration: The centrality of leadership. *Educational Administration Quarterly, 31*(1), 61–85.

Greenfield, W., Leicata, J., & Johnson, B. (1992). Towards measurement of school vision. *Journal of Educational Administration, 30*(2), 65–76.

Gronn, P. (1984). I have a solution ... : Administrative power in a school meeting. *Educational Administration Quarterly, 20*(2), 65–92.

Gronn, P., & Ribbins, P. (1996). Leaders in context: Postpositivist approaches to understanding educational leadership. *Educational Administration Quarterly, 32*(3), 452–473.

Hall, G., & Rutherford, W. (1983, April). *Three change facilitator styles: How principals affect improvement efforts.* Paper presented at the annual meeting of the American Educational Research Association, Montreal.

Hallinger, P. (1992). Changing norms of principal leadership in the United States. *Journal of Educational Administration, 30*(3), 35–48.

Hallinger, P. (1995). Culture and leadership: Developing an international perspective of educational administration. *UCEA Review, 36*(2), 1–13.

Hallinger, P., & Heck, R. (1996a). Reassessing the principal's role in school effectiveness: A review of the empirical research, 1980–1995. *Educational Administration Quarterly, 32*(1), 5–44.

Hallinger, P., & Heck, R. (1996b). In K. Leithwood (Ed.), *The international handbook of research on education leadership* (pp. 723–783). Boston: Kluwer.

Hallinger, P., & Heck, R. (1999). Can leadership enhance school effectiveness? In T. Bush, L. Bell, R. Bolam, R. Glatter, & P. Ribbins (Eds.), *Educational management: Redefining theory, policy, and practice* (pp. 178–190). London: Paul Chapman.

Hallinger, P., & Leithwood, K. (1996). Culture and educational administration: A case of finding out what you don't know you don't know. *Journal of Educational Administration, 34*(5), 98–116.

Hallinger, P., & Murphy, J. (1986). The social context of effective schools. *American Journal of Education, 94*(3), 328–355.

Hallinger, P., Taraseina, P., & Miller, J. (1994). Assessing the instructional leadership of secondary school principals in Thailand. *School Effectiveness and School Improvement, 5*(4), 321–348.

Hart, A. (1994). Creating teacher leadership roles. *Educational Administration Quarterly, 30*(4), 472–497.

Heck, R. (1991). Towards the future: Rethinking the leadership role of the principal as philosopher-king. *Journal of Educational Administration, 29*(3), 67–79.

Heck, R. (1993). School context, principal leadership, and achievement: The case of secondary school in Singapore. *The Urban Review, 25*(2), 151–166.

Heck, R. (1996). Leadership and culture: Conceptual and methodological issues in comparing models across cultural settings. *Journal of Educational Administration, 35*(5), 74–97.

Heck, R., & Hallinger, P. (1999). New methods to study school leadership. In J. Murphy & K. S. Louis (Eds.), *Handbook of research on educational administration* (2nd ed., pp. 141–162). San Francisco: Jossey-Bass.

Hodgkinson, C. (1983). *The philosophy of leadership.* Oxford, England: Basil Blackwell.

Hodgkinson, C. (1991). *Educational leadership: The moral art.* Albany, NY: SUNY.

Hoy, W. (1994). Foundations of educational administration: Traditional and emerging perspectives. *Educational Administration Quarterly, 30*(2), 178–198.

Hoy, W., & Miskel, C. (1991). *Educational administration: Theory, research and practice* (4th ed.). New York: Random House.

Hoy, W., & Miskel, C. (1996). *Educational administration: Theory, research and practice* (5th ed.). New York: Random House.

Hughes, M. (1988). Comparative educational administration. In N. Boyan (Ed.), *The handbook of research on educational administration* (pp. 655–676). New York: Longman.

Inbar, D. (1977). Perceived authority and responsibility of elementary school principals in Israel. *Journal of Educational Administration, 15*(1), 80–91.

Jantzi, D., & Leithwood, K. (1996). Toward an explanation of variation in teachers' perceptions of transformational school leadership. *Educational Administration Quarterly, 32*(4), 512–538.

Johnson, N., & Holdaway, E. (1990). School effectiveness and principals' effectiveness and job satisfaction: A comparison of three school levels. *The Alberta Journal of Educational Research, 36,* 265–295.

Keith, N. (1996). A critical perspective on teacher participation in urban schools. *Educational Administration Quarterly, 32*(1), 45–79.

Kmetz, J., & Willower, D. (1982). Elementary school principals' work behavior. *Educational Administration Quarterly, 18*(4), 62–78.

Kuhn, T. (1962). *The structure of scientific revolutions.* Chicago: University of Chicago Press.

Lambert, L. (1995). Constructing school change. In L. Lambert (Ed.), *The constructivist leader* (pp. 52–82). New York: Teachers College Press.

Leithwood, K. (1994). Leadership for school restructuring. *Educational Administration Quarterly, 30*(4), 498–518.

Leithwood, K., Begley, P., & Cousins, B. (1992). *Developing expert leaders for future schools.* Bristol, PA: Falmer Press.

Leithwood, K., & Duke, D. (1999). A century's quest to understand school leadership. In J. Murphy & K. S. Louis (Eds.), *Handbook of research on educational administration* (2nd ed., pp. 45–52). San Francisco: Jossey-Bass.

Leithwood, K., & Hallinger, P. (1993). Cognitive perspectives on educational administration: An introduction. *Educational Administration Quarterly, 29*(3), 296–301.

Leithwood, K., & Stager, M. (1989). Expertise in principals' problems solving. *Educational Administration Quarterly, 25*(2), 126–161.

Leithwood, K., & Steinbech, R. (1991). Indicators of transformations leadership in the everyday problem solving of school administrators. *Journal of Personnel Evaluation in Education, 7*(4), 221–244.

Lewellen, T. (1992). *Political anthropology: An introduction* (2nd ed.). Westport, CT: Bergin & Garvey.

Louis, K. S., Toole, J., & Hargreaves, A. (1999). Rethinking school improvement. In J. Murphy & K. S. Louis (Eds.), *Handbook of research on educational administration* (2nd ed.), (pp. 251–276). San Francisco: Jossey-Bass.

Lum, J. (1997). Student mentality: Intentionalist perspectives about the principal. *Journal of Educational Administration, 35*(3), 210–233.

Macpherson, R. (1996). Educative accountability policy research: Methodology and epistemology. *Educational Administration Quarterly, 32*(1), 80–106.

Marshall, C. (1993). Politics of denial: Gender and race issues in administration. In C. Marshall (Ed.), *The new politics of race and gender* (pp. 168–174). Washington, DC: Falmer Press.

Marshall, C. (1995). Imagining leadership. *Educational Administration Quarterly, 31*(3), 484–492.

Marshall, C., Patterson, J., Rogers, D., & Steele, J. (1996). Caring as career: An alternative perspective for educational administration. *Educational Administration Quarterly, 32*(2), 271–294.

Mawhinney, H. (1999). Rumblings in the cracks in conventional conceptualizations of school organizations. *Educational Administration Quarterly, 35*(4), 573–593.

Maxcy, S. (1995). Responses to commentary: Beyond leadership frameworks. *Educational Administration Quarterly, 31*(3), 473–483.

Ogawa, R. (1991). Enchantment, disenchantment, and accommodation: How a faculty made sense of the succession of its principal. *Educational Administration Quarterly, 27*(1), 30–60.

Ogawa, R., & Bossert, S. (1995). Leadership as an organizational quality. *Educational Administration Quarterly, 31*(2), 224–243.

Ortiz, F. (1992, April). *Women's ways of becoming leaders: Personal stories.* Paper presented at the annual meeting of the American Educational Research Association, San Francisco.

Ortiz, F., & Marshall, C. (1988). Women in educational administration. In N. Boyan (Ed.), *Handbook of research on educational administration* (pp. 123–142). New York: Longman.

Ouston, J. (1999). School effectiveness an school improvement: Critique of a movement. In T. Bush, L. Bell, R. Bolam, R. Glatter, & P. Ribbins (Eds.), *Educational management: Redefining theory, policy, and practice* (pp. 166–177). London: Paul Chapman.

Paige, R. M., & Mestenhauser, J. A. (1999). Internationalizing educational administration. *Educational Administration Quarterly, 35*(4), 500–517.

Peterson, K. (1978). The principal's tasks. *Administrator's Notebook, 26,* 1–4.

Pitner, N. (1988). The study of administrator effects and effectiveness. In N. Boyan (Ed.), *Handbook of research on educational administration* (pp. 99–122). New York: Longman.

Pounder, D., Ogawa, R., & Adams, E. (1995). Leadership as an organization wide phenomenon: Its impact on school performance. *Educational Administration Quarterly, 31*(4), 564–588.

Regan, H. (1990). Not for women only: School administration as a feminist activity. *Teachers College Record, 91*(4), 565–577.

Reynolds, D. (2000). School effectiveness: The international dimension. In C. Teedlie & D. Reynolds (Eds.), *The international handbook of school effectiveness research* (pp. 232–256). London: Falmer.

Robinson, V. (1996). Problem-based methodology and administrative practice. *Educational Administration Quarterly, 32*(3), 427–451.

Rutter, M., Maugham, B., Mortimore, P., Ouston, J., & Smith, A. (1979). *Fifteen thousand hours: Secondary schools and their effects on children.* Cambridge, MA: Harvard University Press.

Salley, C., McPherson, R., & Baehr, M. (1979). *A national occupational analysis of the school principalship.* Chicago: Industrial Relations Center, University of Chicago.

Sara, N. (1981). A comparative study of leader behavior of school principals in four developing countries. *Journal of Educational Administration, 19*(1), 21–32.

Schmidt, W. H., & Prawat, R. S. (1999). What does the third international mathematics and science study tell us about where to draw the line in the top-down versus bottom-up debate? *Educational Evaluation and Policy Analysis, 21*(1), 85–91.

Scott, W. (1992). *Organizations: Rational, natural, and open systems* (3rd ed.). Englewood Cliffs, NJ: Prentice-Hall.

Silins, H. (1994). The relationship between transformational and transactional leadership and school improvement outcomes. *School Effectiveness and School Improvement, 5* (3), 272–298.

Slater, R. (1995). The sociology of leadership and educational administration. *Educational Administration Quarterly, 31*(3), 449–472.

Tarter, C., Bliss, J., & Hoy, W. (1989). School characteristics and faculty trust in secondary schools. *Educational Administration Quarterly, 25*(3), 294–308.

Teedlie, C., & Reynolds, D. (2000). *The international handbook of school effectiveness research.* London: Falmer.

Teedlie, C., Stringfield, S., & Reynolds, D. (2000). Context issues within school effectiveness research. In C. Teedlie & D. Reynolds (Eds.), *The international handbook of school effective-ness research* (pp. 160–185). London: Falmer.

Tierney, W. (1996). Leadership and postmodernism: On voice and qualitative method. *Leadership studies, 7*(3), 371–383.

Wagner, J. (1993). Ignorance in educational research: Or, how can you not know that? *Educational Researcher, 22*(5), 15–23.

Walker, A., Bridges, E., & Chan, B. (1996). Wisdom gained, wisdom given: Instituting PBL in a Chinese culture. *Journal of Educational Administration, 34*(5), 12–31.

Wolcott, H. (1973). *The man in the principal's office: An ethnography.* New York: Holt, Rinehart & Winston.

part II:
The Influence of Societal Culture on Schools and School Leadership

6

Leadership, Learning, and the Challenge to Democracy

The Cases of Hong Kong, the United Kingdom, and the United States

JOHN MACBEATH

Introduction

This chapter begins with five challenges to leadership, all of which in some way serve to explain an increasing demoralization among teachers. This is portrayed by some commentators in the United Kingdom and the United States as a crisis of confidence in national leadership, but to what extent do these same critiques apply equally to Hong Kong? The language of outcomes, accountability, quality assurance, and excellence find a common register.

Hong Kong is itself an integral part of the global concern pressure for higher standards while simultaneously engaged in effecting a paradigm shift toward a new radical learning to learn agenda. The bridge between in-school learning and out-of-school learning is, it is argued, an important focus for schools and schools leadership because it is here that preparation for lifelong learning receives its sternest test.

While cultural, religious, and historical factors separate East and West it is easy to both oversimplify the differences and gloss the commonalities. With these caveats in mind, the question engaged with is: "what can we learn from the common search for effective leadership in a time of change?"

A Time of Challenge and Change

"Why," asks Michael Fielding, is there such disillusionment amongst so many involved in education at a time when a still hugely popular government has insistently and persistently proclaimed education as its main priority? (Fielding, 2001). And, quoting words written nearly 70 years ago, why is it that "We have immense power, and immense resources; we worship efficiency and success; and we do not know how to live finely?" (Macmurray, 1935, p. 76).

The reference is to the Blair government (United Kingdom) and its espousal of three key priorities—education, education, and education. But it is not only the British government that has raised the profile of education. In the United States, Bush wanted to be known as the "education president," and in the shaping of the new Hong Kong, education has assumed a preeminent role. But in all three countries educational leadership at the beginning of the third millennium is constrained within policy objectives not always of their own choosing. While there are very significant differences of culture and history within these three countries they are, nonetheless, bound together by the common bond that is globalization, by the common bond of their fiscal friends and by the alliance against collective adversaries.

Within a political context, increasingly global in nature, increasingly hege-menous, what is truly "effective" leadership? How can it be genuinely learning-centered? How can leaders help to create the conditions in which their students and their teachers can "live finely," can give their attention to the things that matter, can be the building blocks of a better more democratic social order?

The Diminishing Globe

In the 1970s Marshall McLuhan coined the term "global village" to denote a world that is becoming progressively smaller. The "network society" and "information capitalism," as described by Manuel Castells (1996, 1999), depict a world that even McLuhan could not have foreseen. In this globalized market economy, value-for-money has become the preeminent concern, and inputs are justified in terms of measurable outputs—in the new mantra of the last decade, "outcomes." As educational leaders it is vital to know what lies at the root of this brave new reality that they are expected to manage and where its momentum might lead if is not countered with a principled professional vision.

Demythologizing

For present and future leaders it is a priority to dissect established belief systems so as to avoid being carried passively forward toward reform on the back of untested assertion and political myth making. The following are five of those myths:

- of teacher subversion
- of the business model
- of objective measurement
- of economic productivity
- of "levering up" standards

Teachers as Agents of Subversion

The "crisis in the classroom" that Charles Silberman reported in the early 1970s appears, three decades later, not to have diminished, but the political rhetoric, in the United Kingdom at least, has been forced to change by the realization that the more teachers are blamed and shamed the greater will be the recruitment and retention dilemma.

Although she cannot be ascribed sole credit for seeding distrust of the teaching profession, Margaret Thatcher targeted teachers as one the primary causes of social and economic malaise, criticizing their motivation, their effectiveness and Leftist politics, casting them and their unions as the enemy within. It was a view she shared with Reagan as well as other right-of-center world leaders. It was to become something of an international crusade brooking no dissent from "academics" who were seen as the subversive force that had led teachers astray with ideas that were "woolly," "progressive," "caring," and, most heinously of all, "child-centerd."

The damaging effect of this attack on the teaching profession was explicitly recognized by the outgoing British Secretary of State David Blunkett in 2001. Reflecting on the first term of New Labour, he admitted that the anti-teacher legacy that his government had inherited had not been turned around in four years of New Labour.

> My biggest regret is that we weren't able to win over the teaching profession as quickly or as extensively as I would have wished. The 10 years of change and conflict that had taken place up until the time I took over had really created a backcloth which soured their attitude toward what politicians were trying to do and made our challenges seem like an additional burden. That, coupled with the changes we've brought in, has felt like a major increase in workload and the challenge for the new parliament will be not only to reduce workload—I've set that in train now—but also to learn the lesson that you do need to take time to get people to respond to you. (Blunkett, 2001, p. 22)

Significantly, political leaders in Hong Kong did not follow this same damaging path. Yet, while not indulging in such a rhetorical crusade there was, nonetheless, a keen recognition that there would need to be an urgent and large scale upskilling of the teaching force if Hong Kong was to meet the demands of the new millennium. Their close watching brief and alliance with Western systems resulted in a reshaping of policies and priorities and an Education Commission, reporting in 2000 with a radical vision of the a future in which teachers would play a key and much changed role. While blame was not laid at the door of teachers the message was one of radical reappraisal of teaching.

All in all, despite the huge resources put into education and the heavy work-load endured by teachers, learning effectiveness of students remains not very promising; learning is still examination-driven and scant attention is paid to "learning to learn." School life is usually monotonous, students are not given comprehensive learning experiences with little room to think, explore and create. (Education Commission, HKSAR, 2000, p. 4)

The responsibility for change was laid at the door of school leadership and, as common to all three national systems, leaders have to weigh the danger of leaving teachers behind in the urgency of their reformist zeal and opening a growing divide between leadership and teachers. Fullan's 1997 study of Canadian principals (quoted in Fullan, 2001) found a progressive loss of trust and confidence in the principals' effectiveness by teachers, as reported by principals themselves. Sixty-one percent reported a decrease in effectiveness, 72 percent reported a lack of trust, while 91 percent felt that principals could not fulfill all the obligations laid on them.

The following quote is from a teacher as reported in A Study on the Effectiveness of Public-sector Secondary Schools in Hong Kong (Lee et al., 2001). The study suggests why the above may be so:

Sometimes he thinks of something and then he wants you to do it quickly, like when he sees what good things other schools are doing, he would bring it back and then say "you have to do it in your subject." But people only achieve and arrive at what they are gradually. (p.42)

This finds an echo in Leithwood and colleagues' work (2000) on large scale reform. They concluded that for reform to be effective it required three vital ingredients—will, meaning, and situation. That is, teachers need to have the desire and motivation for change, they need to see meaning in it for them and their students, and it must be sensitive to their contexts and situation.

There is a slow and belated realization that teachers are the nation's greatest and only ally in the war against poverty and ignorance and that they are the ultimate gatekeepers of change.

Such sentiment is found in the Education Commission's proposals for reform of the education system: "The EC has proposed a direction for the reform, but the 'paradigm shift' can only be realized with the active participation of frontline educators. (Education Commission, HKSAR, 2000, p. 40).

The Business Myth

It was during the years of Thatcher-Reagan that the incursion of private enterprise into education grew most rapidly. It was not new in the United States where, since the early 1970s, there had been various attempts to put the running of schools and school systems into the hands of private enterprise. Performance contracting enjoyed a brief and high profile life in the early 1970s with companies such as Ohio-Westinghouse contracting with school districts to "deliver" results, which they did, but ultimately no more successfully than teachers who contracted equally successfully to also deliver raised test scores if that was going to be the test of an education.

Thatcher put her trust in private enterprise to showcase models of efficiency in the running of schools and local authorities. Government departments were happy to give large amounts of money to consultants and private agencies that they would never give to people within the education system. Under the Blair administration this ideology is still pitting private corporations against local authorities in contracting out services, with the effect that the large companies poach local authority staff at higher wages because they lack the educational expertise and are able to pay more handsomely because they are able to charge more handsomely. A high level private consultant can charge upwards of £3,000 a day, a sum which could have purchased 10 teachers.

Referring to the United States, Berliner (2001) said that while business leaders have advocated performance-related pay and data-driven organizations they have been cavalier in disregarding both of these precepts themselves. He cited the American auto industry with extensive knowledge of the Japanese market but consciously, and ultimately disastrously, ignoring the data. He cited the tobacco industry's willful and self-interested denial of data and concluded, "I don't think the business community have earned the right to be listened to on the pay for performance issue" (p. 8) and provided an extensive list of multi-million dollar payoffs to corporate leaders whose performance ruined and nearly ruined companies such as Proctor and Gamble, Mattell, Xerox, Coca-Cola, Conseco.

Similar messages are to be found in the extensive literature of the Asia-Pacific Consortium for Economic Development (apec.org) which lists conference reports and expert papers with a common theme that business and economic interests must drive educational thinking and policy priorities.

The Mythology of Measurement

The quest for objective measurement—the hunt for the unicorn—is allied to this faith in business models of productivity, of inputs and outputs, value added and value-for-money—terms that have slipped insidiously into the daily vocabulary of education. This brings a demand for better, more systematic, quantitative data on school performance. It is a third millennium global Zeitgeist embraced as avidly by politicians in the East as in the West. However unarguable the case for better data and for reliable diagnostic and formative tools, schools find themselves driven by a measurement mania not of their choosing and one at times profoundly dissonant with their own values.

In his book *Standardized Minds*, Peter Sacks (1999) said this in reference to the United States:

> never had so many false claims been made about education in the name of "evidence." Once the crusade reached a nationwide critical mass, any dissent over the path the country was taking with respect to school reform was marginalized, relegated mostly to concerns expressed by some educators and researchers who were discovering the real effects this crusade was having on education. Indeed the "group-think" quality to the reform crusade has been made possible by widespread trust in several highly questionable beliefs sustained by the powerful coupling of business and political interests. It's time for us to dissect those beliefs. (p. 5)

Dissecting those beliefs, Sacks produced data to show that the states that have invested most in high stakes tests are not the ones that are the most educationally effective. Writing at the same time, Labaree (1999) described in devastating critique *How to succeed in school without really learning*. Success in the performance culture is bought at a high price, both for the student who is unequipped for life after school and for the teacher who is obliged to squander energy in endless coaching for the next test.

In respect of the performativy pressure on teachers, the significant difference between West and East is that the Pacific Rim countries rank relatively highly in the mathematics and science league tables while the West—the United States and United Kingdom at least—are ranked lower than is comfortable for politicians and policy makers. The consequence is that teachers bear the brunt of the crusade to raise standards in line with the countries of the Pacific Rim. In this desperate quest for the answer to the success of Hong Kong, Taiwan and Singapore emissaries were sent to study classrooms and report back on the secret of success. The Third International Mathematics and Science Study (TIMSS) study and the book *Learning gap* (Stevenson & Stiegler, 1994)—with its comparison of Japanese, Chinese, and American classrooms—have together reinforced a belief among those in search of the quick fix that it is in interactive whole class teaching that the answer is to be found. While Stevenson and Stiegler do indeed probe the culture of home and community, the simple message abstracted by U.K. and U.S. policy makers was not that answers lie deeply in the culture, the history, and the relationship of home and community but in the bag of tricks that the individual teacher deploys.

While the United States and Britain look to the East, Hong Kong looks outside its borders to the West and to Australasia to find ways of making its classrooms more stimulating, its teachers more adventurous, its teachers more creative. This is, however, underpinned by an ambivalence about performativity on the one hand and learning goals on the other. As Lo (1999) suggested, these give rise to tensions between traditional and Eastern and more Western values. The collective good (harmony) as an ultimate goal, harnessed to the willingness to make sacrifices and put group interests before self, sits uneasily with the competitive individualist ethic of performance comparisons. It is interesting that many teachers in the West, perhaps an older, more educationally liberal generation, experience a similar ambivalence.

The Myth of Economic Productivity

The drive for measurement is allied closely to the belief that raised standards are good for the economy. For Bush, for Blair, for European governments and for governments of the Pacific Rim, politicians regard this link as implicit although there is scant evidence to support the notion of a causal link between school standards and economic advance. The following statement is contained in a recent report from a conference of the APEC (Asian-Pacific Economic Consortium, 2000, apec.org):

> The emphasis on education for its own sake and education for democracy must become subservient to education for economic development. And [s]chool to work partnerships are needed to drive out those who advocate learning for the sake of learning.

We do not need to dig too deep, however, to see the lack of any coherent pattern of relationship in data presented in Table 6.1 from the Institute of Public Policy Research in the United Kingdom (Robinson, 1988).

Table 6.1 Mean Score of Mathematics Attainment and GDP in Ten Countries.

	Mean score in math	GNP per capita
Singapore	643	122
Korea	607	57
Japan	605	128
Hong Kong	588	125
Czech Republic	564	50
Russia	535	26
Ireland	527	76
Thailand	522	39
England	506	100
United States	500	144

Note. From Tyranny of the league tables, parliamentary brief, by P. Robinson, 1998, *May Institute of Public Policy Research, 5*(5), 60.

This presumed relationship between the two sets of data in Table 6.1 rests on a number of unexamined fallacies:

- That high standards are the product of finance and resources rather than culture and history
- That school mathematics is relevant to economic efficiency or competitiveness
- That the average attainment of pupils on any given school subject is related to economic efficiency or competitiveness
- That this information will help shape educational provision in the future

Economies may need high level mathematicians, but that does not imply that the 5 percent that the economy requires are to be found by remorseless teaching of the 100 percent while at school. In California the answer to the state and the country's relative poor performance was to initiate a concerted statewide push on mathematics for all, a singular mission statement that made this the driving priority for all Californian schools. Evaluations have yet to show any improved outcomes (Leithwood, 2000) and are unlikely to ensure that young people are any better equipped to face the future in California's unpredictable and entrepreneurial climate of constant change. United States school students may perform relatively poorly on school math (first in GNP, 28th position in the attainment league table), but that doesn't stop their universities from producing world class mathematicians and scientists.

Levering Up Standards

With this link established in government mythology it follows that economic competitiveness means greater monitoring from the center, monitoring standards, measuring and reporting on performance, holding school to account, levering up standards through legislation and exhortation. For Bush the strategy is clear—carrot and stick: "In his presentation Tuesday, the President underscored early literacy, annual testing, and rewarding or punishing schools based on the results" (Washington Post Times, 2001, p. 5). And with the high rhetoric of reform:

the last several years have been a time of bold change in education. A drizzle of innovation has become a flood of reform—a great movement of conscience and hope. A movement of parents and political leaders, voters and educators, hungry for high standards, tough accountability and real choices. (Washington Post Times, 2001, p. 5)

And so myths are made. The rhetoric across Atlantic and Pacific states has some remarkably similar resonances. From a stock of policy words, speech makers may perm any combination—*tough, bold, standards, accountability, choice, quality, benchmarking, success, attainment*—to suggest but a few unarguably good things of which we are undoubtedly all in favor. Much of this is, however, empty rhetoric, hollow of meaning.

The assumption is that governments can lever up standards. The belief is that politicians and administrators can deliver shocks to the system, jolting teachers into improved performance. In the United Kingdom the Office for Standards in Education (OFSTED) had as its strapline, "Improvement Through Inspection." That has now been quietly laid to one side as the realization grows that inspectors do not raise standards, nor do they empower teachers. It is something that teachers have to do for themselves. They do it for themselves with a quality of support that allows challenge to be accepted and acted upon.

The Challenges for Educational Leadership

These five mythologies present common challenges for leadership in Hong Kong, United States, and United Kingdom. These will be worked out differently in their different contexts, but the change story is one to follow with close interest over the next few years. At the heart of it will be how these school systems respond to the paradigm shift from teaching to learning, from passivity to activity, and from dependence to independence.

Learning for Life and Changing Times
All three countries recognize that school learning will never be the same again. All three countries acknowledge that there is a paradigm shift from a teacher-centered school to a learner-centered education, and all three share common dilemmas of how to get there from here.

In Hong Kong as in the United Kingdom and the United States, curricular reform has been a continuing process, a constant endeavor to find the valance, coherence, and progression that will build, which throws this traditional restructuring into question:

> the focus of the curriculum reform suggested by the Education Commission (2000) is not on specific changes in the subjects or the syllabus, but rather an overall reform of the rationale behind learning and teaching. It aims at placing students' learning at the centre of the education system and making students the masters of learning, in the true spirit of the "student-focussed" principle. (Education Commission, HKSAR, 2000, p. 40, para. 6.29)

This is a radical departure from the traditional view of curriculum as packaged and delivered. It seeks to explore a deeper issue, the very rationale for teaching and learning in the twenty-first century and the increasingly contested relationship between teaching and learning. The threefold paradigm shift of the teacher is described in the document as:

- from someone who transmits knowledge to someone who inspires students to construct knowledge;
- from someone who implements the curriculum to someone who participates in the development of school-based curriculum; and
- from someone who executes policies to someone who leads and contributes to the reform.

While similar visionary sentiments are also to be found in British and American documents, in these two countries there has been a tightening of the curriculum, greater rather than lesser prescription for teachers. In the United States, designer packages provide teachers with sequential programs to follow, sometimes in very specific detail with training in technique an essential part of the package. Many of these, such as "Success for All" (Slavin, Madden, Dolan, Wasik, Ross, & Smith, et al., 1994), claim a high degree of success. In England the highly prescriptive numeracy and literacy strategies are also seen as a success and with Key Stage testing at 5, 7, 9, 11, 14, and 16, there is little room for departure from the National Curriculum.

If there is a yawning gap between where we are and where we want to be it will not be closed by policies that are retrogressive rather than progressive, policies that seek refuge in the past rather in the future, that offer tighter structures rather than flexible and responsive inimical to tension deep learning (Entwistle, 1987). The conception of learning as linear, as ruthlessly sequential, is antithetical to inquiry learning, which is typically intuitive, spontaneous, and usually messy.

Moving from a performativity agenda to a learning agenda requires a change in mindset. It requires a shift from the left hand to the right hand column in Table 6.2.

The movement from a performativity to a learning paradigm requires that school leaders take charge of the agenda, that they have a conviction about where the balance should lie, that they know what is happening in classrooms, and that they know who to entrust with the learning for change goal. In Hong Kong many secondary school principals have left that task to middle management, to heads of departments. Yet it is at this level that the blockage to radical reform often lies, the careful guarding of an inviolate subject domain resting on decades of success and satisfied inertia. While British and American principals might also agree that it is at this level that reform or rethinking is typically impeded, principals and headteachers have to rely on their subject heads to deliver the subject performance in an internally competitive climate that strongly reinforces subject status.

Table 6.2 Comparing a Performance and a Learning Orientation.

Performance	Learning
Believe that ability leads to success	Belief that effort leads to success
Concern to be judged as able, concern to perform	Belief in one's ability to improve and learn
Satisfaction from doing better than others	Preference for challenging tasks
Emphasis on normative standards, competition, and public evaluation	Deriving satisfaction from personal success at difficult tasks
Helplessness: evaluating self negatively when task is difficult	Using self-instruction when engaged in a task

Note. From Learning about learning enhances performance, by C. Watkins, 2001, *Research Matters*, 13, 2.

In a time of rapid change, high stakes external accountability, and heavy demands on staff, teachers will tend to welcome off-the-shelf packages that do not require them to think or prepare, and they will be grateful to leaders who make their life easier. That may, however, be no more than a palliative and may leave teachers dissatisfied with their lack of professional ownership of their own practice.

Commenting on the strength of the harmonious staff culture in one Hong Kong school, Lee et al., (2001) nonetheless offer this important caveat:

> However, the emphasis of harmonious relationships with fewer conflicts and disputes hinders the generation of new ideas among teachers. It also exerts a strong norm for teachers to follow the existing practices. This culture would become an obstacle for the school to cope with the coming educational changes. (p. 51)

For school principals or management teams this is the most difficult challenge. It is one of Senge's (1990) organizational learning disabilities, which he characterises as "Nothing fails like success."

Learning Out of School

A useful and focused starting point may be with the perenially troublesome area of homework. At first sight it may seem to have very little to do with life-long learning or the radical constructivism suggested by the Hong Kong Commission, but policies on homework and the quality of what students do says a lot about the learning culture and change capacity of a school. Stevenson and Stiegler's (1994) comparisons of American, Japanese, and Chinese students reported strong cultural differences not only in the amount of time spent on homework (American pupils spend less time on average) but in attitudes to, and support for, home learning. Their findings were that Chinese parents exerted greater pressure than their American counterparts, with an accompanying tendency for American parents to worry more about the deleterious effects of homework on their children.

Nonetheless, the addiction to homework is deeply embedded in all three systems and high level generalizations such as these tend to miss the range of variance within countries. In Hong Kong secondary schools, Lee et al. (2001) identified a serious problem of lack of support, lack of interest, and lack of pressure from parents in lower band schools and lower socioeconomic communities. American and British studies, on the other hand, have found among certain groups of parents high levels of pressure on children to study and spend time on homework. Despite the socioeconomics of the community the perception persists at large that good schools give homework, and this is as common to U.S. and U.K. schools as to those in Hong Kong (Dimmock, O'Donoghue, & Robb, 1996; Walberg, 1985). By the same token the school that eschews homework or is lax in its approach is generally looked upon less favorably by parents who implicitly treat this as one of the hallmarks of a "good school." Policy makers have not been slow to understand this and the importance of homework is written indelibly into public documents.

However, the debate over the purpose and value of homework is a continuing one and vital for a school staff to engage in critically. Does homework in fact help enrich and extend learning, develop independent learning skills and good habits as is so often claimed for it? Its critics (Krolovec & Buell, 2001) argued that is does none of these and is, in fact, divisive, inimical to family life, and effective only in stretching the distance between have and have not. Those who "do" are more likely to perform well at school, whether because they actually learn more or simply because they enjoy the benefits of being "good students" and avoiding the disapproval and sanctions reserved for those who don't play by the rules.

The debate tends to polarize homework, as conventionally conceived and self-driven "authentic" learning, as if these two concepts are essentially and irrevocably at odds. Learning out of school can, with imagination be engaging and enjoyable and can be designed to encourage the development of learning and thinking skills.

However intrinsically engaging, self-initiated learning, freed from the direction and cajoling of the teacher, continues to benefit the motivated and to disenfranchise those who never quite get round to it. Those who do generally enjoy the support and encouragement of a parent or other adults, while those who don't have little or no source of support and are easily distracted by other more immediately engaging pursuits.

This is not only true of the United States or the United Kingdom but equally in Hong Kong where fishing people, managers of small businesses working long and unsocial hours, and parents who have no schooling beyond elementary see themselves as unable to help their children (Lee et al. 2001). This lack of a bridge between home education and school learning leads in two main policy directions. One, is to educate and involve parents in their children's learning, the other, to provide after hours programs targeted specifically at students who have no support at home.

At school level, initiatives aimed at educating parents assume remarkably similar forms. In all three countries there are schools in which courses are run specifically for parents, on Information Communication Technology (ICT), in child development, on curriculum and curriculum change. There are schools in all three countries that engage in home visiting by teachers or social/community workers and in all three countries parent–teacher meetings are held to discuss children's progress and future goals. Indeed there is far greater similarity among parent-friendly schools in Hong Kong, the United States, and the United Kingdom, than between the most and least parent-friendly schools within any one of these countries—however different their cultural context. And all share the common dilemma of getting to see, or have impact on, those parents whose children are most in need.

A second set of strategies center on complementary provision. Again such initiatives tend to be specific to individual schools but with common features across cultures. There are many Hong Kong schools where the end of the school day does not mark the end of the learning day. An hour or two after the end of school there are still teachers in classrooms, students sitting with them in one-to-one tutorial, or groups of students working together in mutual support groups, around them a buzz of extracurricular activities.

As the focus moves more toward skills for team working and lifelong learning, "extra" curricular assumes a less marginal significance. Activities such as sport, music, hobbies and games come to be seen less as enjoyable diversions or relief from real learning but as vital opportunities for enhancing self-confidence, developing teamwork, leadership, independence, and interdependence.

In the United States and the United Kingdom after school programs take myriad forms but are generally more formally structured and often targeted on those most in need of complementary support. While it is not unknown for teachers to stay on after school, disputes over pay and conditions lost the goodwill of teachers, and supplementary programs tend nowadays to come only with extra payment attached.

Miller (2001), referring to the United States, finds that after school programs tend to expose the inadequacy of traditional homework practices. They are able to demonstrate an alternative model of independent learning in which there is a more informal relationship between teachers and learners, where teaching takes a back seat and inquiry and collegial learning comes to the fore. This has also been true of the United Kingdom where the dilemma for schools is how to transfer the quality of learning after hours into the mainstream school curriculum. While much of this would also hold true for the informal more student-centered work that goes on voluntary basis in many Hong Kong schools after hours, it would not necessarily be characteristic of tutorial centers and out-of-hours tuition, which can be heavily tutor-directed and examination orientated.

In the U.K., complementary programs under the generic title of "study support" have experienced a new vitality under New Labour. The Labour government made a significant investment in study support—usually learning after school but often in the form of breakfast clubs, weekend, Easter, and summer schools. These programs, designed to complement, enrich, and extend learning, have been targeted at disadvantaged students who get little support at home. A four-year independent evaluation of study support programs, comparing students who went with those who didn't, found not only strong evidence of added value in achievement and attitudes to school but also a greater likelihood for learning to be seen as a shared enterprise.

Tang's finding (1996) that Chinese students tend to collaborate spontaneously outside the classroom may be seen as a significant difference between East and West, but out-of-hours programs in the United Kingdom have provided a context for a much higher degree of spontaneous collaboration among students.

In the U.K. evaluation of study support, the most successful schools were those in which leadership had been instrumental in creating a culture where out-of-school learning was seen as integral to learning policies, fed directly back into the classroom and flowed back out. It was built-in not bolt-on. In-school and out of school learning were treated as a seamless activity, and "homework" had ceased to be a discrete, lonely, and unloved activity. This is perhaps no startling insight since the most consistent finding of school effectiveness research in the United States, the United Kingdom and Hong Kong (Lo, Tsang, Chung, Chung, Sze, Ho & Ho 1997; Teddlie, 1995; MacBeath & Mortimore, 2001) comes to a similar set of conclusions as to the relationship between home learning and school learning.

The message for school leaders is clear. Leadership needs to be brave in confronting deeply held views of homework, by parents and teachers alike. In doing so it can also lay bare some of the even more deep lying fallacies of what learning is and where and how it occurs. The challenge is nor merely the reeducation of parents, but of teachers and students too, often locked into a tripartite collusion from which escape is problematic because it is threatening to the comfortable stable state.

The most significant unlearning that faces teachers has to do with conceptions of "ability" and "intelligence." Although Hong Kong teachers may be less guilty than their Western counterparts of such unexamined notions, there is some evidence (Lee et al., 2001) that Hong Kong teachers too can set expectations too low because of their reading of a student's home and social background. A recent UNESCO study (Wilmms & Somers, 1999) in South America found that key factors in improving outcomes were:

- high level of parental involvement,
- principals with a high degree of autonomy,
- schools which place emphasis on regular evaluation, and
- teachers who do not attribute success and failure to family background

Taken together, these four factors have relevance far beyond South America and are closely interrelated. Redefining the roots of success and failure is at the center of new ways of thinking about the place and purpose of learning. It involves rethinking both the limitations and potential of the classroom as the primary locus for learning. It requires a more profound understanding of family and social capital (Putnam, 1999) and how that interlinks with school structure and capacity. Imaginative developments presuppose principals and management teams with a high degree of autonomy to explore, innovate, take risks, and break the rules and long-standing conventions.

Schools That Place Emphasis on Regular Evaluation

The trend to greater school autonomy is a common policy trend in all three countries. In the United States it is known as site-based management, in the United Kingdom local management of schools, and in Hong Kong school-based management. All place greater power and responsibility in the hands of the principal. All bring with them an enhanced need to move away from external quality assurance to a system of evaluation that is internal, ongoing, and focused on learning.

Yet there is a paradox in this devolution of power to the school site. While quality assurance is the primary responsibility of the school itself it sits within a context where quality assurance is a strong political commitment. While "quality" is a concept that everyone can sign up to—perhaps because it is such an inclusive and slippery concept—the "assurance" half of the terminology is much more contested. It begs the question of who is in charge of "assuring," who is seen as the intended audience, and what the focus of that process is.

Quality assurance from external sources comes in a number of forms. It takes the form of published reports, in some cases on individual schools, in some cases an aggregate of schools. Elsewhere (in England and Scotland, for example) it takes the form of performance tables published by newspapers and/or by the government. In some instances external agencies, universities, or private enterprise are commissioned by governments to evaluate a school or school initiative, sometimes over a period of time so as to provide a picture of progress, change or value added. It may also take the form of awards to school or to individual teachers, sometimes with high profile public accolades such as Teachers of the Year in the United States or the televised Platos Annual Teaching Awards in England (modelled by David Putnam on the Hollywood Oscars) and the Quality Education Fund Schools Awards in Hong Kong.

These accolades for individual schools and teachers are a complement in Hong Kong and the United Kingdom to school inspection, born out of a recognition of a need to celebrate success as well as pinpointing weakness. The United Kingdom and Hong Kong follow a very similar approach to school inspection, using virtually identical performance categories and indicator sets to evaluate the quality of classroom teaching and of whole school effectiveness and improvement. Individualized school reports and annual aggregated reports by the Chief Inspector are common to both countries. Inspections increasingly rely on schools to have conducted their own internal audits, or evaluations, and to have in place systems for appraising teachers.

This can act as a straitjacket for schools, and many schools in the United Kingdom and Hong Kong treat it as such and respond defensively and with dependency on external evaluation. Other schools, as yet almost certainly a minority in both countries, take charge of their own quality assurance and have the confidence and conviction to meet the external view with their own robust criteria and data. They know their strengths, and they do not need the inspector's finger to point to their weaknesses and area for development.

This is where effective leadership receives its most stringent test. Learning-centered leadership starts from the premise that schools are heterogeneous places. They are not ever completely or perennially effective. They are subject to flux and change. They are reborn with every new influx of students and with every teacher who arrives or leaves. They experience crises, often not of their own making, and their quality can never be described by a score, a simple label, or a position on a comparative table. They are perceived and received differently by their different stakeholders. They are simultaneously good and bad schools, exhilirating places for some and threatening unhappy places for others. Effective leaders are those most able to encourage and to manage diversity and conflict and capture that in their ongoing self-evaluation.

Grasping this important truth is the hallmark of the "Smart School" Perkins (1995), the "Learning School" (Schratz & Steiner-Löffler, 1998), and the "Intelligent School" (McGilchrist, Reed, & Myers, 1998). These are all schools that are open to surprise, and are welcoming of the hidden intelligence that resides in pupils, teachers, and parents. These are schools that both challenge conventional wisdom and are open to challenge themselves. These are schools which recognize how little we know about learning and how much we still have to learn at both individual and organizational levels:

> Learning starts from the joint acknowledgement of inadequacy and ignorance.... There is no other place for learning to start. An effective learner, or learning culture, is one that is not afraid to admit this perception, and also possesses some confidence in its ability to grow in understanding and expertise, so that perplexity is transformed into mastery. (Claxton, 1998, p. 201)

One of the most important insights that arises from a decade of work on school self-evaluation (MacBeath,1999; MacBeath, Jakobsen, Meuret, & Schratz, 2000) is that when teachers have the tools of self-evaluation they move into new realms of understanding of the nature of learning and teaching and their interrelationship, and that their students are a teacher's and a school's most valuable resource.

A decade ago Michael Fullan posed the question what would happen if we treated pupils as if their opinion mattered? (1991). As Soo Hoo (1993) put it, their views are "a treasure in our own backyard," which we have too often ignored or undervalued:

> Somehow educators have forgotten the important connection between teachers and students. We listen to outside experts to inform us, and, consequently overlook the treasure in our very own backyards, the students. (p. 389)

The student perspective does not, of course, stand alone. It is one source of evidence. It has to be set alongside evidence from other sources—from teachers, from parents, from achievement measures, and from examples of pupils' work. Self-evaluation is a synthesis of these various sources. It is, as Ernest House (2000) described it, "an all-things-considered synthesis." It cannot be presented as ultimate or objective "truth." It is the best, most honest, most considered judgement we can arrive at in the circumstances.

When leadership is open to learning from students, from staff, and from parents it provides a powerful model for staff. If leadership is receptive to learning about itself, it paves the way for teachers to listen more openly to feedback from their students. With this outlook teachers find just how different learning can be for different people and what a different place the classroom is depending on from where teachers are able to open up dialogue with their classes about when, where and how pupils learn best and, with the benefit these conversations provide about learning, the extent to which are able to identify ways of making learning more effective—in and beyond the classroom.

With such confidence, transparency, and integrity schools can steer their own course, confront authority, and educate beyond the boundaries of their own physical site. In 1995 Howard Gardner defined a number of criteria of effective leaders that such schools need.

- a readiness to confront authority
- risk taking
- resilience in the face of failure
- confidence in one's own instinct and intuition
- the ability to see and keep in mind the big picture
- being driven by a moral commitment
- a sense of timing allowing one to stand back, reflect, and learn from experience

It is a set of qualities that provides a guiding frame for leaders confronting the challenges of the new learning agenda, the new professionalism, and the internal school-driven commitment to its own quality assurance.

Conclusion

Despite the differences of context and culture, school leaders in Hong Kong, the United States, and the United Kingdom face similar challenges. The policy community looks to them to transform the culture of learning and teaching in their schools, and to embed professional development and continuous self-evaluation not simply into the structures, plans, and priorities but into the hearts of teachers. At the same time, while attempting to broaden the perspective of teachers and parents, they have to manage an international competitive agenda that narrows the goals and constricts the field of practice. Confronting the performativity myths is an important first step for leaders if they are to avert the risk of teachers being swept along in a tide change with no anchor to hold them to what is important, what is valued, and what is a real priority for the young people whom they are expected to serve. The second step is to instate a learning policy that works across the boundaries of home and school and puts center stage the skills and habits that help students to become confident independent, and interdependent, lifelong learners.

References

Berliner, D. (2001, April). *The John Dewey lecture.* Paper delivered at the American Educational Research Association, Seattle, WA.

Blunkett, D. (2001, January). *Teacher Magazine,* p. 22.

Castells, M. (1996). *The rise of the network society.* Oxford, England: Blackwell.

Castells, M. (1999) *End of millennium.* Oxford, England: Blackwell.

Cheng, Y. C. (1999). The pursuit of school effectiveness and educational quality in Hong Kong. *School Effectiveness and School Improvement,* 10(1), 1–16.

Claxton, G. (1998). *Hare brain tortoise mind.* London: Bloomsbury.

Dimmock, C., O'Donoghue, T., & Robb, A. (1996). Parental involvement in schooling: An emerging research agenda. *Compare, 26*(1), 5–20.

Education Commission, HKSAR. (2000) *Learning for life: Learning through life: Reform proposals for the education system in Hong Kong.* Hong Kong: Author.

Entwistle, N. (1987). *Understanding classroom learning.* London, Sydney: Hodder and Stoughton.

Fielding, M. (Ed.). (2001). *Taking education really seriously: Four years hard labor.* London: Routledge.

Fullan, M. G. (1991). *The new meaning of educational change.* London: Cassell.

Fullan, M. G. (2001). *The new meaning of educational change.* New York: Teachers College Press.

Gardner, H. (1995). *Leading minds: An anatomy of leadership.* London: Harper Collins.

House, E. (2000). *Schools for sale.* New York: Teachers College Press.

Krolovec, E., & Buell, J. (2001). End homework now. *Educational Leadership, 58*(7), 39–42.

Labaree D. F. (1999). *How to succeed in school without really learning.* New Haven, CT: Yale University Press.

Leithwood, K. (2000). *The return of large scale reform.* Toronto: Ontario Institute of Education, University of Toronto.

Lo, L. N. K. (1999). Knowledge, education and development in Hong Kong and Shanghai. *Education Journal, 27*(1), 55–91.

Lo, N. K.; Tsang, W. K.; Chung, C. M., Chung, Y. P.; Sze, M. M.; Ho, S. C.; Ho, M. K. (1997). *"A Survey of the Effectiveness of Hong Kong Secondary School System."* Final Report of Earmarked Grant Research Projects: RGC Ref. CUHK 28/91 & RGC Ref. CUHK 160/94H) Supported by Research Grants Council. (278 pages)

MacBeath, J. (1999). *Schools must speak for themselves.* London: Routledge

MacBeath, J., Jakobsen, L., Meuret, D. & Schratz, M. (2000). *Self-evaluation in European schools: A story of change.* London: Routledge.

MacBeath, J., & Mortimore, P. (2001). *Improving school effectiveness.* Buckingham: Open University Press.

Macmurray, J. (1935). *Reason and Emotion.* London: Faber

McGilchrist, B., Myers, K., & Reed, J. (1998). *The intelligent school.* London, Paul Chapman.

Miller, B. (2001). The promise of after school programs. *Educational Leadership 58*(7), 39–42.

Perkins, D. (1995). *Smart schools.* New York, The Free Press

Putnam, R. (1999). *Bowling alone: The collapse and revival of American community.* New York: Touchstone.

Lee, J. C. K., Chung, Y. P., Lo, L. N. K., Wong, H. W., Tsang, H. W., Dimmock, C., Walker, A., Pamg, N. S. K., Cheung, W. C., Ma H. T. W., Tang, Y. N., Ko, M. L. R., Lee, L. M. F., & Lai, M. H. (2001). *Study on the effectiveness of public sector secondary schools (phase 2)* (individual and cross case reports). Hong Kong: Centre for University and School Partnership and Hong Kong Institute of Educational Research, The Chinese University of Hong Kong.

Robinson, P. (1998). Tyranny of the league tables, parliamentary brief. *May Institute of Public Policy Research, 5*(5), 60.

Sacks, P. (1999). *Standardized minds.* New York: Touchstone.

Schratz, M., & Steiner-Löffler, U. (1998). *Die lernende schule: Arbeitsbuch pädagogische schulentwicklung.* Weinheim, Germany: Beltz.

Senge, P. (1990). *The fifth discipline: The art and practice of the learning organization.* New York: Doubleday.

Silberman, C. E. (1970). *Crisis in the classroom: The remaking of American education.* New York: Random House.

Slavin, R. E., Madden, N. A., Dolan, L. J., Wasik, B. A., Ross, S., & Smith, L. (1994). *Success for all: Longitudinal effects of school-by-school reform in seven districts.* Paper presented at the Annual Meeting of the American Research Association, New Orleans, LA.

Soo Hoo, S. (1993). Students as partners in research and restructuring schools. *The Educational Forum, 57,* 386–393.

Stevenson, H. W., & Stiegler, J. W. (1994). *The learning gap: Why our schools are failing and what we can learn from Japanese and Chinese education.* New York: Touchstone.

Tang, C. (1996). Collaborative learning: The latent dimension in Chinese students' learning. In D. A. Watkins & J. Biggs (Eds.), *The Chinese learner: Cultural, psychological and contextual influences* (pp.183–204). Hong Kong: Comparative Education Research Center, University of Hong Kong.

Teddlie, C. (1995). *ISERP case studies, USA sites, Comparison of four differentially effective schools.* Baton Rouge, LA: Louisiana State University College of Education.

Walberg, H. J. (1995). Homework's powerful effects on learning. *Educational Leadership, 42*(7), 76–79.

Washington Post Times. (2001, May 15), p. 5.

Watkins, C. (2001, Spring). Learning about learning enhances performance. *Research Matters, 13,* 2.

Wilmms, D., & Somers, M. A. (1999). *Schooling outcomes in Latin America.* Geneva: UNESCO.

7.

Educational Change in Thailand

Opening a Window onto Leadership as a Cultural Process

Philip Hallinger and Pornkasem Kantamara

Over the past decade policy makers have increasingly focused on the need to develop system capacities for educational reform and change. This focus on *change* represents a global response to the widening gap between the traditional capabilities of educational systems and emerging demands of the information age (e.g., Caldwell, 1998; Cheng & Wong, 1996; Dimmock & Walker, 1998; Hallinger & Leithwood, 1996; Murphy & Adams 1998). Throughout the world, reform policies are reshaping the context for school management and highlighting the role of school-level leaders as change agents (see Caldwell, 1998; Cheng & Wong, 1996; Dimmock & Walker, 1998; Hallinger, Chantarapanya, Sriboonma, & Kantamara, 1999). Consequently, in London, New York, Bangkok, Hong Kong, Melbourne, Singapore, and Beijing, developing the leadership capacities of school administrators has taken center stage as an educational priority (e.g., Davis, 1999; Feng, 1999; Hallinger, 1999; Hallinger & Bridges, 1997; Li, 1999; Low, 1999; Reeves, Forde, Casteel, & Lynas, 1998; Tomlinson, 1999).

While a global consensus has formed around the need for more adept change leadership in schools, the knowledge resources on which to build these capacities remain uncertain and unevenly distributed.

> Over the past few decades the knowledge base about ... change has grown appreciably. Some scholars feel that we know more about innovation than we ever have.... But although we have surely learned much, there remain two large gaps in our knowledge: training and implementation. (Evans, 1996, p. 4)

Evans' observation is especially salient in nations outside Europe and North America where the indigenous literature on school leadership and change is often less mature (e.g., see Bajunid, 1995, 1996; Cheng, 1995; Hallinger,

1999; Walker, Bridges, & Chan, 1996; Walker & Quong, 1998). Thus, when formal training is provided, school practitioners in non-Western nations often learn Western frameworks that lack cultural validity. This has led to calls for development of an "indigenous knowledge base" on school leadership, particularly among Asian scholars (for commentaries on the need for such studies see Bajunid, 1995, 1996; Cheng, 1995; Dimmock & Walker, 1998; Hallinger, 1995; Hallinger & Leithwood, 1996, 1998; Heck, 1996; Walker et al., 1996; Walker & Quong, 1998; Wong, 1996).

These calls for culturally-grounded research set the context for our own research and development effort aimed at understanding change leadership in Asian cultures (see Hallinger & Kantamara, 2000; Hallinger, 1999). In an earlier paper we took the position that leading organizational change is fundamentally a cultural process (Hallinger & Kantamara, 2000). While this is not an original proposition, most scholars to date have employed organizational culture as the conceptual framework for understanding change (Bolman & Deal, 1992; Evans, 1996; Fullan, 1993; Kotter, 1996; Sarason, 1992; Schein, 1996). We instead employed national culture as the conceptual lens (Hallinger & Kantamara, 2000; see also Brislin, 1993; Hofstede, 1991). In that article, using Thailand as a case for our theoretical examination of the change process, we drew the following conclusion.

[W]e have barely touched perhaps the most intriguing aspect of this topic: the interaction between these traditional cultural norms that shape behavior in Thai educational organizations and global change forces. That is, earlier we asserted that the effective change leader in Thai schools would need to be both adept at negotiating the traditional culture and knowledgeable in the ways of "modern" educational reforms.

Experience suggests that the scarcity of this dual set of skills among Thai school leaders is only exceeded by the paucity of theoretical or practical knowledge in supply by academics. While this compounds the already difficult tasks of educational reform in Thailand, we believe that it holds fascinating challenges for those practitioners and scholars willing to accept the charge. (Hallinger & Kantamara, 2000, p. 55)

In this chapter, we build on this theoretical analysis by reference to an exploratory case study of change leadership in Thailand. The earlier analysis focused solely upon speculating on how traditional cultural norms might shape the process of change in Thai schools. Here we examine the change process as experienced in Thai schools that successfully undertook complex systemic reforms that reflect the direction of what we refer to as "modern Thai education." By this we mean Thai schools that are seeking to meet global educational goals (e.g., computer literacy, English proficiency, problem-solving capacity, social responsibility, mastery of disciplinary knowledge) and that are using some subset of globally-disseminated educational practices (e.g., school-based management, parental involvement, IT, cooperative learning).

The purpose of the chapter is twofold. First, we explore how Thai school leaders successfully respond to the demands of traditional cultural norms even as they transform schools into "modern" Thai organizations. Second, we reflect on these findings from Thailand in the light of a cross-cultural perspective on educational change. The findings demonstrate the significance of cross-cultural research by expanding traditional (i.e., Western) perspectives on organizational leadership and change.

Leading Educational Change in Thailand

Like other areas of public administration in Thailand, the educational system is highly centralized (Hallinger et al., 1999; Hallinger & Kantamara, 2000; Ketudat, 1984; Meesing, 1979). In Thailand's educational system, participants assume that orders from above are orders for all concerned. This has resulted in what even senior Ministry of Education officials have acknowledged, with mixed feelings, is a "compliance culture" (see also Sykes, Floden & Wheeler, 1997; Wheeler, Gallagher, McDonough, & Sookpokakit-Namfa, 1997). Over the past decade the constraints imposed by this institutional culture on educational reform have become increasingly apparent. Consequently, the Ministry of Education (MOE) has recently adopted policies that seek to implant "empowering" educational reforms into Thai schools (Ministry of Education 1997a, 1997b; Sykes et al., 1997). These include school-based management, parental involvement, social-constructivist teaching practices, and the use of new learning technologies.

In their countries of origin, implementation of these "global" school reforms has been difficult, long, and uncertain (e.g., Caldwell, 1998; Evans, 1996; Hargeaves & Fullan, 1998; Murphy & Adams, 1998). Not surprisingly, these reforms have found an even more tentative welcome in the strongly hierarchical social and institutional culture of Thailand's schools. More so than in the West, the values and assumptions underlying these "modern" educational practices run counter to traditional cultural norms of Thai society (Hallinger et al., 1999; Hallinger & Kantamara, 2000; Sykes et al., 1997; Wheeler et al., 1997).

This is not to say that Thai educators have not been asking for change. Indeed, there is widespread recognition that the current system is inefficient and ineffective at meeting the demands of the emerging era. Even so, when faced with implementing these challenging new approaches to management, learning, and teaching, Thai educators remain subject to traditional Thai cultural values, assumptions, and norms.

We therefore assert that implementation of these "modern" educational reforms will fail unless Thai leaders demonstrate a deep understanding of how traditional cultural norms influence the implementation of change in Thailand's social systems. We further contend that being Thai no more guarantees understanding how to foster real change in Thai schools than being American does in the United States or being Chinese does in Hong Kong. Thus, we begin this inquiry into leading change with a summary of key facets of Thai culture (see Hallinger & Kantamara, 2000, for a more complete explication).

A Cultural Perspective on Change in Thai Schools

Geert Hofstede, an engineer and industrial psychologist, conducted a six-year social study in the late 1960s to explore cultural differences among people from 40 countries, including Thailand. Hofstede defined culture as the collective mental programming of the people in a social environment in which one grew up and collected one's life experiences (Hofstede, 1980, 1983; 1991). He identified four dimensions on which national cultures differ: power distance, uncertainty avoidance, individualism-collectivism, and masculinity-femininity. According to Hofstede's cultural map, Thailand ranks high on power distance, high as a collectivist culture, high on uncertainty avoidance, and high on femininity. In an earlier paper, we concluded the following points.

High Power Distance

The high power distance characterizing Thai culture shapes the behavior of administrators, teachers, students, and parents to show unusually high deference (greng jai) toward those of senior status in all social relationships. This results in a pervasive, socially-legitimated expectation that decisions should be made by those in positions of authority (i.e., Ministry administrators for principals, principals for teachers and parents, teachers for students). High power distance also creates a tendency for administrators to lead by fiat. There is a cultural assumption that leading change entails establishing orders—which will be followed—and applying pressure in special cases where it is needed.

Collectivist

The collectivist facet of Thai culture shapes the context for change by locating it in the group more than in individuals. While it is still individuals who must change their attitudes and behaviors, Thais exhibit a stronger "We" than "I" mentality. They look primarily to their referent social groups in order to "make sense" of their role in change (Holmes & Tangtongtavy, 1995). Moreover, staff are more likely to "move in the direction of change" as a group than as individuals.

Uncertainty Avoidance

The high level of uncertainty avoidance means that Thais are strongly socialized to conform to group norms, traditions, rules, and regulations. They evince a stronger tendency to seek stability and to find change disruptive and disturbing than those in "lower uncertainty avoidance" cultures.

Feminine

The feminine dimension leads Thais to place a high value on social relationships, to seek harmony, and to avoid conflict. Since conflict is a natural by-product of change; this exerts a further drag on the already slow process of change. Thais also place great emphasis on living and working in a pleasurable atmosphere and on fostering a strong spirit of community through social relations. Anything that threatens the harmonious balance of the social group (e.g., change) will create resistance. In this current research effort, we assumed the challenge of exploring empirically the salience of these propositions in Thai schools.

Methodology

Several potentially conflicting characteristics complicate research into school leadership in Thailand and other rapidly developing countries in this era.

Thailand's Ministry of Education (MOE) is promulgating reform policies that seek to change the normative practices of Thai schools in terms of management, the role of parents and community, teaching, and learning (MOE, 1997a, 1997b).

The social-economic context surrounding Thai schools is in a period of rapid transition. This emerging context is characterized by rising expectations and dissatisfaction with the educational system among a growing middle class and a concerned business community (Hallinger, 1998; Hallinger & Kantamara, in press).

To date, new reform policies have reached relatively few schools, and Thailand's leaders are under pressure to consider how they will "import" these innovative practices into more schools (MOE 1997a, 1999b; Sykes et al., 1997).

Given these trends, understanding "what worked" in terms of leading Thai schools in 1980 or 1990 will provide an incomplete picture of what it takes to lead change in the year 2,000 (Drucker, 1995). This rapidly evolving context created a problematic situation given our goal of illuminating the process of change in Thai "schools of the future." We settled on a research strategy that would study schools that had demonstrated success in implementing the type of "modern" educational reforms envisioned by Thai policy makers for all schools.

Our case study focused on a subset of 139 schools that participated in a systemic school reform project undertaken by the MOE between 1993 and 1997: the Basic and Occupational Education and Training (BOET) (MOE 1997a, 1997b). The BOET project's goal was, "To expand access to and improve the quality of basic and occupational education programs so that traditionally disadvantaged groups will be better served" (MOE, 1997b). This was accomplished largely through local collaboration and technical assistance designed to assist these project schools in implementing the types of innovations in management, teaching, and learning noted above. The BOET program was funded by the United Nations Development Program (UNDP) and implemented in 13 provincial sites in the four regions of Thailand.

We selected three schools from among the 139 schools two years after completion of the project (i.e., spring 1999). The three schools were nominated by the project director as having successfully implemented and maintained the desired reforms over a seven-year period. Moreover, the principals who led these schools during the project were still working at them in the spring of 1999. The three schools were located in different regions of Thailand (North, South, Central). They were coeducational schools of moderate size (200–350 students) serving students from preschool to 9th grade. Teaching staffs ranged from 15 to 17 teachers per school. Staff qualifications were similar across the schools, with all teachers having at least a special diploma and a few teachers at each school possessing a bachelor's degree. The directors (two male and one female) each held a B.A.

Participation in the BOET project meant that these schools received more resources than "typical" Thai schools. Despite this difference from the challenge facing Thai schools in general, they still met our most important criteria. They had started at a typical baseline of performance compared with other schools in their regions. Initially, the schools had been selected for participation in the BOET project because their norms of practice reflected a range typical of other Thai schools. They were implementing the same educational reforms envisioned for all Thai schools by the MOE (i.e., parental involvement, school improvement planning, IT, school-based management). Over a seven-year period, the schools had overcome a typical set of change obstacles faced in Thai schools and still managed to sustain the implementation of these complex reforms. While this sample of three schools would not provide a definitive perspective on the salience of our conceptual analysis, it seemed well-suited to the requirements of an exploratory empirical effort.

Data Collection and Analysis

We contacted principals from the three schools to obtain their participation in "a study of educational reform." Two days were spent at each of the schools.

A researcher observed and conducted focus group interviews with teachers. More extensive individual interviews were held with each of the principals. The interviews were semi-structured and designed to elicit staff perceptions of the change process that the school had undertaken. Each interview typically lasted from one to two hours.

We employed thematic analysis of the data focusing specifically on two areas: obstacles and change strategies. Initially we looked for patterns within the three schools and compared the perceptions of the teachers with those of the principal. Then we compared data across the schools in order to generate common categories. Finally, we referred back to our conceptual framework on cultural change to generate additional perspectives on the data. Due to space limitations, we limit our report of findings to a summary and discussion related to the change strategies employed in the schools.

Results

When comparing the findings across the three schools, several common categories emerged from the data: leadership style, group orientation and teamwork, pressure and support for change, spirit and celebration, and accountability.

Leadership Style

As suggested above, the predominant tendency of Thai school administrators is to rely heavily on position power when implementing new policies or programs. In light of this, we were surprised to find that all three directors used decidedly participatory management styles. Although it manifested in different ways, each of the directors took specific steps:

1. to build widespread support for the vision of change;
2. to reduce the "status gap" between themselves and their stakeholders; and
3. to gather information that reflected a broad range of perspectives from stakeholders prior to and during the adoption of school changes.

This was demonstrated in their approaches to building visions for change in the schools. Contrary to the top-down vision approach favored by many Thai leaders, these principals involved all stakeholders—students, teachers, parents, community members—in setting the direction for change.

One of the directors, Mr. Lek, went to unusual lengths for a Thai leader to ensure that everyone had an opportunity to voice their thoughts on school matters. Annually, he asked all students to fill out an evaluation form on their teachers. Lek summarizes the results, and the staff use the data to identify the needs of the school. In addition, he holds individual teacher conferences during which he shares the classroom-based information. He noted, "In the first couple years there were only compliments for the teachers, because the students tended to 'greng jai' them. But more recently they have begun to offer critical comments as well."

The teachers also evaluate the director in writing once a year. Lek claimed to find this method helpful because most teachers were too greng jai to give him direct verbal feedback. The teachers noted that allowing them to evaluate him represented a powerful form of modeling. It indicated that Lek supported continuous improvement for all staff, not just teachers.

A second director, Ms. Jintana, gives each parent a form on which to write their opinions of the school. The forms are anonymous and divided into different sections: teachers, students, school administrator, and care provided for students. She distributes the results to all teachers so that they can become aware of how the community views the school.

The third director, Mr. Suchin, noted the importance but also the difficulty in obtaining broad participation in developing a school improvement plan. Consistent with Thai tradition, staff, students, and parents were initially afraid to express their opinions even when he encouraged them to do so. Few people, teachers and villagers alike, felt comfortable speaking up in group forums. A Thai who speaks up in the company of a mixed social group runs the risk of appearing to think he/she is better than others. They felt much more comfortable letting the senior person present—the school director—decide for them. With students, the problem was even more pronounced. They refused to speak up at all because they were bound to greng jai everyone; all other members of the committees were senior. Suchin reduced this problem by inviting their seniors (or "roon pii") who recently graduated to attend the meetings and to work with them as coaches. This began to bridge the gap between ages. Suchin noted that the most important thing is for the school leader to find ways to help people see that it is okay for them to voice their thoughts and ask questions.

Through involvement in a variety of projects, these norms began to change in all three schools. Representatives of students, graduates, staff, and community members felt more comfortable participating in the process of developing school improvement plans that were based on locally identified needs. However, this change only occurred slowly and over a period of several years. Teachers at all three schools gave much credit for their success to the school directors. they elaborated that the directors would often participate in tasks with their staffs, an unusual step for Thai principals. All three directors were more involved in activities with their staff than is typical. All led by example, a key facet identified among change leaders (e.g., Evans, 1996).

Group Orientation and Teamwork

The three directors worked hard to create a sense of family in their schools. One director noted, "I want my staff to work as brothers and sisters with a sense of mutual responsibility and a high level of trust, even in the face of the conflict that comes with change." This also reflected the high value that the principals placed on teamwork as a focus for change.

In one school, staff identified how peer coaching, in formal and informal ways, provided support in the midst of change. Teamwork had both technical and emotional dimensions. Given the feeling of living as brothers and sisters, senior teachers (or "pii") helped their junior teachers (or "nong") in learning to use curricular and instructional innovations. The family atmosphere promoted trust among colleagues and somewhat reduced the sense of uncertainty that comes naturally with change.

Access to special budget allocations afforded the staff the opportunity to participate in numerous group planning and development activities: planning meetings, workshops, seminars, site visits to other schools, and study tours. These seemed to have a positive impact on change in two ways. First, they afforded the staff—as a group or subgroups—with opportunities to "make meaning" out of the new (Evans, 1996; Fullan, 1990, 1993). These also enabled staff to gain access to moral and technical support from a broader array of sources: program staff, colleagues, teachers from other schools, and consultants.

Pressure and Support for Change

When the BOET project was initiated, all three directors explicitly avoided forcing teachers to join. Instead, they sought initial participation on a voluntary basis and then expanded the program concurrent with increased staff interest. They all used a similar strategy of encouraging the more active and knowledgeable teachers to participate in the change effort first. This allowed sceptical colleagues to observe their colleagues as well as the reactions of students. This reduced the stress associated with change and defused the fear that they were "guinea pigs for another top-down MOE project." Over time, many of the initially sceptical teachers decided to join the project activities as well.

There were of course some teachers who paid little attention to the new initiatives. Moreover, while they were indifferent to the new programs, they were not averse to criticizing other staff's efforts. The directors relied on a combination of support and peer pressure to foster change with these staff members (Evans, 1996; Kotter, 1996).

As suggested above, this project provided a high degree of technical support. Teachers were able to attend numerous workshops in areas targeted by the innovations. In the BOET program human resource development was

provided for teachers, students, community members, and school administrators all at the same time. Moreover, they had multiple opportunities to visit
other schools and see the new management, instructional, and curricular
processes at work prior to and during implementation. Professional development and implementation activities went well beyond the typical one-shot
workshop.

The directors employed a variety of strategies with staff who simply would
not work toward implementation of the project goals over a long period of
time. Suchin, for example, noted that he relied more on persuasion than orders
to foster change. He used both group meetings and individual conversations
to explain the rationale of the initiatives and to encourage staff participation.
Sometimes he assigned sceptical staff members with particular responsibilities to make them feel special and also to encourage a sense of responsibility.

Jintana would meet with a particularly resistant teacher personally
outside of the school to have a jap-kao-kui-gun or "touch-the-knee" talk. This
is an informal "open-heart" talk to discuss an issue, problem, or concern about
the new. Or the director might ask an informal leader among the staff
member's colleagues to talk with a resistant colleague or even to act as a mentor.

With the most resistant teachers, the directors also used administrative
pressure, especially from outside the school. For example, Lek used high status
"resource people"—the district/provincial teacher supervisor, BOET task force
consultants, UNDP representatives—to legitimate the project as a larger
priority of the educational system.

Over time, public recognition of the schools' success also became a
source of positive pressure for change. For example, over a period of several
years, one school became a model for the use of student portfolios. Teachers
came from other schools around Thailand to observe how its teachers used
portfolios. Even teachers who had continued to resist the use of student portfolios gradually began to take a closer look. Positive recognition of the school's
successful innovation among "outsiders" validated the school's efforts and
created positive pressure for sustaining the change effort.

While parents and community members typically play a limited role in
Thai schools, a goal of this project was to increase collaboration between
schools and their communities. The principals were key players in navi-
gating the potentially treacherous waters as teachers, parents, and community members came together. Jintana noted: "We need to open our door, go
to the people, and accept them first. Some things we do not know as well as
the community . . . teachers do not know everything." This attitude and the
practices associated with it represent a major departure from traditional
Thai schools and norms (e.g., high power distance). It is also interesting to
note that as collaboration between schools and their communities increased,
these external groups became a new source of positive pressure for change.

Spirit and Celebration

Thai culture's feminine dimension places a strong emphasis on social relationships in the workplace. A key outgrowth of this norm lies in the importance of paying attention to spirit in the workplace. To be productive Thai people must find some degree of fun in their work. Harmonious group relationships are a necessary condition for effectiveness in Thai organizations (Holmes & Tangtongtavy, 1995). This takes forms that differ in both subtle and obvious ways from Western schools. In these schools it was apparent in the degree to which group-oriented socializing occurred in the context of the school's change implementation activities.

For example, the schools used several different kinds of celebrations to publicize, reinforce, and share the fruits of change. Student fairs, teacher fairs, and BOET-sponsored study visits in Thailand and abroad all became vehicles for celebrating the collective effort. Many people prepared for these events, which became occasions for fun, or "sanook." But it was also the shared effort putting the fair together successfully that energized the staffs.

At Suchin's school, when parents were invited to a school fair displaying their children's products they felt very proud. Moreover, parents began to hear stories about how "their teachers" were training teachers in other schools. This made them curious about what the school was doing and further stimulated their interest. It also reinforced the public impression that the school was providing a high quality education. Increased pride and spirit—gumlung jai—among the public became a source of new energy to sustain the teachers during the difficult effort to change.

Accountability

The BOET program provided regular monitoring and evaluation of the school's progress. The teachers noted that the follow-up visits by BOET staff were different from traditional infrequent monitoring conducting by MOE officials. When a teacher supervisor visits a school, he tends to only check whether the school is following the annual plan and if the teachers write their lesson plans. MOE monitoring of schools follows a checklist mentality and has been characterized as "hit and run visits" (Hallinger et al., 1999). Few teachers feel the visits are helpful. Worse yet, they feel threatened rather than supported, as the purpose often seems to be to find fault in their teaching.

The BOET program visits focused on formative evaluation and made staffs feel that people cared what the school was doing with their money. Was it worth it or not? How were school projects progressing? Was any help needed? The result was a more positive attitude of staffs toward accountability.

One strategy that fostered staff learning while also promoting implementation and accountability was action research. This approach gave practical support to long-term implementation and seemed to increase teachers' sense of responsibility. In sum, this actively formative approach toward program accountability made staff feel that policy makers were "jing jung"—serious—about the project. This is seldom the case in the traditional system (e.g., see Hallinger et al., 1999).

Discussion and Conclusions

Our earlier analysis of educational change in Thailand's cultural context led to several propositions about leading change in Thai schools (Hallinger & Kantamara, 2000). Here we seek to extend these propositions using the findings of this exploratory study. Note that results from this single case study cannot confirm the propositions; they merely elaborate on their face validity.

Leading School Change in the Thai Cultural Context
(1) Target formal leaders and obtain their support early in the change process. If administrative support is an important condition for educational change in Western countries (Evans, 1996; Fullan, 1990, 1993; Kotter, 1996), our theoretical and empirical analyses suggest that it is a sine qua non in Thailand. The "high power distance" that characterizes Thai culture invests the principal with significantly more position power as well as culturally legitimized, informal influence. Both carried over to the principal's role in leading change. The teachers at all three schools made it clear that their principals played a critical role by creating an initial stimulus for change and actively supporting implementation. The leader's role as a catalyst for change seems even more necessary given that these schools were undertaking reforms that ran counter to deeply-rooted Thai cultural norms. Thus, early, firm support from the principal seems necessary for catalyzing and sustaining the transformation of Thai schools into "modern organizations."

(2) *Formal leaders must use strategies that counter traditional norms of deference and bring staff concerns to the surface so they may understand and address staff resistance.* The high power distance prevalent in Thai culture creates an intriguing problem for change leaders. It would appear that Thai leaders may need to "disarm" themselves of the most powerful tool at their disposal—power—in order to promote lasting change. This is consistent with a Buddhist principle familiar to Thai people: "In order to get something that you really want, you need to want it less."

In the face of the principal's power and status, the Thai tendency to greng jai or show deference forestalls the initial impulse of staff to ask important questions about the innovation. Consequently, Thai leaders often fail to surface the concerns and questions of staff at the outset. They may come to believe they have achieved consensus where none exists. These principals demonstrated an implicit understanding of this fact as they employed a variety of "disarmament" strategies designed to reduce the power distance between themselves and their constituencies.

The tendency of staff to greng jai by responding with surface politeness also drives resistance underground. The result is a polite, surface compliance seasoned with varying degrees of passive resistance. This also means that managers fail to tap the most important resource they possess in the change implementation process, the knowledge of their own staff. As Maurer has observed:

> Often those who resist have something important to tell us. We can be influenced by them. People resist for what they view as good reasons. They may see alternatives we never dreamed of. They may understand problems about the minutiae of implementation that we never see from our lofty perch. (1996, p. 49)

Resistance is a natural by-product of the change process (Bolman & Deal, 1992; Evans, 1996; Maurer, 1996; O'Toole, 1995; Senge, 1990). It is something leaders must learn to work with—not something to sweep under the rug, to bludgeon into submission, or even to "overcome" through argument. To successfully foster change in organizations, leaders must learn to look for and use resistance. Yet, as suggested above, the high power distance in Thai culture creates a dynamic in which resistance is unconsciously smothered.

To our surprise, these principals evinced a more participatory mode of leadership than we typically see in Thai schools. This extended to personal perspectives (e.g., vision), behaviors (e.g., modeling), leadership tools (e.g., surveys, annual written evaluation-feedback forms, open meetings), and to the strategies used to foster staff interest and involvement in the change projects. While these directors emphasized the importance of breaking down cultural norms of deference, they also continued to maintain traditional values of mutual respect and sincerity. More in-depth case studies that describe the manner in which leaders walk this fine line of cultural transformation would add greatly to our understanding of change leadership more broadly.

(3) Obtain and cultivate the support of informal leaders and leverage the resources of the social network to create pressure and support for change. As noted above, Thailand is a highly collectivist culture. Thai people learn to use their social groups as the primary sources of reference for understanding their place in society. Not surprisingly, these principals made extensive and varied use of the social networks in and around their schools to foster change. The principals targeted informal leaders in the initial implementation of the reform project and maintained close contact with them throughout. Their colleagues

often looked to these leaders for direction and reassurance. Accessing the resources of the social network of the school, and in this case the community, created support for change. For example, staff outings gave the staff a chance to gain a group perspective on the innovations under consideration. Surprisingly, parental and community pressure emerged as a factor that exerted considerable influence on teachers over time. This project mandated a level of community participation hitherto unknown in Thai schools. A range of activities that increased contact among staff and community members (e.g., planning meetings, fairs, celebrations, study visits) also created pressure (e.g., higher expectations) as well as support (e.g., pride) for change. Thus, we would suggest that the informal network of the school and its community is as important—if not more important—in Thailand as in Western schools.

(4) Use formal authority selectively to reinforce expectations and standards consistent with implementation of the innovation. As suggested above, these principals walked a fine line in the use of their authority. They understood the need to downplay their authority if there was any hope of stimulating meaningful participation among staff, students, and community members. Thus, they began the change project by seeking the participation of volunteers and encouraging the use of "democratic" group processes. Even so, over time they did use a variety of strategies that increased the pressure for implementation. Some were quite direct, while others were indirect. Thus, they were not afraid to use the authority of external educational constituencies (e.g., project staff, provincial administrators, experts), the expectations of the community, and peer pressure to foster change.

(5) Find ways to inject fun, encourage the spirit, and celebrate shared accomplishments in the workplace while maintaining accountability. All three directors identified the importance of fostering a family spirit of mutual responsibility and assistance when speaking of visions for their schools. The skill of their leadership and that of their colleagues lie in finding an acceptable balance between the pressures for change (e.g., accountability) and group harmony. Organizational rituals such as study visits, fairs, and celebrations became important opportunities for creating meaning and sustaining the momentum of change. The staff in all three schools would claim that in an effective school, sanook (fun) and gumlung jai (moral support/spirit) go hand in hand with productivity.

Implications for Cross-Cultural Studies of Leadership

We emphasize that this report represents an early step in a long-range program of research and development on leadership across cultures. Moreover, this study's abundant limitations point the way for future research. For example, the addition of comparison schools from another culture would add greatly to the richness and power of this analysis.

As a preliminary effort, however, this study confirms the complexity of understanding leadership processes across cultures. Two decades ago Bridges (1977) claimed that leadership entails getting results through other people. If this is the case, then we can only understand the nature of leadership by exposing the hidden assumptions of the cultural context. This will open new windows through which to view educational leadership.

The culture of Thailand creates a unique context in which to lead educational change. According to Hofstede's cultural map (1991), however, Thai culture also shares similarities with other Southeast Asian nations. In particular, other Southeast Asian nations tend to rank high on both collectivism and power distance. Thus, for example, high power distance also shapes the context for leading educational change in Singapore and in Hong Kong (Hallinger, 1999). To the extent that this is the case, school principals in these nations might find a need for similar "disarmament strategies" in efforts to foster change.

This analysis further suggests that a culture's strengths are also its limitations. In the case of leading change, high power distance enables leaders to achieve initial compliance more easily. However, it can become a limitation when the goal is deeper implementation of complex innovations that require staff to learn new skills. This is an intriguing problem that only cross-cultural comparison can illuminate.

This perspective on leadership seems especially salient during an era in which global change forces are changing the face of education throughout the world. An ever-expanding array of Western management innovations are traversing the globe and finding their way into traditional cultures. Not unlike the response of a living organism to a virus, the instinctive response of many organizations to these innovations is to attack with self-protective mechanisms. Thus, even as policy makers embrace foreign educational policy reforms, change engenders more suspicion than enthusiasm at the point of implementation. Successful implementation will require sophisticated leadership, especially where the underlying assumptions are foreign to prevailing norms of the local culture.

A special caveat is in order before we close. We emphatically restate the cautions of other scholars against the tendency to believe that change in cultural processes can be achieved quickly, even in the presence of the most skilled leadership (Evans, 1996; Fullan, 1990, 1993; Kotter, 1996; Ohmae, 1995; O'Toole, 1995; Sarason, 1982; Schein, 1996; Senge, 1990). As futurist Kenichi Ohmae has observed: "The contents of kitchens and closets may change, but the core mechanisms by which cultures maintain their identity and socialize their young remain untouched" (1995, p. 30). Schools were never designed with the goal of rapid change, and the transformation of traditional schools into "modern" organizations will require a long-term perspective and persistence (Tyack & Hansot, 1982).

References

Bajunid, I. A. (1995). The educational administrator as a cultural leader. *Journal of the Malaysian Educational Manager, 1*(1), 12–21.

Bajunid, I. A. (1996). Preliminary explorations of indigenous perspectives of educational management: The evolving Malaysian experience. *Journal of Educational Administration, 34*(5), 50–73.

Bolman, L., & Deal, T. (1992). *Reframing organizations.* San Francisco: Jossey-Bass.

Bridges, E. (1977). The nature of leadership. In L. Cunningham, W. Hack, & R. Nystrand (Eds.), *Educational administration: The developing decades* (pp. 202–230). Berkeley, CA: McCutchan.

Brislin, R. (1993). *Understanding culture's influence on behavior.* New York: Harcourt Brace.

Caldwell, B. (1998). Strategic leadership, resource management and effective school reform. *Journal of Educational Administration, 36*(5), 445–461.

Cheng, K. M. (1995). The neglected dimension: Cultural comparison in educational administration. In K. C. Wong & K. M. Cheng (Eds.), *Educational leadership and change: An international perspective* (pp. 87–104). Hong Kong: Hong Kong University Press.

Cheng, K. M., & Wong, K. C. (1996). School effectiveness in East Asia: Concepts, origins and implications. *Journal of Educational Administration, 34*(5), 32–49.

Davis, B. (1999, June) *Credit where credit is due: The professional accreditation and continuing education of school principals in Victoria.* Paper presented at the Conference on Professional Development of School Leaders, Center for Educational Leadership, University of Hong Kong.

Dimmock, C., & Walker, A. (1998). Transforming Hong Kong's schools: Trends and emerging issues. *Journal of Educational Administration, 36*(5), 476–491.

Drucker, P. (1995). *Managing in a time of great change.* New York: Talley House, Dutton.

Evans, R. (1996). *The human side of change.* San Francisco: Jossey-Bass.

Feng, D. (1999, June). *China's principal training: Reviewing and looking forward.* Paper presented at the Conference on Professional Development of School Leaders, Center for Educational Leadership, University of Hong Kong.

Fullan, M. (1990). *The new meaning of educational change.* New York: Teachers College Press.

Fullan, M. (1993). *Change forces.* New York: Teachers College Press.

Hallinger, P. (1995). Culture and leadership: Developing an international perspective in educational administration. *UCEA Review, 36*(1), 3–7.

Hallinger, P. (1998). Educational change in Southeast Asia: The challenge of creating learning systems. *Journal of Educational Administration, 36*(5), 492–509.

Hallinger, P. (1999, June). *Learning to lead change: Seeing and hearing is believing but eating is knowing.* Paper presented at the Conference on Professional Development for School Leaders, Center for Educational Leadership, University of Hong Kong.

Hallinger, P., & Bridges, E. (1997). Problem-based leadership development: Preparing educational leaders for changing times. *Journal of School Leadership, 7,* 1–15.

Hallinger, P., Chantarapanya, P., Sriboonma, U., & Kantamara, P. (1999). The challenge of educational reform in Thailand: Jing Jai, Jing Jung, Nae Norn. In T. Townsend & Y. C. Cheng (Eds.), *Educational change and development in the Asia-Pacific region: Challenges for the future* (pp. 207–226). Rotterdam, The Netherlands: Swets & Zeitsinger.

Hallinger, P., & Kantamara, P. (2000). Leading at the confluence of tradition and globalization: The challenge of change in Thai schools. *Asia Pacific Journal of Education, 20*(2), 46–57.

Hallinger, P., & Leithwood, K. (1996). Culture and educational administration: A case of finding out what you don't know you don't know. *Journal of Educational Administration, 34*(5), 98–119.

Hallinger, P., & Leithwood, K. (1998). Unseen forces: The impact of social culture on leadership. *Peabody Journal of Education, 73*(2), 126–151.

Hargreaves, A., & Fullan, M. (1998). *What's worth fighting for out there.* New York: Teachers College Press.

Heck, R. (1996). Leadership and culture: Conceptual and methodological issues in comparing models across cultural settings. *Journal of Educational Administration, 30*(3), 35–48.

Hofstede, G. (1980). *Culture's consequences: International differences in work-related values.* Beverly Hills, CA: Sage.

Hofstede, G. (1983). The cultural relativity of organizational practices and theories. *Journal of Business Studies, 13*(3), 75–89.

Hofstede, G. (1991). *Cultures and organizations: Software of the mind.* Berkshire, England: McGraw-Hill.

Holmes, H., & Tangtongtavy, S. (1995). *Working with the Thais: A guide to managing in Thailand.* Bangkok, Thailand: White Lotus.

Ketudat, S. (1984). Planning and implementation of the primary education reform in Thailand, Prospects. *Quarterly Review of Education, 14*(4), 523–530.

Kotter, J. (1996). *Leading change.* Boston: Harvard Business School Press.

Li, W. C. (1999, June). *Organizing principal training in China: Models, problems and prospects.* Paper presented at the Conference on Professional Development of School Leaders, Center for Educational Leadership, University of Hong Kong.

Low, G. T. (1999, June). *Preparation of aspiring principals in Singapore: A partnership model.* Paper presented at the Conference on Professional Development of School Leaders, Center for Educational Leadership, University of Hong Kong.

Maurer, R. (1996). *Beyond the wall of resistance.* Austin, TX: Bard Books.

Meesing, A. (1979). Social studies in Thailand. In H. D. Mehlinger & J. L. Tucker (Eds.), *Social studies in other nations* (pp. 31–43). ERIC Reproduction Document Service No. ED. 174 540.

Ministry of Education. (1997a). *Introducing ONPEC.* Bangkok, Thailand: Author.

Ministry of Education. (1997b). *The experience from the Basic and Occupational Education and Training Programme.* Bangkok, Thailand: Author.

Murphy, J., & Adams, J. (1998). Reforming America's schools 1980–2000. *Journal of Educational Administration, 36*(5), 426–444.

Ohmae, K. (1995). *The end of the nation: The rise of regional economies.* New York: Free Press

O'Toole, J. (1995). *Leading change.* San Francisco: Jossey-Bass.

Reeves, J., Forde, C., Casteel, V., & Lynas, R. (1998). Developing a model of practice: Designing a framework for the professional development of school leaders and managers. *School Leadership and Management, (18)*2, 185–196.

Sarason, S. (1982). *The culture of the school and the problem of change* (Rev. ed.). Boston: Allyn & Bacon.

Schein, E. (1996). Culture: The missing concept in organization studies. *Administrative Science Quarterly, 41,* 229–240.

Senge, P. M. (1990). *The fifth discipline.* New York: Doubleday.

Sykes, G., Floden, R., & Wheeler, C. (1997). *Improving teacher learning in Thailand: Analysis and options Bangkok* (#21/2540). Bangkok, Thailand: Office of the National Education Commission.

Tomlinson, H. (1999, June). *Recent developments in England and Wales: The professional qualification for headship (NPQH) and the leadership program for serving headteachers (LPSH).* Paper presented at the Conference on Professional Development of School Leaders, Center for Educational Leadership, University of Hong Kong.

Tyack, D., & Hansot, E. (1982). *Managers of virtue.* New York: Teachers College Press.

Walker, A., Bridges, E., & Chan, B. (1996). Wisdom gained, wisdom given: Instituting PBL in a Chinese culture. *Journal of Educational Administration, 34*(5), 98–119.

Walker, A., & Quong, T. (1998). Valuing differences: Strategies for dealing with the tensions of educational leadership in a global society. *Peabody Journal of Education, 73*(2), 81–105.

Wheeler, C., Gallagher, J., McDonough, M., & Sookpokakit-Namfa, B. (1997). Improving school-community relations in Thailand. In. W. K. Cummings & P. G. Altbach (Eds.), *The challenge of Eastern Asian education: Implications for America* (pp. 205–319). Albany, NY: State University of New York Press.

Wong, K. C. (1996, April). *Developing the moral dimensions of school leaders.* Paper presented at the meeting of the APEC Educational Leadership Centers, Chiang Mai, Thailand.

8

Shaping the Curriculum in Hong Kong

Contexts and Cultures

PAUL MORRIS AND LO MUN LING

Introduction

Schooling, and the curriculum specifically, have been portrayed as both an extension of a society's culture (Reynolds & Skilbeck, 1976) and a forum in which a variety of interest groups within a society compete to promote their conception of valid knowledge (Goodson, 1994). This chapter explores the relationship between curriculum and culture through an analysis of the career of the Target Oriented Curriculum (TOC), which is the most comprehensive attempt to date to reform the curriculum of Hong Kong's primary schools. We shall trace the reform from its inception to its enactment in a school and identify how it was shaped by the multitude of interest groups that influenced its creation and subsequent adaptation in classrooms. The competition to define the nature of the curriculum was intense because the reform was systemic, comprehensive, radical, rushed, and introduced into a Chinese community by a departing colonial government within a period that was intensely politicized

As Peshkin (1992) noted, "culture" is a ubiquitous, amorphous, overused, and over-defined term—to the extent that a conception to match nearly any purpose can be found. With reference to Hong Kong and other East Asian societies, "culture" has frequently been used in the context of education to explain the differences between the academic achievements of Asian and Western societies. Specifically, Confucianism and/or Asian values have been identified as key features of the culture of East Asian societies and an explanation for the high levels of academic achievement of Asian pupils compared to their Western counterparts (Reynolds & Farrell, 1996). Such analyses focus on what Linton (1936) termed the universal component of culture, which depicts societies as homogeneous and underscores the significance of the many smaller and specialized groups whose ways of thinking and acting are more akin to those of sub-cultures. Our preferred conception of culture is that of Metz (1983), who defined it as "a broad, diffuse and potentially contradictory body of shared understandings about what is and what ought to be" (p. 237). The reference to "what ought to be" captures the imperative and normative tone of curriculum reforms, whilst the stress on the diffuse and contradictory nature of culture moves beyond its portrayal as a singular and systematic set of beliefs.

Analyses of the nature of culture in Hong Kong also suggest that the doctrine of Confucianism has not been its central feature. Leung (1996), for instance, argued that there was no indigenous Hong Kong culture in the nineteenth century, and the traditional culture brought from the mainland consisted of the social customs and family socialization patterns "of the struggling masses whose concerns were security and survival rather than the grandiose Confucian ideals of moral cultivation and self-perfection," and so "amorality, materialism and a pragmatic orientation eventually prevailed over Confucian ethics in the evolution of Hong Kong culture." Hong Kong's distinctive indigenous culture has, more recently, been described as "egotistical individualism" (Lau & Kuan, 1990) and an interaction of the themes of survival, affluence and deliverance (Chan, 1993). In terms of the impact of moral principles on behavior, Lau and Kuan (1988) described the preferred option as one of "situational morality," meaning that ideas of what is right and wrong vary according to context, and are not predicated on a universal set of moral beliefs. In brief, an interpretation of the curriculum/culture fit solely reliant on a Confucianism/Western dichotomy would fail to capture the diverse and fragmented nature of this society.

The career of the TOC involved a clash between an innovation based on Western cultural precepts and a Chinese/Confucian culture, but the process was also more complex and fragmented, and was characterized by the competition between groups that operated within distinct arenas. We have identified three different, but interactive arenas that were critical in shaping the nature and impact of the reform as it progressed from intention to practice. These could be seen to embody distinct sub-cultures or cultural orientations (Peshkin, 1992) in that the various interest groups that operated in each arena, whilst promoting their own visions of schooling, shared common understandings of their purpose, ways of acting, the nature of their audience, and a distinctive discourse.

The first is the relatively private arena of policy making in which different sections within the state bureaucracy were predominant. Secondly, there is the national political arena, which involves the various public contexts in which a multitude of interest groups react to education policy initiatives, and promote both their visions of schooling and their interests. They include teachers' unions, the media, politicians, and school management bodies. This arena was characterized by its role in providing an opportunity for public advocacy and promotion of all those groups who seek to gain public support during a period that was increasingly critical of established institutions. The third arena is located within and across schools and involves those groups directly engaged in the process of implementation. Whilst those operating in this arena shared a common concern for the real world of classrooms and playgrounds, there were critical differences between them—especially those associated with the three major primary school subjects (Chinese, English, and mathematics), the organizational culture of individual schools and the power of participants.

In the subsequent sections we focus on each of the three arenas and identify the various interest groups, their shared values, and how these affected the TOC as it evolved from a plan and was enacted in schools and classrooms. The three arenas broadly correspond to the stages through which policy in highly centralized educational systems traditionally passes (namely: state-centered initiation and promotion, public debate and modification, and local implementation) and reflect the many manifestations of curriculum that Eisner (1979) identified (the explicit, implicit, and null).

Before proceeding, it is necessary to provide a brief description of the goals of the TOC. Figure 8.1 illustrates how the reform documents both portrayed the existing primary school curriculum and the changes they envisaged. The rationale was strongly influenced by a social constructivist view of learning. Two premises of the TOC were pertinent—the value of formative and criterion-referenced assessment, and the need for pupils to learn through tasks a set of generic competencies. Despite this, two key features of primary schooling remained in place—the use of an academic aptitude test at Primary Six to allocate pupils to different types of secondary schools, and the organization of the curriculum and teachers around the three school subjects.

The Policy-Making Arena

The genesis of TOC is unclear, but it seemed to evolve more from a coalescing of factors than from the linear processes of goal-directed, or problem-solving decision-making described by Walker (1990) and Cheng and Cheung (1995). The process was more akin to those described by Kingdon (1984), March and Olsen (1984) and Weiss (1980) who respectively described policy as emerging from a "primeval soup," a "garbage can," and from "decision creep." Kingdon's (1984) portrayal, in which three process streams—*problems, the political context,* and *expertise*—converge, often in random ways, provides an appropriate interpretative framework. The framework requires supplementing with a fourth stream to recognize the influence on the genesis of policy making,

Figure 8.1 The TOC: Key dimensions of the reform.

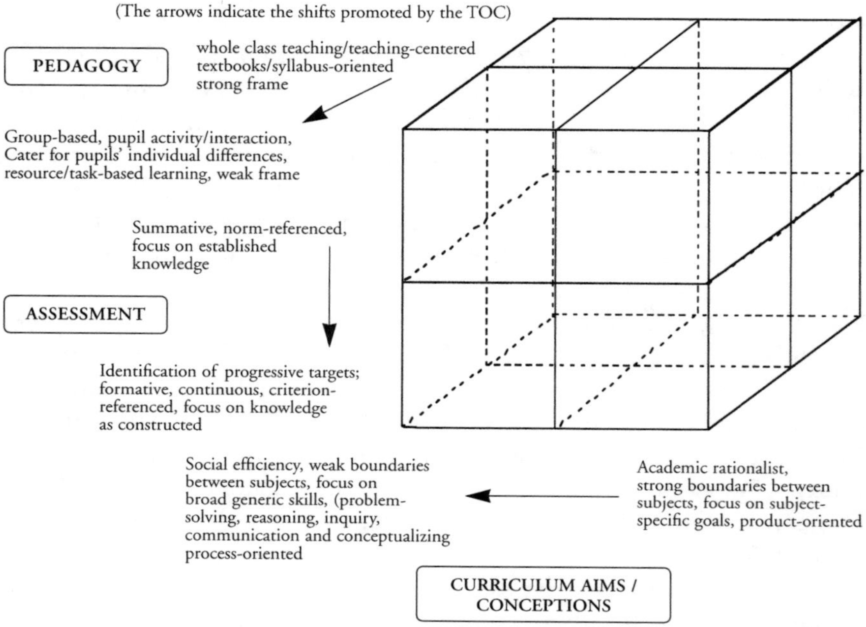

(The arrows indicate the shifts promoted by the TOC)

PEDAGOGY — whole class teaching/teaching-centered textbooks/syllabus-oriented strong frame

Group-based, pupil activity/interaction, Cater for pupils' individual differences, resource/task-based learning, weak frame

Summative, norm-referenced, focus on established knowledge

ASSESSMENT

Identification of progressive targets; formative, continuous, criterion-referenced, focus on knowledge as constructed

Social efficiency, weak boundaries between subjects, focus on broad generic skills, (problem-solving, reasoning, inquiry, communication and conceptualizing process-oriented

Academic rationalist, strong boundaries between subjects, focus on subject-specific goals, product-oriented

CURRICULUM AIMS / CONCEPTIONS

Note. From *Target oriented curriculum evaluation project interim report* (1996, p. 46), by P. Morris et al., INSTEP, Hong Kong: Faculty of Education, The University of Hong Kong.

especially in small states, of *global* (or more specifically Western) *developments* and their capacity to provide both external precedents and justifications for reform.

Since Hong Kong achieved compulsory primary and then junior secondary schooling, in 1971 and 1979 respectively, policies shifted from addressing questions of provision to a focus on more curriculum-oriented issues. A range of specific *problems* had, for some time, captured the attention of the media and policy-making community. Many of these were identified in an internal report of the Education Department (1989) and included: the highly central-ized nature of curriculum development; a perception of declining standards of language proficiency; the lack of clear objectives and targets for learning; a dissatisfaction with didactic teaching styles; the competitive nature of schooling; and a concern that the changing nature of the economy (from manufacturing to service industries) required a significant reform of the school curriculum.

The *political context* includes swings of national mood, election results, ideological priorities and changes of administration. The TOC emerged from a climate that was dominated by the aftermath of the Tienanmen Square massacre. The colonial government was portrayed by an increasingly critical local media as a "lame duck" administration pandering to the wishes of the mainland. In parallel, the Democratic Party emerged as a powerful political force and independent source of criticism of the government. The colonial government was thus keen in its last decade to demonstrate strong leadership, and reform of education was one of the few domains of policy in which its room for maneuvering was less subject to external constraints than other areas, such as the political or economic systems. The fact that the government's tenure was to end on July 1, 1997 also served to significantly change the constraints to and horizons of policy making. The maintenance of the long established doctrine of "positive nonintervention" and a minimalist approach to investment in public services were no longer paramount as the long term consequences of decisions would be borne by the post-handover government.

There were three key interest groups in the policy-making arena in government. Firstly there was the Education and Manpower Branch (EMB), which is the policy-making body, and secondly, Education Department of Hong Kong (ED), which supervises schools and implements policies. The third composed a group of expatriate *experts* in English language education located in the Institute of Language in Education (ILE) whose task was to develop a comprehensive curriculum based on the policy proposals. A less fractious relationship developed between the education policy-making and executive branches of government than was evident prior to 1989 (Morris, 1996). These groups possessed a shared understanding of both the urgent need, given the political context outlined above, to produce a statement of the government's curriculum policy intent that was visionary, radical, and wide-ranging, and a highly critical perspective on the features of the existing curriculum, especially the prevailing pedagogic style. The task was therefore conceived of as partly symbolic in nature and the discourse was both rhetorical and critical, as the principal goal was to create a vision that represented the government's commitment to reform.

The process was facilitated by the international availability of a number of models of curriculum reform that involved an attempt to promote forms of outcomes-based education (OBE) (Spady, 1994). These served as a source of justification of ideas and of expertise. Generally, all those operating within this arena were cognizant of the pattern of *global developments* in curriculum reform. For example, members of the development team had worked on OBE reforms elsewhere (Australia, the United States, and the United Kingdom), and EMB and ED staff were members of international educational agencies such as the Organization for Asia Pacific Economic Cooperation (APEC) and the Organization for Economic Cooperation and Development (OECD).

Despite these shared understandings there were critical tensions within this arena as the interest groups described above promoted distinct conceptions of the nature and purposes of the new curriculum. One group saw it as a vehicle for introducing a regular system of testing that would serve to provide a mechanism for assessing pupils' performance, improve the accountability of schools, and provide a means to select pupils who were able to attend English-medium schools. This conception had minimal implications for the other components of the existing curriculum and it was most strongly associated with the EMB and their allies, drawn mainly from the business/commercial sector. The second conception was most strongly associated with the ED and saw the reform as a long-term means to improve the existing curriculum through incremental changes to the existing core subjects. The third conception saw the reform as designed to radically restructure all key elements of primary schooling, and subsequently of secondary schooling. In contrast to the other conceptions, it envisaged an integrated curriculum, the reduction of the existing boundaries between school subjects, and the abolition of the selective system of assessment at Primary Six. The group most strongly associated with this conception was the TOC developmental team. Given the private nature of this arena, these contradictions and tensions were hidden from public scrutiny.

The resulting public statement of intent (Education Commission of Hong Kong, 1990) that emerged was a compromise that satisfied the needs of all three interest groups insofar as it was derived from a highly derisory portrayal of prevailing practices and couched in a rhetoric that provided broad support for all three conceptions (enhanced accountability, improved teaching, and systemic reform). Consequently, the basic contradictions about the purpose of curriculum reform between the groups were effectively deferred, but emerged subsequently when policy intents were translated into policy actions and in their implementation in schools. Overall, the culture of the policy-making arena was characterized by its sensitivity to the shifting political context, a focus on symbolic action, a discourse that was critical and rhetorical, the reproduction and nonresolution of key contradictions, and its linkages with international trends.

The National Political Arena

Initially the public response to the policy proposal (ECR4) was muted as the teachers' unions and associations representing school principals focused on the recommendation that whole day primary schools replace bisessional schools. Attention focused on the TOC when the nature and full implications began to emerge with the publication of a range of explanatory documents. The discourse became increasingly critical and derisory as the expectations of the reform became clearer and as teachers reacted to the wholesale critique of their existing practices, which was employed as a central justification for change. The media played an active role in the debate, and the TOC was labelled "Totally Objectionable Curriculum." The broad picture that emerged was one of a top-down reform, based on the UK National Curriculum, being hastily imposed on schools without adequate consultation by a colonial government. Further, the intention to use the new assessment system to stream pupils into English- or Chinese-medium schools was interpreted as a crude attempt to surreptitiously segregate pupils and enhance the status of English.

No other educational reform had been the subject of such intense public scrutiny and criticism. This was facilitated by the changing political environment that emerged in the early 1990s—the return to Chinese sovereignty was dominating the agenda, the electoral franchise was being broadened, Britain and China were in conflict over the pace of democratization, and a generation of politicians were emerging who required broadly based public support. Those who were successful in the subsequent elections were mainly drawn from the Democratic Party. The TOC provided an opportunity for candidates to satisfy what emerged as key elements of political success, namely to distance themselves from both the colonial government and the government of China.

The main interest groups that contributed to the debate were the teachers' union, subject associations, school management bodies, academics, and politicians. The central thrust of the critique was both pragmatic and ideological. The pragmatic concerns emerged mainly from teachers and principals, and focused on poor levels of resourcing, the complexity and radical nature of the reform, its impact on teachers' workloads, and its unclear relationship with the existing features of schooling, especially the system of selective assessment that operates at Primary Six. Teachers were bemused and concerned as to the complexity and lack of clarity of the TOC, especially in terms of its expectations as to how pupils were to be assessed and what was to be done to help those identified as having learning difficulties.

At a more ideological level, the critiques reflected more fundamental tensions within Hong Kong society generally—including the elite–egalitarian divide; Chinese traditional values versus modern (Western) values; top-down versus local decision making; and child-centered versus subject-centered education. Schools with elite intakes feared a change to the status quo. A group of mathematics teachers and teacher educators was critical of the TOC for its failure to introduce more fundamental reforms to the primary school mathematics curriculum. They argued that by basing the TOC on the existing curriculum, which focused on developing memorization and accuracy skills, an essentially traditional curriculum was maintained. Others portrayed the TOC as an attempt by the departing colonial government to diminish traditional Chinese values and to bequeath Hong Kong schools a curriculum based on Western cultural precepts. The specific Chinese values that were portrayed as threatened by the TOC were the centrality of moral education within the subject Chinese and the value of competitiveness among pupils as a source of motivation and as a preparation for adult life (Morris, Lo, Chik, & Char, 2000).

There was also concern that the TOC was derived from a conception of pedagogy derived from English as a second language that was inappropriate for Chinese language and mathematics education. These concerns of subject specialists were exacerbated by the lack of consistency and confusion amongst many of those civil servants charged with the task of translating the policy into the curriculum of the three school subjects. As Clark (1999) noted, whilst the English curriculum was revised to incorporate the principles of the TOC, Chinese and mathematics responded by introducing very minor adjustments to the existing curriculum.

This highly critical public reaction to the TOC initiative slowly became less hostile, and this was a consequence of a variety of factors. Firstly, the government began to provide resources and training to support teachers, and this signalled that the reform was not solely symbolic in purpose. Secondly, the definition of what TOC required became increasingly flexible—thus terms such as "introducing TOC elements," and the "essence" and "spirit" of TOC were employed, which allowed the government to minimize evidence of noncompliance and claim that schools were implementing it regardless of the reality. In parallel, the government became less critical of teachers and of long established pedagogic styles. Thirdly, some of the more innovative school principals and teachers used the TOC as an umbrella for school and classroom improvements, and this resulted in the reform receiving some positive publicity. Essentially it provided an external source to legitimize internal change, and this was facilitated by its comprehensiveness and increasingly flexible nature.

Overall, therefore, the TOC served as a symbol not only of the government's vision for education, but also as a symbol of the departing (colonial) government. The culture of this arena was thus characterized by its public and politicized nature, and a discourse that was confrontational, critical and focused on pragmatic and local issues. This contrasted markedly with the global, private and rhetorical orientation in the policy arena.

The Schools Arena

In the third arena, the culture was more complex as schools were asked to resolve the contradictions inherited from the policy-making arena within a context that, following the reform's reception in the national arena, was critical, highly politicized, and shifting. Thus, as relatively open systems, the schools were influenced by and reflected the tensions of the other arenas, and these were played out against the distinctive culture of individual schools, school subjects and the tasks of implementation.

In order to understand the ways these interacted, we focus on the Paul Cheung Memorial Primary School, which adopted the TOC in 1995. The implementation of the TOC in the school was studied for three years (Lo, 2000). Local primary schools have a long tradition of operating with strong hierarchical power structures, and in this school the Head operated, and was regarded, as the supreme leader. He made the decision to adopt the TOC, senior teachers disseminated the decision, and the other teachers perceived they had no choice but to comply. Although, some teachers had gathered information from the media about the genesis of the TOC and voiced concern about whether it was feasible to import a curriculum reform from overseas countries that were themselves having problems. Their voices were soon silenced as discussion centered on means of implementation. The policy-making arena in the school, which consisted of the Head and some senior teachers, saw the purposes of the TOC in a way akin to that of the EMB, but their focus was to improve the control and accountability of teachers. The Head explained:

> TOC has very definite aims and targets that the teacher has to fulfil. This gives better control to the school to ensure that teachers are doing a good job.... I see TOC as an opportunity for teachers to reflect on their actions and decide whether they want to dedicate themselves to education ... or they should quit.

In the first year, the Head and senior teachers interpreted the TOC, then produced lesson plans and teaching schedules for teachers to follow. In general, teachers took a fidelity approach to curriculum implementation and expected their leaders to provide prescriptions. Thus a strong alignment existed between the administrative policy and teachers' expectations and some changes were made, although these tended to involve compliance with the administrative requirements introduced by the Head. Although teachers were shielded by senior staff from the requirements of the policy-making arena, they were fully aware of the critical discourse in the national political arena. Consequently, two contradictions manifested themselves: one pedagogic, the other related to assessment.

Most teachers operated in a culture that adopted a technical, scientific view of teacher competency and wisdom, in which experts generate knowledge and there are definite right or wrong answers, which could be acquired through a transmission model of teaching. They had succeeded within such a model, and they brought it to their classrooms. Conversely, the TOC required pupils to be active learners and to construct their own knowledge. The new pedagogy contradicted teachers' beliefs and they were doubtful of its effect. As one teacher said:

> I was thinking that we were educated by the traditional method, and we are able to cope with novel situations. I heard people from other schools saying this too: all of us are from traditional education and we found nothing wrong with it. A person would naturally learn to fit into new environments. That's the feedback they gave me. With this new pedagogy, it is difficult to predict whether these children will grow up to be better.

However, on the premise that policy makers and Head knew best and that as ordinary teachers they were insufficiently knowledgeable or senior to make comments on policies, they tried hard to comply but found themselves entangled in the contradictions between the expectations of the new pedagogy and the traditional classroom culture. For example, the traditional classroom was quiet and pupils were obedient. When they tried the more pupil-centered method, pupils got excited and the noise level rose. Some teachers were unable to tolerate this and were frequently observed breaking up activities to restore order. Many teachers became exhausted and depressed, and some complained that they felt de-skilled. Whilst most teachers conceded that pupils were generally happier, they also believed that they did not learn as much. A few teachers, however, did think that pupils were learning better because it was more meaningful.

The proposed assessment system was another source of tension with the prevailing culture. Teachers had a strong belief in the function of schooling as a ladder to higher education, highly paid jobs, and success in life. As one explained:

> Hong Kong is a competitive society. If we prevent children from competing, how can they survive? I cannot imagine how they can compete with others when they are not used to competing in school.

Schools were perceived to be both part of the selection process, and designed to train pupils to compete with and excel over others. The corollary of this was that fairness and objectivity were regarded as critical elements of assessment. A teacher elaborated:

> I do not have confidence in my own professionalism. I fear that I would not be fair when giving marks. Some children are very naughty and you tend to give him lower marks even if they are good at speaking. It is fairer with exam-

inations and written tests. With impression marks, I am afraid that it is difficult for the teacher to be impartial. (Morris et al., 1999, p. 19)

Traditional norm-referenced and summative tests served these purposes well, while the TOC, which promoted criterion-referenced and formative assessment, was considered contradictory to the culture of the school and society. Consequently, in the first year, implementation of the reform in the school could be described as only surface and had limited impact on classrooms.

The Head perceived successful implementation as dependent on teachers' expertise and resource availability, and saw very different patterns across the subjects. He explained:

Maths is the best, they have done everything for us, teachers are confident in Maths because there is good support. Support from English is very good too, but teachers are not confident in English because of their own weak knowledge base. Chinese is the worst. I fear TOC will fail with Chinese if no change is made. I can see little difference between what is proposed for TOC and the traditional Chinese syllabus. There should be more research on the learning of Chinese to establish the priority of learning experiences based on learning theories.

In the second year, the Head focused on generating observable outcomes like assessment records, but also mandated a number of measures to enforce the implementation of the TOC—some of which had a more direct impact on classrooms. The measures included a mentoring system for teachers and peer classroom observations. These reduced the capacity of teachers to create an illusion of change by simply producing documents like teaching schedules indicating learning targets and lesson plans. They began to try out aspects of the TOC pedagogy and some found great satisfaction in adopting a more student-centered approach. A hybrid form of teaching strategy emerged, which combined the traditional teacher-centered strategy with a more pupil-oriented method. The result was a form of whole-class interactive teaching (Mok & Ko, 1999). Feedback from pupils indicated that they enjoyed the opportunities to interact, and a more collaborative culture began to develop amongst teachers, who spent time jointly planning their teaching strategies and supporting each other. Their conceptions of teaching slowly shifted toward a belief that knowledge could be generated from practice. They also realized that they actually knew more about teaching than the "experts" from the ED. The portrayal of the school as a model, receiving positive publicity, reinforced this process.

But this only applied to the lower level of the school (i.e., Primary grades

One to Three). Although the school claimed to have implemented TOC to all levels, up to Primary Six, the situation was very different for the upper classes. Since pupils still had to be allocated to secondary schools according to their academic ability, teachers were reluctant to take the risk of experimenting with new teaching strategies in the face of this high stake examination. Thus, with the upper classes, teachers only complied with the requirement of reporting assessments in a Target-Oriented Assessment (TOA) format, but there were no real changes in classroom practices.

In terms of assessment, a hybrid also emerged (Morris et al., 2000). A greater variety of assessments were used, but the selective function remained unchallenged. Teachers were able to prevent any impact on their own classrooms by complying with certain administrative requirements of the Head (e.g., undertaking criterion-referenced testing and the completion of report cards). However, this data was subsequently converted to percentage marks and norm-referenced. Teachers became sceptical about the workload generated by these conversions and the filling in of assessment forms, which they viewed as administrative matters that did not contribute to improving pupils' learning. Concerns about pupil learning replaced more self-oriented concerns (e.g., workload) as a central feature of the discourse of teachers in the school.

Thus, two very different cultures coexisted and were in tension: the top-down culture of the management—characterized by clear power relations and hierarchical control—remained, but a more democratic and collaborative culture was emerging amongst groups of teachers as they developed hybrid systems of pedagogy and assessment. With the emergence of a group of teachers in middle management, the micro-politics of the school also changed. The adoption of the TOC caused a rapid expansion of the academic committee at the expense of other committees, especially the counseling and guidance committee, which was previously the core of the school's organizational structure. Later, when the head of the academic committee was promoted to deputy head, some teachers were concerned that others might be reaping more than their fair share of the benefit of the hard work of all teachers.

As the organizational culture and teachers' professional development took different paths in response to the introduction of the TOC, the power struggle amongst middle managers became more apparent. The tensions that were emerging were brought to the fore by a critical incident during the summer preceding the third year—when the Head was absent due to illness. During this time, teachers extended their collaboration and professional autonomy and began to make decisions affecting their work. Unfortunately, the Head overruled most of their decisions from his sickbed. The tension was aggravated when, on returning to school at the beginning of the third year, he announced without consultation, that each teacher should write every term a 150-word profile for each pupil he/she taught. As many teachers were teaching several classes, this meant that on average each teacher would write over 100 profiles each term. As teachers were already sceptical about the value of the TOA, they felt that this was the last straw and they refused to comply. They raised the matter with the school supervisory board, which sympathized with the teachers and the decision was deferred.

Subsequently, teachers felt that the Head, supported by some senior teachers in middle management, used his power to hurt those whom he perceived to be the ringleaders of the resistance (e.g., issuing warning letters for very minor offenses). Some teachers started to reappraise their situation—they felt oppressed and that power was being abused, and so sought support from the school supervisors, who again restrained the power of the Head. A new culture emerged in which teachers began to discuss every policy before making a decision whether to support it or not, and this resulted in some policies being rejected. Some teachers realized that it was their solidarity that had brought about this change, and they became more supportive of each other. These formed a strong team, which adopted what Carr and Kemmis (1986) termed a critical perspective, and this moved the school toward a conflict and bargaining model of management (Elmore, 1997).

In parallel with these shifts, the discourse of teachers also changed. In the initial period it was essentially concerned with implementation and resource matters as they struggled to comply with the Head's prescriptions. In the third year, the discourse shifted to one in which issues of power, fairness, and resistance became central.

Overall, the impact of the reform on the culture within the school was marked and multifaceted. Teachers were clearly learning and changing through the process of interpreting the reform. In terms of professional development, some teachers moved from a restricted to a more extended form of professionalism. Some have also moved from an empirical, analytical to a practical, interpretative perspective, and some have adopted a critical perspective. In terms of organizational culture, the school shifted from a top-down systems management model toward a bottom-up conflict and bargaining model. In terms of curriculum change, it evolved from focusing on infrastructural and procedural changes toward changes in teaching and learning in some classrooms.

Conclusion

Clearly, all sub-cultures are rooted in the larger culture of society, but a reliance on the universal aspects of culture tends to portray societies as homogeneous and static. The portrayal in this chapter intentionally underlines the discrepancies across and commonalties within the sub-cultures of each of the arenas identified. Our analysis has attempted to trace, albeit briefly, the complex, segmented, and changing nature of the sub-cultures within three different arenas that affected the TOC, and the key interest groups within each arena. These arenas served distinct functions and constituted sub-cultures insofar as their constituent interest groups operated with shared meanings and ways of acting.

The policy-making arena was shielded from public scrutiny, but its sub-culture was characterized by a shared understanding of the need for reform; a strong influence from global trends; and a reliance on a discourse that was rhetorical as to intentions, but critical and derisory of established practices, and that masked contradictory conceptions of its purpose. The public national agenda was dominated by the local political context, and this contributed to a sub-culture that was confrontational, critical, and dismissive of the reform, as it was seen as a symbol of the departing colonial state and impractical. The schools' arena inherited the contradictions in-built in the policy stage, and its personnel were fully cognizant of the critique that the TOC received in the public arena.

Our focus on an innovative school shows how the reform influenced and was affected by both the organizational and professional cultures within the school as they attempted to grapple with curriculum change. An autocratic and top-down organizational culture created the conditions for changing the curriculum, the culture of teaching, and of teachers. The outcome was professional growth and eventually resistance as the organizational culture was unable to cope with the changed culture of teachers. Clearly, different patterns and outcomes emerged in other schools as they struggled with trying to reconcile the contradictions inherited from the policy arena and the hyper-politicization of the public national arena against the background of the culture of each specific institution.

References

Carr, W., & Kemmis, S. (1986). *Becoming critical.* London: Falmer Press.

Chan, H. M. (1993). Popular culture and democratic culture: Outline of a perspective on the 1991 Legislative Council Election. In S. K. Lau & K. S. Louie (Eds.), *Hong Kong tried democracy* (pp. 346–368). Hong Kong: Hong Kong Institute of Asia-Pacific Studies, The Chinese University of Hong Kong,

Cheng, Y. C., & Cheung, W. M. (1995). A framework for the analysis of educational policies. *International Journal of Educational Management, 9*(6), 10–21.

Clark, J. (1999, February). *Conceptions of TOC.* Paper presented in a symposium on the Findings and Recommendations from TOC Research Studies, International Conference on Teacher Education, The Hong Kong Institute of Education.

Education Commission of Hong Kong. (1990). *Education Commission Report 4: The curriculum and behavioral problems in schools.* Hong Kong: Hong Kong Government Printer.

Education Department of Hong Kong. (1989). *Report of the working group set up to review language improvement measures.* Hong Kong: Hong Kong Government Printer.

Eisner E. (1979). *The educational imagination.* New York: Macmillan.

Elmore, R. E. (1997). Organization models of social program implementation. In M. Hill (Ed.), *The policy process: A reader* (2nd ed., pp. 241–271). Hertfordshire, United Kingdom: Prentice Hall/Harvester Wheatsheaf.

Goodson, I. (1994). Subjects for study: Towards a social history of curriculum. In I. Goodson & S. Ball (Eds.), *Defining the curriculum: Histories and ethnographies* (pp. 25–44). London: Falmer Press.

Kingdon, J. (1984). *Agendas, alternatives, and public policies.* Boston: Little, Brown.

Lau, S. K., & Kuan, H. C. (1988). *The ethos of Hong Kong Chinese.* Hong Kong: The Chinese University Press.

Lau, S. K., & Kuan, H. C. (1990). Public attitudes toward laissez-faire in Hong Kong. *Asian Survey, 30*(8), 766–781.

Leung, B. (1996). *Perspectives on Hong Kong society.* Hong Kong: Oxford University Press.

Linton, R. (1936). *The study of man.* New York: Appleton Century.

Lo, M. L. (2000). Learning without tears? The relativity of a reform and its impact. In B. Adamson, P. Morris, & T. Kwan (Eds.), *Targeting the curriculum* (pp. 47–48). Hong Kong: Hong Kong University Press.

March, J. G., & Olsen, J. P. (1984). The new institutionalism: Organizational factors in political life. *American Political Science Review, 78,* 734–749.

Metz, M. H. (1983). Sources of constructive social relationships in an urban magnet school. *American Journal of Education, 91*(2), 202–245.

Mok, I. A. C., & Ko, P. Y. (2000). Beyond labelling: Teacher-centered and pupil activities. In B. Adamson, P. Morris & T. Kwan (Eds.), *Targeting the curriculum* (pp. 175–194). Hong Kong: Hong Kong University Press.

Morris, P. (1996). The management of participation in the policy-making process: The case of the Education Commission in Hong Kong. *Journal of Education Policy, 11*(3), 319–336.

Morris, P., Adamson, R., Au, M. L., Chan, K. K., Chan, W. Y., Ko, P. Y., Lai Au Yeung W., Lo, M. L., Morris, E., Ng, F. P., Ng, Y. Y., Wong, W. M., & Wong, P. H. (1996). *Target oriented curriculum evaluation project interim report.* INSTEP. Hong Kong: Faculty of Education, The University of Hong Kong.

Morris, P., Adamson, R., Chan, K. K., Che, M. W., Chik, P. M., Lo, M. L., Ko, P. Y., Kwan, Y. L., Mok, A. C., Ng, F. P., & Tong, S. Y. (1999). *Target Oriented Curriculum: Feedback and assessment in Hong Kong primary schools: Final report.* Hong Kong: Faculty of Education, The University of Hong Kong & Curriculum Development Institute.

Morris, P., Lo, M. L., Chik, P. M., & Chan K. K. (2000). One function, two systems: Constraints to changing assessment in Hong Kong primary schools. In B. Adamson, P. Morris & T. Kwan (eds.), *Targeting the curriculum* (pp. 195–216). Hong Kong: Hong Kong University Press.

Peshkin, A. (1992). The relationship between culture and curriculum: A many fitting thing. In P. Jackson. (ed.), *Handbook of research on curriculum* (pp. 248–267). New York: Macmillan.

Reynolds, D., & Farrell, S. (1996). *Worlds apart? A review of international surveys of educational achievement involving England.* London: OFSTED, HMSO.

Reynolds, J., & Skilbeck, M. (1976). *Culture and the classroom.* London: Open Books.

Spady, W. G. (1994). Choosing outcomes of significance. *Education Leadership, 51*(6), 18–22.

Walker, D. (1990). *Fundamentals of curriculum.* New York: Harcourt Brace Jovanovich.

Weiss, C. (1980). Knowledge creep and decision accretion. *Knowledge, 1*(3), 381–404.

9

Leadership in High Achieving Schools in Singapore

The Influence of Societal Culture

Leslie Sharp and Saravanan Gopinathan

Walker and Dimmock (Introduction, this volume) note that investigations that analyze the relationship between culture and educational leadership promise to add much to our understanding of the ways that schools in a variety of national cultures function. By making theory building more holistic and better grounded in real conditions, issues regarding both the preparation of leaders and in turn their management of schools are expected to be better understood. Their view of culture and schooling is that culture is seen as interacting with economic, political, and sociological factors to shape schools, and they warn against an overzealous search for causality. This is a view we endorse.

In this chapter we present a way of understanding the role of culture, leadership, and schooling in Singapore from a sociopolitical perspective. We have consciously avoided using the well-known Hofstedeian framework as we believe that a sociopolitical perspective offers a richer detailing of culture in interaction with schooling. Our argument is that "societal culture" in Singapore can usefully be understood as an evolving mix of what we term "traditional" and "modernizing" cultures, which are in turn complexly related to dominant political and economic processes. Notions of leadership, including school leadership, are a central strand in this discourse. A decentralization of the education system beginning in the mid-1980s is particularly significant for an understanding of recent developments in school leadership in Singapore. It opened up spaces for autonomous action in what had previously been a highly centralized education system. To illustrate our analysis we draw on a study of two improving government secondary schools in Singapore.

The Sociocultural Context of Schooling in Singapore

Any attempt to understand the significance and function of schooling in Singapore must begin with an appreciation of the sociopolitical context. By the late nineteenth century Singapore was already a plural society with Chinese and Indian immigrants outnumbering the Malays. Thus, the challenge of managing an ethnically and culturally complex population predates independence in 1965—the first half-decade of the twentieth century saw the colonial power, the British, attempting to control a rising tide of Chinese cultural and nationalist chauvinism; issues such as the medium of instruction and control over schools were hotly contested and used in the political sphere as symbols of authenticity. Cultural contestation thus gave education tremendous significance within politics; in post-independence Singapore the socializing role education has to play in the formation of a national identity has remained important, even as the nature and significance of culture continues to be actively debated in the wider society.

Singapore received the unexpected and unwanted gift of independence in 1965 following its ejection from the Malaysian federation. The years in Malaysia had seen political turbulence, in large part due to the struggle for political and economic power between ethnic groups leading to racial riots; the successful management of issues of ethnicity, language, religion, and culture in Singapore were thus crucial political imperatives. Additionally, Singapore was a small, economically underdeveloped nation with a Chinese-dominant population in a geopolitical area of Malay Muslims. However, while Singapore looked in part to education to contribute to the development of a socially cohesive and economically productive society, the education heritage itself was one of an underdeveloped, segmented, and underfunded system held hostage by various political factions (Gopinathan, 1974).

The nascent state's primary aim was to establish viability and sovereignty, resulting in the "politics of survival" as one commentator called it (Chan, 1972). Though the dominant political party, the People's Action Party, was a party in which all ethno-cultural groups were represented, and the party had endorsed the continued use of English in the schools and made Malay the national language, the political leadership saw, and continues to see, Singapore as a plural society in which ethnic cleavages persist. It argues that rather than opt for a shallow multiculturalism, the state should accept the reality of primordial attachments (Mutalib, 1992) and treat it as a resource. Thus the dominant feature of political discourse in relation to culture is that of culture with a capital C (Goodenough, 1981)—the tradition-bound collection of values, beliefs, folk traditions, and customary practices that is represented in the rituals and literary and religious classics. In this context it would be unthinkable to think of Chinese culture without Confucius coming to mind, and of Confucianism as the very touchstone of Chinese culture and identity. Thus, traditional cultures are seen as repositories of wisdom, their very survival over millennia an indication of their resilience and worth, and significantly, possession of which was seen as distinguishing Asians from others. In Lee Kuan Yew's memorable phrasing

> it is basic we understood ourselves: what we are, where we come from, what life is or should be about and what we want to do ... only when we first know our traditional values can we be quite clear that the Western world is a different system, a different voltage, structured for purposes different from ours. (Lee, 1972, p. 1)

Interestingly, this need to differentiate the Asian/Singaporean worldview from that of the West, to locate state and group identity within an "Asian" culture was being emphasized well before globalization's homogenizing tendencies were recognized. And yet this view of culture, at least within education, was not unproblematic—in the early twentieth century, Chinese educational reformers saw repudiation of this tradition as necessary for modernization, and many students in Chinese schools in Singapore were political and social activists, which alarmed a government that was trying to assert itself as the only legitimate power source. It is also the case that in spite of a Confucian-based values education program for Chinese pupils, thousands of Chinese youth in Singapore know more about pop idols both Western and non-Western than they do of Confucius' life and wisdom.

The political establishment's view of culture as high tradition and its utility as a unique resource sits cheek by jowl with a modernizing culture, which is driven by economic imperatives. Singapore needed western capital, technology, and markets—hence the emphasis on English, science, and mathematics in the school curriculum. Singapore was always an important node in international trade—modern Singapore was after all founded by a representative of the British East India Company. This openness to the West is tied to the state building project. Singapore was not to end up as a dusty tropical port but rather to be a modern global city—a commercial, economic, and, more recently, a intellectual hub for the region. The philosophy that guided this vision has all the hallmarks of modernism, represented by a vision of progress, clear goals, a commitment to systematic planning, and target setting, and managed by a highly trained and competent bureaucracy. And the amazing transformation of the state and city in just three decades speaks to how well the vision has been realized. Discipline, effectiveness, and efficiency are everywhere evident. Singapore is then, in the economic domain, a good example of a state that is determinedly modern, having effectively embraced the values of industrial society to learn and benefit from experiences elsewhere and now especially keen to embrace the market and the global economy, the better to advantage itself in the race for competitive economic advantage. Singapore now has one of the world's most competitive economies. The success of East Asian economics in the 1980s was attributed by some Western analysts as being due to Confucian values, a view that served to endorse and strengthen the Singapore government's view of the value of traditional cultures.

We should not see the functioning of traditional and modernizing cultures in Singapore as opposed. It could be argued that what the ruling elite did was to treat culture, both traditional and modernizing, as tools, and thus to appropriate suitable elements in the pursuit of the wider vision. Values in traditional culture were to be embraced but without the oppressive feudal elements; thus while loyalty to kin and family was to be strengthened, nepotism was to be avoided. That view that cultural components can be used for larger purposes is seen in the argument that traditional culture provides for stability in the midst of necessary change. Also, its mobilizing potential—that is, pride in an enduring civilization—was recognized as useful for the major societal changes the government intended to bring about. In similar fashion, the government has set about to fashion a modernizing culture deemed appropriate to Singapore's needs. While it has been happy enough to opt for a market-driven economy, benchmark Singapore's services and infrastructure against cities in the West, and enthusiastically embrace modern technology, it has been clear in opposing social trends like permissiveness in modern mass culture, in the erosion it sees in the work ethic, or the decline in the family as a vital social unit.

Views of Leadership

It would not have been possible to overcome Singapore's constraints without inspired leadership and it is possible to argue that aspects of both modernizing and traditional culture are reflected in the way leadership is represented in the discourse. In many ways Lee Kuan Yew, Singapore's long serving Prime Minister (1965–1991) and now Senior Minister, exemplifies key elements of the cultures. Lee's emphasis on the value of traditional culture and the need to modernize are crucial to the ways policies have been created. Terms such as visionary, realist, tough, unsentimental, pragmatic, and conservative can all be equally well-applied to aspects of his life and work. He is at ease on the global stage and can the next day be equally effective at a mass rally; he is both the cosmopolitan and the heartlander. Lee is also the leader who, by virtue of his achievements, actions, impartiality, and commitment, claims moral authority for his views and influence in Singapore society. The Confucian view of leadership in government, that of honorable men doing their duty, of improving the lives of their people, and thus winning trust and respect, is mirrored in many government leaders' statements about leadership. It might be said of Lee's leadership that it is trust in action, hard earned and highly valued.

Lee and his colleagues in government in the mid-1960s sought to amass political power at the center in order to better deal with the many political and developmental problems the fledgling state faced. The government built up institutions like the People's Association to better network and to mobilize the population in support of government initiatives. Though periodic elections are held, the People's Action Party has always been returned with huge parliamentary majorities. It has selected and nurtured a civil service that has a deserved reputation for integrity and effectiveness, which enables the party to deliver on its election promises. However, the government is now beginning to feel some pressure to allow for more civic action and participation. A better educated, better traveled population wants more consultation, choice, and involvement. New technologies now make it less possible to control the flow of information to citizens. The nature of the global economy makes overcentralization and bureaucratically-managed states less responsive and thus less effective. Recessions in 1986–1987 and in 1998 have underlined the need for greater liberalization in economic and financial matters.

The view of Singapore as a distinctly Asian society in which traditional culture and values will play a significant part in building and maintaining rootedness is very evident in the education system. Bilingualism and values education are key features of the education system. The teaching of the mother tongues (Chinese, Malay, Tamil) is justified on the grounds that language is a key carrier of values and thus representative of ethnicity; mother tongues are assigned to pupils on the basis of race (Gopinathan, 1988b). The teaching of values, which is done in the medium of the mother tongue in primary schools, is intended to provide pupils with moral moorings to allow them to be shielded against the ill effects of westernization, (Gopinathan, 1988a, 1995). The government has also allowed, indeed encouraged, several traditional Chinese-medium schools. Though these schools follow the national curriculum and students are efficiently bilingual, what is unique about them is the Chineseness they represent, which the schools celebrate. At the same time there has been unwavering commitment to the teaching of English, mathematics, and science. English is the dominant medium of instruction, and mathematics and science teaching has been so effective that Singapore students led all other countries in science and mathematics achievement in the third international science and mathematics study.

Views of leadership are also well reflected in the way school leadership is viewed. First, the significance of education in the nation building project, and the vital roles principals play is seen in the following:

every principal should no longer be an anonymous one.... Headmasters and teachers must feel the spirit of nation-building ... its urgency and its importance—otherwise all the best laid plans and all the circulars will go astray. (cited in Wee & Chong, 1990, p. 40)

In much the same way that Lee Kuan Yew and his colleagues had to centralize power to manage the development process, the Ministry of Education (MOE), inheriting a divided school system, had to seek centralization to assert control to ensure policy implementation. This centralization enabled the government to impose order on the school system and lay the foundations of an effective, well-resourced national school system, which was achieved by the late-1980s. The key to effective schools was strong leadership. The physical and cultural construction of the new government schools went hand in hand. Key correlates of effectiveness were put in place during this period. By the mid-1980s many of the reforms that would only be attempted in developed countries later in the decade were already in place in Singapore (Sharpe & Gopinathan, 1996). We would argue that the bulk of this transformation was a top-down process, which had major implications for the role of the principal as primarily implementing given policies.

The mid-1980s economic setback raised questions about overcentralization and set in motion a process of decentralization in education and a movement toward greater consultation and downsizing of government (Ho & Gopinathan, 1999). This was to have implications for traditional notions of leadership in general and, in the case of education, for the role of the principal. The "Towards Excellence in Schools" report, for example, spelled out the general direction of the required changes and the establishment firstly of independent schools and later, autonomous schools, and demonstrated a genuine desire of the government and the MOE to provide school principals with greater autonomy. The economic shock had set in process a movement away from the role of the principal as predominantly a manager or administrator in a predominantly bureaucratic, centralized education system to that of an educational leader with growing executive powers.

Our assertion is that the two exceptional principals in our Improving Schools study took advantage of these processes. Decentralization created a space that they were amongst the first to take advantage and test the boundaries of.

The Improving Schools Project

The Improving Schools project (Mortimore, Sharpe, Leo, Gopinathan, Stoll, & Mortimore, in press) was undertaken in 1996 and involved a comparison of two improving secondary schools in each of four locations—Great Britain,

Hong Kong, Shanghai, and Singapore. Its main intention was to discover what the schools' successes were, how they had achieved them, those strategies that had been tried but had not worked, and the continuing challenges of the schools. Two government "neighborhood" secondary schools in Singapore—Queensway and Xinmin—were chosen to take part in the study by the Ministry of Education, largely on the basis of their outstanding performance in the "value-added" performance tables, published in Singapore since 1992. With below average academic intakes, both schools had made significant improvements, particularly in their "0" level results and in the numbers of pupils going on to post-secondary school education. For example, at Queensway the number of students graduating with a minimum number of three "0" level passes in the Express stream improved from 95 percent in 1990 to 100 percent in 1995, and for a minimum of five "0" level passes from 66 percent in 1990 to 91 percent in 1994. By 1994, 96 percent were going on to some form of post-secondary school education, the majority of them to the polytechnics. Even when the new principals took over the schools, then, the academic results were relatively good. However, what distinguished them from other, similar schools were the improvements that were subsequently achieved.

Queensway and Xinmin, the two government schools that we studied, are set in the same modernizing and traditional context of other, less achieving schools. Nevertheless, in the late-1980s they were rather nondescript and did not stand out as being especially successful. The appointment of new principals to each school in 1991, however, began a five- or six-year process of startling and sustained school improvement. This improvement, we believe, has to be accounted for by the initiatives taken by the new school principals.[1] Societal culture, as articulated from above, provided them with a cultural and social stock of readily available recipes that were already showing their worth in raising the general standard of Singapore schools (Neville, 1994). But it was how the principals were able to capitalize on, and develop, these preexisting frameworks that accounts for the outstanding performance of their schools.

A wide range of data was collected by the research teams[2] over a period of five months. The schools supplied extensive documentation; interviews were conducted with the principal, vice principal, teachers, pupils, and parents; pupils completed an National Foundation for Educational Research (NFER) pupil questionnaire that was administered additionally in a nation-wide sample of secondary schools; and a total of 15 pupils were tracked over one school day each. The first step was to ascertain from the principal and vice principal what they perceived to be their school's successes and how they had achieved them. Next, through a process of triangulation, these accounts were compared with those of teachers, pupils, and parents. Finally, through further interviews, observation, and analysis of documentation, an explanatory conceptual framework was generated.

There were clear differences in the routes that each school had taken to improve as well as in the leadership strategies adopted by the two principals. Before turning to these, however, some general observations are in order about the similarities, especially in relation to the notion of societal culture.

In their report on Queensway the year before the study, school inspectors had commented that the school "ticked with clockwork efficiency." Both schools, we found, were indeed rationally organized, as one principal put it, to "engineer success." Clearly in this respect the schools were operating as microcosms of the larger modernizing culture and the principals enthusiastically acting as change agents. As we shall argue, however, though the clockwork had in many respects been imported from outside, the ticking and the efficiency was a school accomplishment. Similarly, there were ample signs in the formal curriculum, in Extra Curricula Activities (ECAs), in ceremonies such as the daily flag-raising, and in symbols such as the prominent photographs of the President and the First Lady, that the broader societal cultural mix had stamped itself on the two schools, much as it had done elsewhere in other schools on the island. Of particular note were the uniformed ECA groups, such as the police, the St John's Ambulance, and other cadet corps.

It was not this cultural inheritance per se that made the schools exceptional, however, but its interpretation, emphasis, reinforcement, validation, and general mobilization at the level of the school. Just as the curriculum did not speak for itself, but needed teachers to articulate it and bring it to life, so too with the framework of objectified culture (Bourdieu, 1997). Though the presence of this relatively standardized culture was of vital importance, it was its management and enhancement in the schools that put it to work in the interests of the pupils (Schein, 1992). It was how it was aligned and adapted to the needs of the pupils that mattered.

What both principals understood was that their pupils, above all else, had to be convinced of the truth of the cultural messages around them. Both principals realized that their pupil intakes were below average academically; that the vast majority had not made the schools their first choice; that their parents were in the main poorly educated and in the lower income bracket; and that many already perceived themselves to be school failures. Not only did they need to be convinced of their academic worth; many also did not have a place to study and did not know how to study.

To address these problems, as the vice principal of Queensway put it, it was necessary to "win the pupils over." In both schools the drafting of a mission statement and mottoes was an early step in constructing what the Xinmin principal described as a "culture of effort." It reads, "Our mission is to ensure that every individual pupil in the school can be taught and will want to be taught." This down-to-earth statement meant, he emphasized, that "No one should be left to rot; no one should be condemned." What impressed our business partners, however, was the high level of awareness of this mission in the school, something that he had not encountered in industry. This was due in large measure to the way that the mission had been operationalized into simple mottoes and emblems. At Queensway, for example, the motto was "Success Through Diligence," characterized by an emblem showing a spider diligently spinning its web. The emblem appeared everywhere in the school—on books, papers, badges, noticeboards, and in the hall. All of the pupils we spoke to knew that it meant that if you worked hard enough and long enough you would succeed. The constant exhortation never to give up was repeated on a daily basis . "If you want a good school," the Xinmin principal announced at assembly, "don't look outside. Build one here."

To meet the pupils' needs for a place to study and practice in studying, both schools devised a range of school-based programs. These were programs in addition to the normal curriculum. Being double session schools, a prerequisite was to find extra time and extra space. Operating an open-gate policy and providing study tables along corridors and in the school grounds were two of the strategies adopted. By the time of our study, the majority of the pupils at both schools were spending the best part of the day on the school premises. This effectively provided them with single session schooling. Special programs included a Mastery Learning Strategy, Peer Tutoring and Study Groups, Structured Remedial Lessons, Time Management, Learning to Learn, and Word Processing, to name a few. Additionally, outside agencies were brought in to provide enrichment courses. In such ways the schools provided structure and support, as well as direction, for their pupils.

The incorporation of the pupils into the life of the school was paralleled by a heavy commitment of time from the teachers. The head of science at Queensway estimated that 70 to 80 percent of the morning session teachers arrived at 7:30 A.M. and stayed until 3:00 P.M. Most heads of departments arrived at 7:15 A.M. and did not leave before 5:00 P.M. Only the two principals spent longer at the school, arriving at 7:00 A.M. and leaving at 7:00 P.M. In addition to classroom teaching, the teachers also served on an average of two committees each, and at Xinmin there was a policy of heads of departments shadowing each other so as to provide cover for duties when required but also to familiarize them with school organization and policy.

It is clear that the culture and organization of both case study schools reflected the mix of traditional and modernizing culture of the wider society. The underlying maxim that "all children can learn and succeed," often associated with the Effective School literature, is deeply embedded in Asian culture. So too with the idea that success comes from working long enough and hard enough and systematically enough (Biggs, 1995; Lee, 1996). However, if the broader cultural heritage was to have any impact on the pupils, the principals recognized that a considerable amount of work had to be done in both the instrumental an expressive dimensions of school culture (Hargreaves, 1995). It was necessary to begin with the visible level of the culture they were attempting to encourage—the technology, art, logos, crests, and vocabulary. Accompanying this were the establishing of norms and articulation of associated values. Eventually, as the Xinmin principal put it, these "technical" and "symbolic" forces would give way to a "cultural force" necessary for deep culture to take its hold. To have an impact, then, the sacred beliefs of the broader society needed to be worked into the life of the schools. Furthermore, if pupils were to be won over, and the leadership to be trusted, there needed to be clear evidence for both the pupils and the teachers that all the effort was worthwhile. Over time this was to come for both schools when the principal was able to point to the better-than-expected examination results and performance tables. Making an initial difference, however, was the main challenge to begin with.

As we have seen, both principals had taken advantage of the spaces for autonomous action that were beginning to be opened up by the process of decentralization in the late 1980s. In particular they had recognized that there was greater freedom to devise and mount their own school programs, to be more flexible in the use of school facilities, and to experiment with different leadership styles. They were in Goldring's term, "dynamic principals" (Goldring, 1996). In this respect, both emphasized the important influence on them of their year-long principal training program at the National Institute of Education. This program, which was introduced in 1984 and sponsored by the Ministry of Education, had introduced them to the school leadership literature and provided on-the-job training under the mentorship of a successful secondary school principal (Chong & Boon, 1997). Its introduction in itself was a clear sign for those looking carefully enough that the MOE had recognized the need for what the principal of Queensway called "a new breed of principal."

Although they had shared the experience of the training program, the strategies adopted by the two principals varied quite markedly. An element of chance seemed particularly important at Queensway, whereas at Xinmin the principal had been more prepared to test the limits of the newly emerging autonomy. A chance complaint about noisy pupils playing football across the road from Queensway had prompted the principal to open up the school gates before and after school so that pupils could play football in the school grounds. Though the school had no grounds to speak of, except for a cracked tarmacadam area with rusted goal posts, the idea caught on with the pupils. It led to the provision of stone tables and umbrellas and a process of the school spilling out into its grounds to take advantage of the tropical climate. Neither had the principal been the source of the peer tutoring and group study strategy that was to make use of the extra tables and that was generally thought to have played a major part in improving examination results. This program, which was unique to the school, had been suggested by a science teacher who had been on a Work Improvement Teams (WITS) course, and sponsored by the head of the science department. Seeing its success, other heads of departments had taken over the scheme. This represented what the principal described as his "consultative management style." Indeed, there was further evidence of this in such diverse practices as the extensive committee structure, the regular meetings between the principal and pupils, a pupils' suggestion box, and the general practice of pupils taking more responsibility for the running of the school. All of this generated a huge amount of paper in the form of charts, minutes, handbooks, and annual internal Self-Appraisal and Action Reports in addition to the usual fare of syllabuses, schemes of work, and ongoing assessment. The aim, explained the principal, was to put in place "a rational organizational structure dedicated to improved academic results," and this accorded well with emphases in the broader modernizing culture. Possibly because the school was one of the first English medium schools to be established in the early 1960s and because Queenstown was one of the earliest housing estates—symbolic of Singapore's modernization drive—there was less evidence of the influence of traditional culture than at Xinmin.

Xinmin began its existence in 1945 as a privately-run Chinese-medium school and the principal had attended it as a pupil. Following a steep decline in its numbers during the 1960s, as parents began to see the merits of an English-medium education, it was fully integrated into the state system in 1987, moving to its new buildings in 1990. Despite its Chinese history, the school that the principal had taken over had declining rolls, above average levels of truency, poor discipline, and unimpressive examination results.

There was general agreement that the Xinmin principal was exceptional, and by the time of the study he had a good reputation in educational circles. On several occasions during the study he spoke of his philosophy, strategies and motivation. He had grown up in the area, had known poverty and had mixed with local "gangsters." These experiences had taught him how to understand his pupils and given him a burning desire to "make a difference in their lives." He had worked hard to overcome the odds in his life and succeeded, and so could his pupils if they were properly guided and supported. Convinced that traditional Chinese virtues provided the essential philosophy for school improvement, he turned to organizational theorists, notably Sergiovani, for a conceptual and programmatic framework. His burning "passion," as he explained, was to turn his school firstly into the best school in the neighborhood, and then the best neighborhood school in the north of the island. Now that that had been achieved, he had set his eyes on his school becoming the best neighborhood school in Singapore.

The Xinmin principal knew that he had been instrumental in turning his school around, and he was quietly proud of the achievement. There were four priorities: discipline, care of pupils, public image, and improved facilities. Discipline had to be the first priority, he said, because without solid achievement it was impossible to convince people to give the school a chance. Good discipline was necessary for sustained academic effort, which in turn led to academic results without which parents would not choose the school. Accordingly, he introduced a "Red Card Scheme" to tackle pupil misbehavior and set about projecting a better image of the school in the community. One innovation was to arrange for pupils during their physical education lessons to have regular runs in the neighborhood so the parents could see how well-behaved they were. He turned to the local community—some of whom were former pupils and were now respectable businessmen—and raised over $100,000 per year at a time when this practice was rare amongst government school principals. The proceeds were used for multiple projects, such as the purchase of MacDonald's style furniture for the canteen, soft-drink vending machines, and the construction of an air-conditioned lecture theater and plush alumni center. The idea was to create a neighborhood school that the local community could identify with. Being a predominantly Chinese neighborhood, it was noticeable that the color red was extensively used in the school for example on the metal girders that spanned the entrance and the MacDonalds style furniture. Additionally, the school's name was prominently displayed in both English and in Chinese characters on the main school wall overlooking the parade ground where often the school's award-winning Chinese Lion Dance Group performed in full view of the residents in the surrounding high-rise flats. In ways such as these, the Xinmin principal explored the parameters of his newly acquired autonomy from the Ministry of Education.

Testing the boundaries of autonomy had other results: staff who did not fit in had been encouraged to leave, and Teaching Practice places for large numbers of trainees from the National Institute of Education were made available to introduce new blood. By the time the researchers arrived, the principal had gathered a willing staff around him. Accordingly, he explained that he had been able to dispense with his early managerial style in favor of a "transformational" leadership (Leithwood, 1992) style based on tight culture and a more structurally loose organization. More staff were coming forward with their own ideas, and the school had developed an extensive battery of homegrown programs. Clearly the influences operating on the Xinmin principal were a complex mixture of traditional culture and subculture, a modernizing zeal, as well as a wide reading of the leadership literature. The mix did not produce a Chinese school, however. What it did do was mobilize the resources of the community, both material and cultural, into a system of reinforcing elements (Mitchell & Willower, 1992) and put them to work in the construction of an efficient school that all of the different ethnic groups could feel at home in. At their last meeting with the principal, the researchers put it to him that his school was already operating as an autonomous school. Formal autonomous status, he replied, was his next step.

School Culture

The term "climate," rather than "culture" would be a more accurate description of the beliefs and values that underpinned everyday life at each school. The term draws attention to the overt and explicit aspects of surface culture or school spirit, in contrast to more deeply embedded taken-for-granted meanings and values (Owens, 1987). At both schools there was a process of "working at culture." It comprised a daily "drilling" of the pupils in desired values and beliefs, in the hope that one day these would be internalized by the children and, perhaps, at some point in the future become more deeply embedded in the school. Neither principal was under the illusion that the path from climate to culture would be easy, however. At Queensway, there was a recognition that winning the pupils over was a constant challenge with each new intake. The Xinmin principal felt that he had succeeded only in providing the pupils with study skills that enabled them to "work smart." His school, he said, might be effective but it still was not a "good" school. There were some encouraging signs, however, he believed. Pupils returned their plates now in the canteen without having to be told to do so, they automatically took out their books when they arrived at school, they dressed properly, and they no longer hid their books in the library. Belief as well as habit was taking control, he felt.

Conclusion

Societal culture is clearly an important concept for comparative studies of school leadership. It draws attention to distinctive patterns of constraints and possibilities, of required and accepted ways of thinking, acting, and feeling that are fundamentally connected to mastery and control of the social and physical world. We have argued for a sociopolitical analysis of culture that takes as its starting point the social, economic, and political problems that Singapore faced at independence and that are still grappled with today, though in different forms. We have identified two predominant cultural strands, and argued that Singapore culture is best understood as a mix between traditional and modernizing cultures, negotiated and legitimized in terms of national interests. As Chung (1999) pointed out, cultures are dynamic and those that survive in a globalized world are the ones that are sufficiently dynamic to incorporate new ideas and values to meet new challenges. If we are correct, the beginnings of a major realignment of these two cultural strands occurred in the aftermath of the 1980s economic slowdown. The immediate effect of this economic setback on the school system was a process of decentralization. Though this process was most clearly apparent in the creation of independent and autonomous schools, it also created a space for more autonomous school leadership generally, which our two case study principals were amongst the first to take advantage of. Though each principal was able to build on strengths of the school system as a whole, the general view of those we interviewed was that it was their leadership skills, especially their ability to mobilize staff and pupils, that made their schools outstanding (Teddlie & Stringfield, 1993). Both drew on the broader traditional and modernizing cultures in this mobilization effort, as evidenced by the efficiency of their school organizations, attention to discipline, beliefs about hard work and practice, and an unashamedly proactive notion of leadership itself. However, it was in the different ways that these broader cultural influences were put to work in the school that made the schools and the leadership styles distinctive. Thus, whilst both espoused such traditional values as filial piety and hard work, they turned to Western organizational literature for such ideas as consultative management and group work. The Xinmin principal turned to Confucianism for his values and beliefs but to Sergiovani for his understanding and direction. Though paternalistic and a strict disciplinarian, the Queensway principal established an elaborate network of staff and pupil committees that allowed a flatter landscape for the sharing of ideas. Thus, whilst we would disagree with Heck and Marcoulides (1996) that leadership skills amongst Singaporean school principals might not be as developed as in the West, our study supports the conclusion of his survey research that effective schools in Singapore are schools that foster innovation and risk taking, teacher participation in decision making, and positive social relations.

As the millenium approaches, there is generally recognition that there is no one recipe for school effectiveness. However, that does not mean that the search for generalizations is misguided. Societal culture is a useful concept precisely because it points to regularities that provide a general context in which schools are obliged to operate. In Singapore that context provides much higher levels of support for schools than is often the case overseas. Singapore schools can, so to speak, swim with the cultural tide and not against it. This goes some way toward explaining the high standards of Singapore schools in general. But societal culture alone will not explain why some schools, in similar neighborhoods and with similar intakes, stand out as being especially successful. To understand that it is necessary to understand how culture is put to work in those schools.

Notes

1. In the case of Queensway, the changes brought about by the principal who joined the school in 1991 were carried on when his vice principal took over as principal in 1994.
2. Each team was made up of a leading Singaporean businessman and professional and was led by a researcher from the National Institute of Education.

References

Biggs, J. B. (1995, June). *Socialization and education in Confucian-heritage cultures.* Paper presented in the 8th Asian workshop on Child and Adolescent Development: Meeting the Challenge of the 21st Century, Singapore.

Bourdieu, P. (1997). The forms of capital. In A. H. Halsey, H. Lauder, P. Brown, & A. H. Wells (Eds.), *Education: Culture, economy, society* (pp. 46–58). London: Oxford University Press.

Chan, H. C. (1972). *The politics of survival 1965—1967.* Singapore: Oxford University Press.

Chong, K. C., & Boon, Z. (1997). Lessons from a Singapore programme for school improvement. *School Effectiveness and School Improvement, 8*(4), 463–470.

Chung, F. (1999). Universal values and particularistic values in world educational systems. *International Journal of Educational Reform, 8*(2), 108–112.

Goldring, E. B. (1996). Schools as dynamic organizations. *International Journal of Educational Reform, 5*(3), 278–286.

Goodenough, W. H. (1981). *Culture, language and society.* Reading, MA: Addison-Wesley.

Gopinathan, S. (1974). *Towards a national system of education in Singapore 1945–1973.* Singapore: Oxford University Press.

Gopinathan, S. (1988a). Being and becoming: Education for values in Singapore. In W. Cumming, S. Gopinanthan & Y. Tomoda (Eds.), *The revival of values education in Asia and the West.* Oxford, England: Pergamon Press.

Gopinathan, S. (1988b). Bilingualism and bilingual education in Singapore. In C. Paulston (Ed.), *International handbook of bilingualism and bilingual education,* (pp. 391–404). New York: Greenwood.

Gopinathan, S. (1995). Singapore. In P. Morris & A. Sweeting (Eds.), *Education and development in East Asia* (pp. 79–104). New York: Garland Publishing.

Hargreaves, D. H. (1995). School culture, school effectiveness and school improvement. *School Effectiveness and School Improvement, 6*(1), 23–46.

Heck, R. H., & Marcoulides, G. H. (1996). School culture and performance: Testing the invariance of an organizational model. *School Effectiveness and School Improvement, 7*(1), 76–96.

Ho, W. K., & Gopinathan, S. (1999). Recent developments in education in Singapore. *School Effectiveness and School Improvement, 10*(1), 3–9.

Lee, K. Y. (1972). Traditional values and national identity. *The Mirror, 8,* 6–8.

Lee, W. O. (1996). The cultural context for Chinese learners: Conceptions of learning in the Confucian tradition. In D. A. Watkins & J. B. Biggs (Eds.), *The Chinese learner: Cultural, psychological and contextual influences* (pp. 25–44). Hong Kong & Melbourne: CERC & ACER.

Leithwood, K. (1992). The move towards transformational leadership. *Educational Leadership, 49*(5), 8–12

Mitchell, J. T., & Willower, D. J. (1992). Organisational culture in a good high school. *Journal of Educational Administration, 30*(1), 6–18.

Mortimore, P., Sharpe, L., Leo, E., Gopinathan, S., Stoll, L., & Mortimore, J. (in press). *Four case studies of improving schools in Singapore and London.* London: University of London Institute of Education.

Mutalib, H. (1992). Singapore's quest for national identity: The triumphs and trials of Government policies. In B. K. Choon, A. Pakir & T. C. Kiong (Eds.), *Imagining Singapore* (pp. 69–96). Singapore: Times Educational Press.

Neville, M. (1994). *Culture and effectiveness: A naturalistic inquiry in two Singapore secondary schools.* Unpublished doctoral dissertation, The National University of Singapore, Singapore.

Owens, R. (1987). *Organizational behavior in education.* Englewood Cliffs, NJ: Prentice-Hall.

Schein, E. H. (1992). *Organizational culture and leadership* (2nd ed.). San Francisco: Jossey-Bass.

Sharpe, L., & Gopinathan, S. (1996). Effective island, effective schools: Repair and restructuring in the Singapore school system. *International Journal of Educational Reform, 5*(4), 394–402.

Teddlie, C., & Stringfield, S. (1993). *Schools make a difference: Lessons learned from a ten-year study of school effects.* New York: Teachers College Press.

Wee, H. T., & Chong, K. C. (1990). 25 years of school management. In J. Y. S. Kwong & W. K. Sim (Eds.), *Evaluation of educational excellence* (pp. 31–38). Singapore: Longman.

10.

Leadership and Culture in Chinese Education

TONY BUSH AND QIANG HAIYAN

Introduction: Applying the Concept of Culture to National Education Systems

The concept of culture has become increasingly important in the discourse of educational leadership and management. It is usually applied to individual organizations rather than to nation-states. The notion that each school, college, or university is unique underpins and supports the growing significance of culture. The combination of values, beliefs, rituals, symbols, and heroes that represents the specific culture of each organization is thought to differentiate it from other schools, even those in the immediate vicinity.

The emphasis on culture has been accompanied by a heightened appreciation of the importance of context in assessing educational policies, leadership, and practice. The previous assumption of generic leadership skills that could be applied to all educational contexts has been replaced by a recognition of the importance of organizational variables and the need for situational analysis. This emerging respect for context is also beginning to be applied to national and regional educational systems. The vital importance of avoiding cultural imperialism is increasingly emphasized:

> Policies and practices cannot be translated intact from one culture to another since the mediation of different cultural contexts can quite transform the former's salience. (Crossley & Broadfoot, 1992, p. 100)

> The uncritical transportation of theories and methodologies across the world, without regard to the qualities and circumstances of different communities, can no longer be regarded as acceptable. (Hughes, 1990, p. 137)

All theories and interpretations of practice must be "grounded" in the specific context. (Bush, Qiang, & Fang, 1998, p. 137)

The significance of the national context is particularly relevant in considering the Chinese educational system. Through much of its long history, and particularly in the 50 years following the establishment of the People's Republic by Mao Zedong, China was a closed system largely impervious to external influences. Its long and distinguished history, and its own distinctive cultural traditions, mean that it is unwise to seek understanding through the application of theories derived from very different Western countries.

The sheer scale and diversity of educational provision also militates against an approach based on Western models. In 1993, there were 990,000 schools with a total enrollment of more than 180 million students. There is also a marked difference between urban and rural provision, as we shall see later. All this serves to justify the argument that culture is a national as well as an organizational phenomenon. Wang and Mao (1996) show how national cultures are developed and sustained:

> The concept of culture is usually understood as a thinking and acting pattern manifested through activities of a given nation, which makes one nation unique from another.... Education ... is both an activity of cultural transmission and cultural production. It cultivates and produces successors and developers of the culture. Therefore, inevitably, countless ties should exist between culture and education. (p. 143)

Dimmock and Walker (1998) demonstrated the links between national and organizational culture and also stressed the prevalence of sub-cultures in educational institutions. This also serves to emphasize the complexity of the concept of culture and the variety of manifestations that can be expected in assessing its significance in any national context. This diversity certainly applies in China and is reflected in the structure of this article. The next four sections address the following aspects of culture in the Chinese education system:

1. Traditional
2. Socialist
3. Enterprise
4. Patriarchal

We begin with an examination of the impact of China's history on its educational culture.

Traditional Culture

The traditional aspects of Chinese culture are rooted in the pervasive influence of Confucius. The long history of Chinese education, and the enduring power of this teacher-philosopher, is illustrated graphically by the fact that Confucius was born in 551 BC, more than 2,500 years ago. His notion of education changing men for the better (Cleverley, 1991, p. 4) remains at the heart of the purpose of education even in the early years of the third millenium. "Confucianism became the ruling ideology of Chinese society, being especially popular among the elite" (Cleverley, 1991, p. 7).

Wang and Mao (1996) referred to the many schools of thought within Chinese traditional culture but emphasized that Confucianism has been the most important. "The development and characteristics of the system of Chinese education . . . have been greatly influenced by this traditional culture" (p. 144). Wang and Mao (1996) identified four aspects of traditional culture and these will be used to structure the rest of this section.

Worshipping the Traditions

Confucianism has now become part of the folklore in Chinese education, "reflecting the traditional Chinese outlook on life, ethics and morality" (Wang & Mao, 1996, p. 144). A central part of this approach was an emphasis on traditions and the linked patriarchal clan system. This may also be linked to what Cleverley (1991, p. 7) described as "the rigidities of ancestor worship." This emphasis on tradition is also reflected in education, where recitation of Confucian classics was given a high priority. This has led to mechanical memorizing becoming the traditional method of teaching and learning (Wang & Mao, 1996). Wang and Mao also claimed that this approach contributed to China's "closed door" policy. These authors criticized this worship of tradition as disadvantageous for Chinese society and claimed that there is now a desire to balance traditional and foreign cultures.

Adoring Authority

Wang and Mao (1996, p. 145) suggested that respect for authority in China "has deep connections with the rigid social stratification of the clan system in Chinese feudal society." Children were expected to comply with the requirements of adults without question. This is closely linked with the concept of filial piety, "which required absolute obedience and complete devotion to parents" (Cleverley, 1991, p. 3). The principle of total obedience to adults extended naturally from parents to teachers. Children are expected to "respect the teacher's authority without preconditions" (Wang & Mao, 1996, p. 148). This stance clearly influences classroom activity where there is an emphasis on teaching, through lectures and demonstrations, rather than learning through discussion or pupil questions. While inimical to Western emphases on child-centered learning, the evidence suggests that it may be effective. The international comparison of performance in mathematics amongst 13-year-old children shows that Chinese children achieved the highest scores (Reynolds & Farrell, 1996). The respect for authority also extends to relationships between teachers in schools. The principal has positional authority within an essentially bureaucratic system. Moyles and Liu (1998, p. 161) referred to "a hierarchical structure which has deep roots in Chinese culture." This bureaucratic approach strongly influences the management of education. (161) Si (1997, p. 5) showed that there are five administrative levels external to the school and concludes that this structure "is too large and too cumbersome." Dimmock and Walker (1998) drew on Hofstede (1980) to conceptualize differential authority in educational systems. They used the notion of "power distance" (PD) to assess the distribution of power:

> In societies with large PD values, greater inequalities of power distribution are expected in the family, in school, and in the workplace. Thus, in the home, children are educated towards obedience to parents, whose authority is rarely questioned; in school, teachers are respected, learning is conceived as passed on by the wisdom of the teacher, and teacher-centerd methods tend to be employed; and in the workplace, hierarchy means existential inequality, subordinates expect to be told what to do, and the ideal boss is a benevolent autocrat or a kind father figure. (p. 574)

China might be regarded as the archetypal high power-distance society, although there are now suggestions of a modest shift from this traditional position. Wang and Mao (1996, p. 145) regarded respect for elders as "a consistent virtue of the Chinese nation" but added that complete submission is unfavorable to the spirit of democracy. Moyles and Liu (1998) referred to the collegial management styles apparent in Chinese kindergartens, and the collective authority of the teachers through the *jiaoyanzu* provides a countervailing influence to the power of the principal. The respect for formal authority is tempered by acknowledgement of the need to work collaboratively with teachers.

Stressing Collectivism

Dimmock and Walker (1998), drawing on Hofstede (1980), referred to the balance between individualism and collectivism as one important aspect of culture. They defined collectivism as follows:

> In collectivist societies, people place group goals above their personal goals; they are brought up to be loyal to and integrate in strong cohesive groups, which often include extended families.... Family groups are brought up with a we

consciousness, opinions are predetermined by the group, and strong obligations to the family emphasize harmony, respect and shame; at school, learning
... focuses on how to do things and on factual knowledge. (p. 575)

Head and Sorensen (1993) adopted a similar approach, saying that
collectivism is characterized by a tight social framework in which people distinguish between ingroups and outgroups. Loyalty is owed to the ingroups, which
in turn have a duty to look after their members. Wang and Mao (1996) stressed
the importance of collectivism within the Chinese traditional value system,
with collective benefits seen as more important than individual needs. This
approach has clear implications for both schools and employment practice.
Satow and Wang (1994) claimed that "modern Chinese human resource
management practice and thinking are rooted in the cultural traditions of the
country" (p. 3) and showed how this is manifested in the workplace:

Within the Chinese work context, being equal and average, avoiding competition or conflict and the work ethic were among the popularly accepted values
... Group approaches have been a dominating influence on Chinese social and
working life, including team work, group decision-making, group reward, group
cohesiveness and group consultation. Harmonious relationships among team
members and across and/or within organizational levels are emphasized and
considered crucial to successful management." (p. 4)

One of the main ways in which group approaches are manifested in Chinese
schools is through the *jiaoyanzu*, which are groups of teachers, usually subject-
based, focusing on teaching and research. Paine and Ma (1993) claimed that
the *jiaoyanzu* operate on the "assumption that teachers would work together
in virtually every aspect of their work" (p. 676). In many respects, the *jiaoyanzu* appear to embody many features of collegiality, the normatively preferred
model of management in many Western countries (Bush, 1995). This
model is illustrated at Qian Ling junior secondary school, a small rural
secondary school in Shaanxi province in the northwest of China. The English
teacher at Qian Ling, interviewed by the authors in 1997, "values the work
of the English *jiaoyanzu* which operates collegially to discuss teaching materials, provide demonstration lessons and observe and comment on each other's
lessons" (Bush, Coleman, & Si, 1998, p. 189). The collectivist assumptions
of the *jiaoyanzu* operate alongside the bureaucratic elements of school
management, including the hierarchy headed by the principal, and the
teaching deans who have overall responsibility for the *jiaoyanzu*. As in many
Western countries, there may be tension between the collegial and bureaucratic aspects of school management. Paine and Ma's (1993) dialectic article
captures the dilemma. Ma emphasized the collectivist aspects of the *jiaoy-*

anzu, while Paine referred to the enduring significance of the hierarchy. Collectivist norms are also under challenge from the reemergence of clear differences in the reputation and funding of schools. Certain favored urban schools, known as key schools, receive preferential funding and are sought after by ambitious parents. Entry is ostensibly by examination, which inevitably leads to an emphasis on individual rather than collective values. Lewin, Hui, Little, and Zheng (1994) showed that, in practice, other factors influence the admissions process:

> Since key-point secondary schools have had a much higher university admission rate, parents try in a hundred and one ways to send their children to these schools. The "back door" cannot be completely closed. Officially a policy of "every student is equal before the examination score" is adopted. However, when key-point secondary schools enrol their students they are under pressure to provide "exceptional" admissions. (p. 95)

Gasper (1989) claimed that these exceptional admissions provide a route to the best schools for children of senior party and army officials, professionals, and intellectuals. The admissions process provides one example of the importance of individualist norms in a society usually characterized by collectivism.

Emphasizing Ethical and Moral Self-Cultivation

The Chinese traditional culture emphasizes a person's self-cultivation for ethical and moral perfection. The Confucian scholars advocated modesty and encouraged friendly cooperation, giving priority to people's relationships. The purpose of education is to shape every individual into a harmonious member of the society. Educational aims have long emphasized a single developmental criterion that all the children should reach. Children are expected to comply with class rules and restrain their own personality (Wang & Mao, 1996). This aspect of culture links with the emphasis on collectivism.

Traditional Culture and Special Educational Needs

Traditional, and particularly collectivist, values have influenced the development of special education in China. Epstein (1989) claimed that "traditional views which promoted discriminatory practice towards the disabled ... have ... been quite powerful throughout Chinese history" (p. 32). This was related to the worship of ancestors. If a child was unhealthy, ancestors lost their presumed power to protect future clan members and their memory would no longer be worshipped (Epstein, 1989).

Another factor limiting the provision of special education, and influencing its nature, is the collectivist assumption that whole-class teaching should predominate. The importance of classical learning and recitation "further assumed that distinctions in individual learning were insignificant" (Epstein, 1989, p. 32).

The low priority given to special education was clearly in evidence in the study by Merry and Zhao (1998) in the Shaanxi province. "The traditional values of the Chinese educational system have meant that children with special educational needs have not been seen as a priority and in many cases have not been recognized as being the responsibility of the system at all" (p. 207). Provision is inadequate to meet all the potential demand, and the selection processes reinforce notions of collectivism rather than educational need. Merry and Zhao (1998) illustrated this in respect of provision for "deaf-mutes" in the city of Xi'an: "Staff at both the special schools for the deaf described quite rigorous assessment procedures designed to select not those children who needed most help but those who were most likely to be integrated into society eventually" (p. 213).

Socialist Culture

The second major aspect of culture affecting Chinese education is socialism which became influential during the civil war and particularly significant in the three decades following the establishment of the People's Republic. While Confucius is the dominant figure of traditional culture in China, the central influence on the socialist culture was its founder and long-time leader Mao Zedong. Hayhoe (1984) said that "Mao's writings . . . [eventually] became as sacrosanct as the Confucian canons" (p. 33). She summarized the main features of this socialist model of education:

> Knowledge encompassed both the natural and social sciences, but applied politics, based on Marxist-Leninist theory, was a requirement for all students and had a guiding and shaping role for other areas of knowledge. Only when false consciousness had been dispelled and people gained a true understanding of the class nature of society could all other forms of knowledge have a sound basis and be directed towards valid ends. (p. 34)

The communist party took over responsibility for education at a time when only a small proportion of the population was in school and when 80 to 90 percent of the population was illiterate (Hayhoe, 1984, p. 42). Cleverley (1991) referred to the functional nature of socialist education; "educational objectives must serve economic ends" (p. 335). This emphasis has led to an expansion of vocational education at the expense of general secondary education (Lumby & Li, 1998; Yang, 1993). By 1994, 49 percent of all senior secondary students were in vocational or specialized schools (Lewin et al., 1994).

Cleverley (1991) pointed to the links between confucianism and socialism in modern Chinese education and claimed that communism and Confucianism have much in common. "What has happened in Chinese education represents a transmutation of the past as well as a transformation along modern lines" (p. 14). Moral education, for example, involves a blend of Confucian and communist ideals, while socialism also serves to reinforce the collectivist norms of traditional Chinese culture.

The influence of socialism on school leadership and management is embodied in the role of the communist party secretary. Each school is expected to have a post of branch secretary who often wields considerable influence. The party secretary and school branch exist "to make sure that educational policy follows the party's direction and provides political education to faculty and students" (Si, 1993, p. 29).

Lewin et al. (1994) argued that "relations between principal and Party secretary ... remain the most basic and complicated relations in school management ... reforms in school management have been focussed on the problem of who should be the number one person in the school" (pp. 210–211). The 1985 reforms ostensibly ceded responsibility for school management to the principal but, in practice, ambiguity remains: "This shift will not be achieved rapidly.... The tendency for Party organisation to intervene in daily management decisions remains common" (Lewin et al., 1994, p. 211).

The party secretary is the main conduit for socialist values in education but Bush, Coleman and Si's (1998) research in Shaanxi province secondary schools suggests that its influence is low key. One of their case study schools had no party secretary or branch while the principals of two other schools were also the party secretaries: "The Party is clearly an important and omnipresent feature of the education system, as elsewhere in society, but its influence is not overt in the case study schools and none of the principals appear to have been unduly constrained by its presence" (p. 188)

The party's power extends beyond education to other work settings. Wang (1992) referred to socialism as one of three sub-systems in industrial organizations. The communist party system exists "to guarantee and supervise the implementation of the guiding principles and policies of the Party" (p. 14).

The socialist values of the communist party have been integrated with traditional beliefs to create a distinctive Chinese culture. According to Hayhoe (1984) this "derives as much from the admirable achievements of over 30 years of socialist modernization as from the renown of her traditional culture" (p. 45). In the 1990s, the advent of market socialism reinforced another strand of Chinese culture—enterprise.

The Enterprise Culture

The advent and increasing importance of an enterprise culture in China may seem surprising for a socialist country, but it provides an obvious outlet for the innate talents of Chinese people. Predominantly Chinese societies comprise three of the territories or nations (Hong Kong, Singapore, and Taiwan) whose exceptional economic growth in the past 40 years has earned them the collective title of "Asia's four little tigers" (Morris, 1996). China's own economic growth has been impressive, averaging over 10 percent since 1980.

It is evident that China is able to thrive with its unique mixture of communism and enterprise, often described as "market socialism." Williams, Liu, and Shi (1997) referred to the impact of the social market economy on the balance between individual and collectivist values. This has a particular effect on university graduates who are now able to seek employment, notably with multinational companies, rather than wait to be "assigned" a job by the government:

> The belief of the collective will of people (represented by the State) having the supreme power and absolute authority, started to evolve into a belief that individuals should have the right to achieve their personal goals and have the opportunity to excel in their respective professions. (Williams, Liu & Shi, 1997, p. 152)

Lewin et al. (1994) and Cleverley (1991) both referred to the underfunding of education, with the former claiming that less than three percent of gross national product was devoted to education in the 1980s, less than other similar countries. This is partly explained by the low salaries paid to teachers, but government funding alone would still leave schools with inadequate budgets.

Cleverley (1991) referred to the "important decision of the 1980s"—to permit and encourage the investment of private, non-state and local government funds in the education sector. This policy has led many principals to engage in income generation from these sources, as Moyles and Liu (1998) illustrated in respect of preschool education: "Principals ... spend significant amounts of time in promoting their kindergartens to industrialists, local communities, the communist party and others to seek funding for various projects" (p. 163).

This emphasis on nongovernment income has also led many schools to engage in business activity. The rationale for this is both ideological and pragmatic. Engaging in productive work is considered to be important for the political and moral education of all students, a view which reached its high point during the Cultural Revolution when universities were closed and students sent to work in the fields. Since the 1980s, however, the main reason has been income generation.

The income from school-run businesses is a particular feature of Chinese education. Fouts and Chan (1997) related the growth of school businesses to the strategic decision to put much of the public funding into key schools:

> The result of this action was that a very large majority of the schools [had] to see to their own financial welfare. The limited funding available to most schools in China meant that the school factories and the resulting profits became more and more important as the second source of income.... virtually every type of school has embraced the idea of school-run enterprises as a source of additional funding. (p. 41)

There is ample evidence of the importance of school businesses in providing significant funds for education. Fouts and Chan (1997) referred to a school in Guangdong province that receives about one third of its operating budget from school factories, while Lewin et al. (1994) mentioned a primary school that was able to generate a surplus of 60,000 yuan (about £5,000)—a significant sum in China.

The authors' case study secondary schools in the Shaanxi province all earned useful sums from business activity. Two schools in the city of Xi'an earned substantial additional income through letting school-owned restaurants and shops. A rural junior secondary school, however, managed a surplus of just 5,000 yuan from its apple orchard, just two percent of its income (Bush, Coleman, & Si, 1998). Lumby and Li (1998) also pointed to large differences in levels of business income from rural and urban vocational schools. These disparities serve to widen the already significant gap between the quality of provision in urban and rural areas. Good teachers are reluctant to work in the countryside—class sizes are often larger (over 70 in the Qian Ling rural junior secondary school), and rural schools cannot easily compensate for these disadvantages through entrepreneurial activity.

Business activity also provides principals with important resources to spend at their own discretion. Teachers' salaries are fixed, materials and equipment from government income are purchased centrally, and the approval of the education authority is required for any significant spending. The only way to circumvent this tight control is through deployment of entrepreneurial income. Much of the extra income in the Shaanxi province case study schools was spent on augmenting staff salaries (Bush, Coleman, & Si, 1998; Lumby & Li, 1998), further reducing the incentive for teachers to work in rural areas.

The widespread business activities in schools serve to emphasize the integration of traditional, socialist, and market values in education. Despite the apparent contradiction of these very different concepts, it appears unproblematic, and "taken-for-granted" inside schools. At a pragmatic level, school leaders simply accept the mix of values and seek to provide the best education possible within their limited resources.

Patriarchal Culture

The three aspects of Chinese culture discussed hitherto each represent different phases of history but are all still prevalent in contemporary China, including its schools. One dimension has remained significant throughout the 2,500 years since Confucius, and that is the dominance of patriarchal leadership in education and the wider society, including business, government, and the communist party itself. China is by no means alone in experiencing under-representation of women in management positions, within and outside education, but it may be slower than most to acknowledge the issue and to seek remedies.

Cleverley (1991) referred to "a dependent status for women" as one of the Confucian dictums that provides a subordinate role for women throughout their lives:

> According to the three obediences, women must obey the father, obey the husband and, when the husband dies, obey the son.... Females had no property rights, and they were excluded from public office as a matter of course. (p. 7)

The establishment of the People's Republic ostensibly produced a significant improvement in the position of women. The Marriage Law of 1950 declared that husband and wife were companions enjoying equal status and having the same rights to property (Cleverley, 1991). In practice, however, the traditional hegemony of men continued, not least in schools where they hold most of the leadership positions. Research by Coleman, Qiang and Li (1998) showed that there were no women principals in the 89 secondary schools in three counties of the Shaanxi province despite the fact that there were some 2,000 women teachers in those schools. In the 163 primary schools in the same districts, there were only eight women principals although there more than 3,000 women teachers, some 45.2 percent of the total. Coleman et al. (1998) wrote that "the relatively low numbers of women in positions of seniority ... indicates the loss of female potential, expertise and managerial ability to the educational community" (p. 143).

Coleman et al. (1998) attribute these inequalities in part to the continuing dominance of patriarchy. "Such structural oppression may be reinforced by patriarchy within society. It may be that the patriarchal attitudes of traditional Chinese society are still influential and surviving alongside the overriding need to modernise society" (p. 144). In Coleman et al. (1998) research in a range of urban and rural schools in the Shaanxi province, the rhetoric of equality contrasted sharply with the reality of underrepresentation:

> Despite the fact that the overwhelming majority of members of most senior management teams were male, there was universal insistence that men and women were treated equally. A typical response from one secondary school principal was: "of course, for many years, everything is equal." However, in this rural secondary school there were no women in the management team, the principal claiming that "the females in his school lacked the ability to be good leaders." (pp. 145–146)

Coleman et al. (1998) found that three reasons were advanced for the underrepresentation of women in school management (pp. 147–150):

1. As in many other societies, women generally had overall responsibility for domestic tasks and for children and this was often advanced as a reason for their absence from management posts: "if women did not have to do a lot of additional housework they could be equally good leaders" (Male secondary school dean).
2. Tradition and culture stress the need for men to achieve in their careers while women are accorded the domestic and nurturing role: "if the wife achieves much her husband loses face. Most women in China focus their spirit on their family after marriage and must sacrifice their career" (Female secondary school teacher).
3. Women were thought by some respondents to be unsuited for leadership because of their innate qualities. They were regarded as good teachers, because of their nurturing characteristics, but men were said to be better managers, particularly because of their understanding of the "big picture': "men have greater ability and are more effective than women" (Male principal of professional and vocational college).

Coleman et al. (1998) concluded that "major changes in attitudes to female managers, and to the proportion of women who achieve senior positions in schools, are unlikely to occur without addressing the underlying values of patriarchy" (p. 153).

Conclusion: The Enduring Nature of Culture

The concept of culture is widely acknowledged to be difficult to grasp because it is based on values and beliefs that are profound and may not always be conscious. "Beliefs are indeed so deeply buried that individuals do not even know what they are" (Nias, Southworth, & Yeomans, et al., 1989, p. 11). They may also have their origins in the past and be passed on from generation to generation.

Chinese culture is in large part a product of its long history. Confucius, whose ideas remain powerful, was an influential teacher when most European countries were still primitive and North America was sparsely populated. Many of his precepts, including respect for authority, patriarchy, worshipping traditions, and collectivist rather than individual values, are still reflected in the structure of schools and the wider society. The communist revolution added a new dimension to Chinese culture but did not greatly disturb these predominant values and perhaps would have been less successful had it done so. The advent of "market socialism" changed the nature of society and, in particular, tilted the balance between individual and collectivist values. In education, it reinforced the previous trend for schools to supplement their limited state income from school-run businesses. However, the predominant elements of Chinese culture remain in place and continue to influence school leadership, which remains overwhelmingly male, with a balance of hierarchy and collectivism. Cultural change is always problematic and, given the powerful effects of its history, it seems likely that change will be slow and incremental in Chinese education.

References

Bush, T. (1995). *Theories of educational management* (2nd ed.). London, Paul Chapman.
Bush, T., Coleman, M., & Si, X. (1998). Managing secondary schools in China. *Compare, 28*(2), 83–196.
Bush, T., Qiang, H., & Fang, J. (1998). Educational management in China: An overview. *Compare, 28*(2), 133–140.
Cleverly, J. (1991). *Schooling in China.* Sydney: Allen and Unwin.
Coleman, M., Qiang, H., & Li, Y. (1998). Women in educational management in China: Experience in Shaanxi province. *Compare, 28*(2), 141–154.
Crossley, M., & Broadfoot, P. (1992). Comparative and international research in education: Scope, problems and potential. *British Educational Research Journal, 18,* 99–112.
Dimmock, C., & Walker, A. (1998). Comparative educational administration: Developing a cross-cultural conceptual framework. *Educational Administration Quarterly, 34*(4), 558–595.
Epstein, I. (1989). Special education in Japan and China. *Curriculum and Teaching, 4*(2), 27–38.
Fouts, J., & Chan, J. (1997). The development of work-study and school enterprises in China's schools. *Journal of Curriculum Studies, 29,* 31–46.
Gasper, B. (1989). Keypoint schools in China: The persistence of tradition. *Compare, 19,* 5–20.
Hayhoe, R. (1984). *Contemporary Chinese education.* London, Croom Helm.
Head, T., & Sorensen, P. (1993). Cultural values and organizational development: A seven country study. *Leadership and Organization Development Journal, 14*(2), 3–7.
Hofstede, G. (1980). *Cultures consequences: International differences in work-related values.* Beverley Hills, CA: Sage.
Hughes, M. (1990 July). *Improving education and training for educational administrators and*

managers: Urgent needs. Paper presented at the UNESCO International Congress, Mexico City, Mexico.

Lewin, K., Hui, X., Little, A., & Zheng, J. (1994). *Educational innovation in China.* Harlow, Longman: Longman.

Lumby, J., & Li, Y. (1998). Managing vocational education in China. *Compare, 28*(2), 197–206.

Merry, R., & Zhao, W. (1998). Managing special needs provision in China: A qualitative comparison of special needs provision in the Shaanxi region of China and England. *Compare, 28*(2), 207–218.

Morris, P. (1996). Asia's four little tigers: A comparison of the role of education in their development. *Comparative Education, 32*(1), 95–109.

Moyles, J., & Liu, H. (1998). Kindergarten education in China: Reflections on a qualitative comparison of management processes and perceptions. *Compare, 28*(2), 155–170.

Nias, J., Southworth, G., & Yeomans, R. (1989). *Staff relationships in the primary school.* London: Cassell.

Paine, L., & Ma, L. (1993). Teachers working together: A dialogue on organizational and cultural perspectives of Chinese teachers. *International Journal of Educational Research, 19,* 675–697.

Reynolds, D., & Farrell, S. (1996). *Worlds apart: A review of international surveys of educational achievement involving England.* London: HMSO.

Satow, T., & Wang, Z. (1994). Cultural and organizational factors in human resource management in China and Japan. *Journal of Managerial Psychology, 9*(4), 3–11.

Si, X. (1993). *The principles of school management.* Xi'an: Publishing Company of Shaanxi Province.

Si, X. (1997). The management of schools in China. *University of Leicester Professional Development News, 9,* 5–6.

Wang, J., & Mao, S. (1996). Culture and the kindergarten curriculum in the People's Republic of China. *Early Child Development and Care, 123,* 143–156.

Wang, Z. (1992). Managerial psychological strategies for Sino-foreign joint ventures. *Journal of Managerial Psychology, 7*(3), 10–16.

Williams, G., Liu, S., & Shi, Q. (1997). Marketization of higher education in the People's Republic of China. *Higher Education Policy, 10*(2), 151–157.

Yang, J. (1993). Technical and vocational education in the People's Republic of China: Current status and prospects. *The Vocational Aspect of Education, 45*(2), 135–143.

11.

School Leadership in English Schools

Portraits, Puzzles, and Identity

GEOFF SOUTHWORTH

Introduction

This chapter traces the cultural and historical antecedents of leadership in English schools by drawing upon recent research and analyses of headship. Having identified some of the cultural traditions that underpin current policy making, I will argue that

1. School leadership in England continues to be preoccupied with organizational power relations;
2. These relations tend to sustain the domination of leaders in "their" schools; and
3. Such a configuration of authority has implications not only for schooling, but also democracy.

This argument is based on certain beliefs and suppositions including the importance of understanding the values and assumptions that shape leadership in any given context. One of the most robust findings about leadership is that it is contextualized (Leithwood, Jantzi, & Steinbach, 1999). Contingency and situational theories of leadership (Fiedler, 1977; Hersey & Blanchard, 1983) have proved valuable in demonstrating the ways in which leaders are influenced by the circumstances in which they work. These circumstances include organizational and occupational cultures, and much valuable work has been done to uncover how these contour and constrain leadership (e.g. Bolman & Deal, 1992; Nias, Southworth, & Yeomans, 1989; Schein, 1985). However, less work has been done on how the wider societal culture influences leadership. Here political and social values come into play, albeit in implicit and tacit ways. Nor has much work been done to explore the dynamics of this influence. Beliefs about charismatic and heroic leadership, for example, imply that leaders are "free from" such social influences. By contrast,

Giddens' (1979) theory of structuration and agency suggests that social structures pervasively and powerfully shape individual's actions.

Gidden's work is important because while he allows for agency and thus the possibility that individuals can always act otherwise, his notion of structure conveys the idea that unless we are critically aware of our circumstances and the values that hold us prisoner to our perspectives, then social structures create parameters for our actions, not least because these structures inhibit or incapacitate our ability to think of alternatives. In other words, Gidden's structuration theory shows how social structures are not an iron cage that deny individuality, but are a more flexible set of shaping influences.

To understand how cultural forces influence leadership we need to look closely at our social contexts and outside them. Contemporary efforts at internationalization in educational administration have tended to draw superficial comparisons between policies and practices in different countries without developing thorough understandings of the contexts, histories, and cultures within which they have become established. At present the successes of Western capitalism and the preeminence of English as the lingua franca of professional discourse may mask both important and subtle cultural and historical differences. I agree with others that we should now begin to "go beneath the veneer of similitude represented by our current professional discourse" (Bredeson, 2000, p. 7).

Dimmock and Walker (2000) argued that theory and practice in educational management is socially constructed and more strongly contextually bound than some are prepared to admit. To avoid the simplistic borrowing of ideas from elsewhere, as well as to prevent ethnocentric theorizing and prescription, these scholars believe it is essential that educational leadership develops a comparative, international study dimension that embraces cultural and cross-cultural perspectives (Dimmock & Walker, 2000). It is by looking outside our own contexts and frames of reference that we can see alternatives and other options. In this way, comparative work feeds our professional imaginations by showing what our occupational worlds might be otherwise.

Of course, this chapter can provide only an outline sketch of the contextual, historical and cultural features that shape school leadership in England. Within the confines of a chapter it is not possible to provide a comprehensive or detailed analysis of the issues because they are simply too large and too deep. Nevertheless, I will draw upon a number of scholarly and empirical studies that have attempted to trace the cultural roots and influences upon leadership in order to delineate an argument that I hope can be further developed at a later time.

The chapter is organized into five sections. In the first section I catalogue the major reforms introduced in England during the 1990s. In the second I briefly review the policy themes that underscore these reforms. The third focuses on how the reforms relate to headship and how the role of headteachers in England reflects cultural and historical assumptions, values, and beliefs. I argue in this section that the identified beliefs shape headship in particular ways and have implications for leadership and schooling in democratic societies. In the fourth section I argue that the cultural and historical beliefs and values combine with occupational norms and together they create a professional identity that holds in place a particular set of assumptions about headship. In the fifth section I present my conclusions and suggestions for future studies.

Recent Reforms

The last decade of the twentieth century was a time of unprecedented reform and restructuring in English education. Policy makers introduced legislation that caused considerable upheaval in the educational system. The successive waves of reforms were not unique to the English system—education in many countries experienced unprecedented turbulence under the watchful eyes of politicians and a skeptical public (Bredeson, 2000).

The consequential effects of the reforms on the roles and responsibilities of the teachers and headteachers who have been caught up in this whirlwind of change have yet to be rigorously researched using large samples. Given that many individuals have already chosen to leave teaching, it is likely that it is now too late to capture the profession's experience of these change processes. Nevertheless, small scale studies revealed that practitioners found the experience of major reform challenging and difficult because of ideological differences between policymakers and practitioners; the scale and pace of the reforms; the lack of sensible implementation strategies in the early years of restructuring; and the sheer amount of administrative change, personal uncertainty, and professional confusion which resulted and which heads and teachers had to deal with on a daily basis (Southworth, 1995b; Southworth, Pocklington & Weindling, 1998; Webb & Vulliamy, 1996). In other words, educational change became "ubiquitous and relentless," and the concomitant turbulence that the reforms created became so common that it could be characterized as systemic (Fullan, 1993, p. 3).

The major reforms that were introduced fall chronologically into two groups—those introduced by the Conservative Governments of Prime Ministers Thatcher and Major, and those latterly put in place, since 1997, by the Blair administration. The Conservative Government's reforms included:

1. the construction and implementation of a National Curriculum;
2. introduction of a national system of testing pupils at the ages of 7, 11, and 14;
3. the publication of schools' test results and the use of league tables to rate schools' apparent success;

4. open enrollment—that is, the right of parents to choose the school they wish their child to attend;
5. local management of schools (LMS), or as is it is called in the United States site-based management (although the U.S. version is nothing like as extensive as that in England);
6. as part of LMS, each school is funded on the basis of the annual number of pupils attending the school;
7. the creation of the Office for Standards in Education (OfSTED), which set in place the week-long inspection of all schools once every four years (latterly relaxed to once every six years), the publication of the each school's inspection report, the grading of schools including the classification of some schools judged to have "severe weaknesses" (i.e., to be very weak schools) and schools requiring "special measures' (i.e., judged to be failing and in need of rapid improvement or, if that proves unsuccessful, for the school to be closed);
8. the introduction of school development plans, later revised to incorporate the setting of improvement targets;
9. reform of the initial teacher training system; and
10. a national program of training for prospective and newly appointed headteachers;

The Blair government's reforms included:

1. The introduction of a National Literacy Strategy into every primary (elementary) school from September 1998;
2. The introduction into every primary school of a National Numeracy Strategy from September 1999;
3. The extension of the National Literacy Strategy into secondary schools from September 2001;
4. The setting of numerical targets for pupils' attainments in every school, linked to the government's pledge to increase pupils' scores in national assessment tests by the year 2002;
5. revisions to the National Curriculum following a five-year moratorium on curriculum and the designing of a curriculum 2000;
6. the intention to link teacher performance to rewards and pay;
7. the articulation of national standards for headteachers and other school leaders;
8. the creation of a National College for School Leadership, which will be responsible for headteacher training;
9. defining teacher competencies in Information and Communication Technologies;
10. further devolution of funds to schools and reduced financial autonomy for local education authorities (school districts); and
11. the extension of the National Literacy Strategy into the early years of secondary education.

Moreover, the Labour Administration has generally left in place the reforms of the previous Conservative Government. Thus, although there are differences between these two sets of reforms, there are also certain continuities, thereby making it possible to identify some common themes in the reforms.

With the return of the Blair administration for a second term of office, the emphases are much the same. The need to continue the reform process and sustain achievements is stressed and while school improvement remains an imperative, more is being made of the need to transform schools. The notion of transformation is another way of articulating the British government's wish to "modernize teaching" and is part of the larger exercise of developing public sector services.

Reform Themes

The reforms reflect a number of policy-making themes which, in turn, have implications for school leaders. Here I will focus on the following themes:

1. Competition
2. Decentralization and centralization
3. Accountability
4. Policy makers' belief in leadership/headship
5. School improvement

In turn, these themes suggest that the cultures of schooling—that is, the values, beliefs, and norms which underpin and influence practitioners' behaviors— have been and continue to be influenced in certain ways, either explicitly or implicitly.

Throughout the Conservative Government's time in office in the 1990s there was an explicit intention to subject schools to "market forces" by increasing competition among them. The policies for open enrollment, parental choice, the publication of results, and the funding of schools according to the number of pupils attending them were mechanisms for encouraging successful schools to grow while, at the same time, pressuring less successful ones to do better, or perish.

Related to this policy were several others. There was increased devolution of powers to schools, mostly in respect of the discretion they had to manage their own financial affairs. All establishments became "locally managed schools" (LMS). Also, a new type of school was created—the grant maintained school. Grant Maintained (GM) schools elected to opt out of local government (school district) control and become wholly self-determining. GM schools were a more radical variant of LMS since they became financially independent of their local districts. Thus between them, the LMS and GM initiatives created schools that were more or less self-managing establishments.

Such decentralization was, however, coupled to a counterbalancing increase in centralization. The national curriculum provided a common framework for self-managing schools to adhere to. National assessments also limited the scope for experimentation in instructional practices. Centralization circumscribed schools' autonomy by ensuring there was increasing specification in roles and responsibilities, curricula, and assessment practices, while the increased emphasis on external accountability is a theme in itself.

The publication of test data, the use of league tables, and the inspection of schools combine to create one of the strongest accountability regimes in the English-speaking world. Schools may have become self-managing, but they are also monitored closely, frequently, and publicly. Furthermore, the scrutiny of schools is such that it is "high stakes" accountability. A poor OfSTED inspection report tarnishes the school's reputation, frequently lowers morale in the school, and is often but not always (depending on tenure) interpreted as a reflection on the school's leadership, in particular the headteacher, and especially so in primary (elementary) schools.

This latter point is important because all politicians from whichever party share a common belief in the power of leadership. One of the unshakeable tenets, bolstered by school effectiveness research that has been cited time and again by policy makers to the point it has become an article of faith, if not a mantra, is the idea that school leaders—especially headteachers (principals)—can make a significant difference to schools' levels of performance. Headteachers have been portrayed as central figures—key people and pivotal players in the national enterprise of school improvement, which is now at the heart of the Blair government's project. Hence the emphasis on heads' training needs and the creation of a National College for School Leadership which has been established in Nottingham.

For example, within a matter of a few weeks of winning the 1997 election, the Labour Government published "Excellence in Education Schools" (Department of Education & Employment [DFEE], 1997), setting out its specific education policy intentions. The paper heralded a "crusade for higher standards" (p. 4) and promised, in the chapter on standards and accountability, to publish more data than ever before on each school's level of academic performance (p. 25). Also, headteachers were urged to monitor the classroom performance of teachers (p. 26). This reference to headteachers pointed to a belief, common among policy makers, in the influence of headteachers to manage the reforms and improvement efforts in their schools: "The quality of the headteacher is a crucial factor in the success of a school" (p. 29). And:

> The vision for learning set out [here] will demand the highest qualities of leadership and management from headteachers. The quality of the head often makes the difference between success and failure of a school. Good heads can transform

a school; poor heads can block progress and achievement. It is essential that we have measures in place to strengthen the skills of all new and serving heads.

We intend to ensure that in future all those appointed as headteachers for the first time hold a professional headship qualification which demonstrates that they have the leadership skills necessary to motivate staff and pupils to manage a school. (p. 46)

These remarks demonstrate that policy makers' emphasis on high-stakes accountability and school improvement are inexorably tied to strongly held beliefs about the nature and impact of organizational leadership. Furthermore, if "culture" means the values, norms, traditions, customs, rituals and symbols of a group (Deal & Kennedy, 1982; Hargreaves, 1995), then the emphasis placed on headteachers is not only a theme, but one which has symbolic significance. Inspection data, school effectiveness research, and improvement studies have been cited in a ritualized fashion so that policy makers and practitioners alike uncritically believe the correspondence between successful schools and "good" headteachers to be axiomatic and causal. Therefore, while the reform process in England warrants detailed analysis in terms of the policy issues, within the parameters of this chapter it is important to explore the influence and impact of the reforms upon headteachers.

Reforms and Headship

Without doubt the reform program has created numerous changes and challenges for teachers and headteachers alike. In terms of school leadership and, in particular, headship, it seems to me that there have been two changes underway:

1. Increased specification of responsibilities and competencies; most visible in the articulation by central government of national professional standards for headteachers.
2. Increased emphasis on leadership, as well as on management.

I highlight these two sets of change because they point to the emergence over the last decade of what some call New Public Management (NPM) (Hood, 1991; Mahony & Moos, 1998). This new form of managerialism is introduced in different countries in different ways, but is generally based on seven doctrines:

1. hands-on professional management;
2. explicit standards and measures of performance;
3. greater emphasis on output controls;

4. break-up of large organizations operating on decentralized budgets;
5. introduction of competition;
6. stress on commercial styles of management; and
7. stress on doing more for less. (Hood, 1991, pp. 4–5)

These doctrines are certainly evident in the English educational reforms. However, analyses of NPM suggest that it is also accompanied by "old managerialism" with its focus on intensifying systems of direct control (Ball, 1987, p. 259). The idea that old and new forms go along side-by-side is a significant point because it implies that change is not always about jettisoning previous ways of working, but rather of adding to them. Consequently, control in educational organizations becomes a matter of developing "loose–tight" structures and systems. There may be decentralization on some issues yet more centralization in others. For example, in England during the 1990s central control of school budgets was loosened, while central control of the curriculum and of accountabilities were considerably tightened. However, what is most important to note is that neither the old nor the new forms of managerialism suggest that organizational control is relinquished or trans-formed. Leaders are held accountable and thus they are understandably reluc-tant to let go of decisions for which they are held individually responsible.

This perspective parallels Grace's (1995) insightful analysis of school lead-ership in England in the nineteenth and twentieth centuries. Grace argued that the nineteenth-century traditions of school leadership, being an expression of social class power, gave way in the middle of the twentieth century to a more meritocratic conceptualization of the headteacher as professional leader. However, since the late 1980s, another, newer discourse has been used, one which advanced a market culture in education and educational leadership. This commodification of education, with its attendant language of "output," "products," "value added," and "measurable product," describes the curriculum as an entity to be "delivered," and parents and pupils as consumers. It also positions the headteacher more as the chief executive than as the leading professional (pp. 40–41). Grace continued with the following:

> The emergence of the headteacher as entrepreneurial leader and chief executive in the 1980s and 1990s marks, insofar as these become the dominant constructs, the final secularisation and commodification of the educational process. The most important characteristics of effective school leaders are now less to be found in their moral, scholarly or professional qualities than in their "street-wise" capacity to survive and exploit market opportunities for education. (p. 42)

However, while these transitions have been taking place, Grace argued that other patterns have been more enduring:

English schooling culture in the 20th century has always had, at its heart, a major paradox and contradiction. Formally designated as the cultural agency for "making democracy work" and involved, at specific periods, with explicit pedagogical projects to enhance education for citizenship, its own practice has remained largely undemocratic. (p. 46)

The reasons for this are complex, but one major factor is the influence of the hierarchical headteacher tradition:

Although this has been modified over the years into more consultative forms, the fact remains that most headteachers are the operative school leaders and few examples exist of serious organizational democracy involving major decision-making in association with teachers, pupils and other school staff.

This lack of a democratic culture and practice in English school life, it can be claimed, is itself a mediated form of historical hidden curriculum of English political and social culture. Despite an early achievement of formal political democracy in England, social and cultural forms have remained pervaded by aristocratic and hierarchical values; in particular, the notion that there is a leadership class. (p. 56)

In other words, although there has been a great deal of surface change, power relations within schools have proved remarkably constant.

The stability of power relations in schools is a theme in my own empirical research into school leadership. My research is essentially an ongoing, cumulative project. Over two decades I have investigated, through a series of related studies, the role, work, and experience of headteachers. Using qualitative methods (mostly interviews and case studies) I have examined headship from a number of standpoints, including:

1. collegiality (Southworth, 1987)
2. organizational culture (Nias et al., 1989)
3. learning organizations (Nias, Southworth, & Cambell, 1992; Southworth, 1994, 2000)
4. professional identity (Southworth, 1995a)
5. change management (Southworth 1995b)
6. school improvement (Southworth, 1998, 1999b; Southworth et al., 1998)

Together these studies show that primary school headship has shifted in its emphases and concerns over time. For example, there has been an intensification of the demands made on heads and of their workloads. The need to be able to manage productively external change agendas and to demonstrate enhanced levels of performance have also been heightened, while many heads have become interested in "marketing the school," and managing the school's image and reputation, or have become embroiled in entrepreneurial activities.

Yet, running through all these studies is one constancy—the belief in the headteacher as the single-most influential person in the school, which ultimately translates into lone leadership. While changes abound, as I have argued elsewhere (Southworth, 1999b, 1999c), the major continuity is the idea that the head is the pivotal player in the school. Expressed another way, although the *content* of headship shifts and changes, the *character* of school leadership continues.

Further support for this interpretation comes from a review of the literature focusing on school leadership in England. Three major role continuities were identified:

- *The persistence of work patterns*—Variety, fragmentation, and busyness characterizing their work schedules;
- *Ego-identification*—Heads feeling personally responsible for "their" schools; and
- *Power*—Heads being keenly aware of their influence, authority, and control and recognizing themselves as powerful individuals. (Hall & Southworth, 1997)

The recurrence of these themes is so strong that Coulson's early, landmark analyses of primary headship (1976, 1978) are still relevant today. Twenty-five years ago Coulson described how heads identified themselves with the schools they led, regarding them as "theirs" in a very possessive way and being very powerful figures inside the schools they led. Today, they continue to hold a formidable concentration of power and can exercise control over the form and direction of internal developments. Moreover, little attention is paid to other school leaders in the literature, so that the sheer amount of space devoted to heads signifies the central importance of heads to the school's health and success (Southworth, 1995a).

Indeed, primary heads are often in the position whereby they dominate their schools (Southworth, 1995a). And, despite some cosmetic changes, power relations are (generally) remarkably enduring. While autocratic styles of leadership have given way to more consultative ones, consultation should not be confused with democracy; "authoritarianism need not have an ugly face and yet it is authoritarianism for all that" (White, 1982, p. 20).

While conceptions of educational leadership are dynamic, contested, and historically and culturally situated, these conceptions are not simply technical formulations for increasing organizational efficiency and effectiveness, they are also expressions of cultural values (Grace, 1995, p. 192). Furthermore:

The form and nature of educational leadership has implications for the reproduction, modification or transformation of the wider social, cultural and political features of the society in which it is situated. It has implications for the socialization of individuals, the formation of citizens and the structuring of social relations. (p. 192)

Although such generalization can appear to deny that some individuals will and can do otherwise, Gidden's (1979) work, as stated in the introduction, shows the relationship between agency and structure often results in individuals being shaped more by structure than the reverse. Therefore, while there have been important developments in the theoretical discourse of leadership throughout the twentieth century, these have probably not generated corresponding shifts in the practice of leadership. Presently there is much interest in transformational leadership, as well as critical and reflective leadership, but the pressures leaders face every day make them much more pragmatic than philosophic or critical in their leadership actions (Southworth, 1999a).

Although it is now less common to hear heads talk about "my" school, the move to talking about "our" school does not necessarily mark a very radical change. Teachers may have become more involved in decision making at the school level, but pupils, parents and the community remain largely uninvolved. External legal and bureaucratic structures continue to operate as if the headteacher was (subject to the formal responsibilities of the school governors) *the* manifest school leader. Nor should it escape attention that while more consultative approaches appear to have been introduced, latterly the emphasis on the head as chief executive has inhibited, if not blocked, further moves toward participation.

At the close of the twentieth century, contemporary conceptions of headship in England incorporate notions of:

1. individualism,
2. hierarchical organization,
3. positional power,
4. authority dependence, and
5. consumerism.

Despite academics and others calling for more ethical and emancipatory approaches to leadership (Bates, 1989; Foster, 1986; Smyth, 1989) these have not been adopted on a widespread basis. Although in the nineteenth century headteachers were expected to give moral and ethical direction, "contemporary leadership has become, in an important sense, devalued" (Grace, 1995, p. 156).

Pupils and parents are regarded as clients and customers, rather than citizens. Education is legitimized more on economic grounds than for civic or communitarian reasons. Schools are model organizations for their pupils, and the capacity of schools to teach pupils about social values and organization is great. As preparation for life in a democratic society, leadership is not realizing its potential. Schools and their leaders, at best, reflect a very circumscribed notion of democracy. The hidden and not-so-hidden curricula of schooling is that pupils learn to live and work in institutions that are more about autocracy than democracy.

As Grace noted: "English education has a history of power domination rather than of power sharing" (p. 202). And the recent and current reforms in English education continue to create and sustain structures that ensure that schools endure as organized hierarchies and in which the position of the head-teacher is paramount. Thus for historical and cultural reasons headship in England has neither been transformed nor become "transformational." nineteenth- and twentieth-century beliefs underpin its passage into the twenty-first century.

Professional Identity

Some will cavil at the argument that external reforms, cultural norms and societal expectations govern the nature of headship. These critics will regard my line of thinking as too deterministic. Plainly, and in common with others, I believe the work of heads to be greatly influenced by macro-political, economic, and social forces (Bredeson, 2000). However, while these forces are powerful, they are not the only ones that shape headship.

Elsewhere I have argued that headship for many individuals is not only a role, but an identitiy (Southworth, 1995a). An individual's professional identity is socially constructed from interaction with significant others and generalized others (such as reference groups), and from experience in the occupation (teaching and headship) where individuals are socialized into accepting occupational norms, values and beliefs.

Occupational socialization is especially potent in England because head-teachers experience two doses of it that are mutually reinforcing. The first is when they become teachers and learn through their training and from their senior colleagues that classroom control is paramount. The second is when they become headteachers where they learn from their peers and others that they are now in control of the school. Moreover, the selection processes largely ensure that you do not become a headteacher unless you demonstrate the first set of values and acknowledge and accept the second set.

The professional identities of teachers and heads are highly consistent in that norms of individualism, moralism, hierarchy, and control are common to both roles (Southworth, 1995a). The classroom is in many ways a microcosm of the school in terms of power relations, as Waller (1932) noted so long ago. Teachers are dominant in their spheres of influence, their classrooms, where they hold power over the pupils, and in turn, they expect and accept their heads' right to exercise power over them, as teachers, in the organizational sphere.

The nature of schools as organizations frames a set of professional interactions and relationships which produce and reproduce the power relations amongst the adults and pupils. These power relations become so pervasive and taken-for-granted that they become sedimented into the occupational identities of teachers and heads, thereby making domination a norm for those in positions of responsibility in the organization (Southworth, 1995a).

Current work on professional narratives and identity also supports much of the foregoing. Part of the social construction of an occupational identity involves sustaining a narrative about one's work and role. The stories teachers and headteachers tell are ways of making sense of themselves:

> How a headteacher experiences his or her job, how s/he interprets his/her position, what s/he understands about what s/he does, what s/he knows, does not know—are neither simply individual choices nor simply the result of belonging to the social category "headteacher." In the course of doing the job and interacting with others they are negotiated. But headteachers' identities are also a matter of their position and the position of their communities within broader social structures. (Moller, 2001, p. 5)

Research in Denmark, Ireland, Norway, and England suggests that there are connections between identity and practice. In terms of the narratives I hear when researching and working with heads, it seems they are profoundly aware of their responsibilities for the school. The implicit loneliness of the role and their strong feelings of isolation betray a sense of individualism and the role weighing heavy upon them, as well as their tacit belief in their central importance to the school's health and vitality.

In other words, the stories they tell me, others, and *themselves* convey a view of themselves as centrally involved and important. These stories are far more meaningful than the "lifeless lists" (Bredeson, 2000) that functionalists produce of effective leaders because they show us what the job means to those who perform it. Although the stories show that there are change forces at work and that over time the role keeps shifting, there is also a meta-message that remains largely undisturbed. This meta-message is one that sustains the identity of the head as powerful, pivotal, and dominating.

In short, the identities of heads are largely undisturbed because they are characterized by a "dynamic sameness" (Bredeson, 2000). Heads manage organizational changes that require them, on the surface, to alter their leadership, but at the deeper level of power relations they also keep it the same. Heads in England are responsible for virtually everything in the school, especially when it is a primary school. Politicians, parents, and the public appear to want it that way and so too do most heads since it is the opportunity to play a leading role that attracts them to the position. Leadership is still seen as personal because political, social, organizational, and occupational norms all combine to make it that way. This convergence of values and beliefs creates stories, narratives, beliefs, and identities that anchor the role to these norms in self-sustaining ways.

Conclusion

This brief discussion points first and foremost to the need for a more considered and comprehensive exegesis. Although I have drawn upon the work of other scholars whose analyses support my argument and empirical research, much more work remains to be done to synthesize their thinking and my own and to articulate a more elaborate thesis.

There is also a need to include a more complex portrait of headship today than I have done here. The challenges headteachers describe, the mixed metaphors they use to characterize their roles, and the ironical professional stories and anecdotes they tell when interviewed imply that their work is frequently full of dualities, contradictions, and dilemmas. Some, for example, see themselves as caught on the horns of the participation/control dilemma (Ball, 1987). That is, while on the one hand they are urged to involve staff, on the other, they are told they remain in control and are responsible for all that occurs in the school (Southworth, 1987; 1995a). In this chapter I have ignored the professional tensions heads encounter and strive to resolve for themselves, in the schools in which they work, in order to make my line of argument starker. Given these deficiencies, I nevertheless believe that five further conclusions can be made.

First, school leadership does reflect historical and cultural traditions, and it also sustains them. Grace's work is one of the most scholarly and penetrating examples of this in English educational writing. Internationally, the work of Smyth (1989) and his collaborators shows how critical theory can help uncover the underlying assumptions about leadership and schooling. Such studies demonstrate that leadership is a social construct that, while always being refined by successive generations, is also held together by deeper structural beliefs, which have an enduring quality to them. As a construct, leadership in England is a mix of change and continuity, but the continuities provide the foundational beliefs for headship to endure as individualistic and dominating.

Second, the interpretation of headship discussed in this chapter suggests that in England school leadership is based upon a set of traditions that circumscribe the role as

1. individualistic,
2. proprietal,
3. pivotal, and
4. powerful.

This is not to say that some aspects of leadership are not shared with others; they are. But it is also the case that shared leadership is largely contingent upon the individual headteacher's preferences, as studies of the roles of deputy heads in primary schools show (Southworth, 1998). In other words, shared leadership is often a *concession* the headteacher grants to others.

These traditions about power relations in schools reflect hierarchical assumptions about organizational positions. They also reflect power relations in classrooms. While it can be argued that the bureaucratic traditions of school organization are one set of assumptions about leadership, another is the occupational culture and structures of teaching and learning. Power relations in classrooms place the teacher at the very center of transactions. The teacher is the pivotal player, and his/her or his exercise of control and authority sets the tone for almost everything else.

Assumptions about power at both the classroom and the school levels are complementary. Teachers being dominant in their classrooms accept, in turn, the head's right to exercise power over them at the school level. Also, teachers and headteachers legitimate their authority in broadly consistent ways—they have similar feelings of responsibility for others, need to feel in control, and want to be themselves (Southworth, 1995a). Thus a particular set of beliefs about power relations become taken for granted, not least because they are further supported and reinforced by historical and cultural traditions.

Third, these traditions are not immutable. They are sufficiently plastic to absorb contemporary values and emphases. In England over the last decade corporatist and capitalist values of choice, competition, and consumerism have been explicitly added to bureaucratic and managerialist values. While there are some tensions within this admixture, they generally sustain the same expectations of leaders.

Leadership is thus like a palimpsest—that is, a text in which more recent scripts are superimposed on earlier ones. Yet the earlier forms also show through the superimposed text so that a sense of history, antecedence, and layers of meaning are hinted at. Understood as a palimpsest, leadership must be seen as an historical, social, and cultural-specific construction. And like a palimpsest, we must look for the stories on the surface of the page and for those which lie beneath the surface and which underscore the script. Current interests in headteachers' narratives may help this kind of analysis advance and develop.

Fourth, although at present there is global interest in the role of leaders as change agents, with consequent concerns about developing the leadership capacities of headteachers and principals, it is central to my argument and the metaphor of the palimpsest, that such global interest should not ignore cultural differences. What I have described here is an indigenous view of leadership, and we need many more of them to develop an "indigenous knowledge base" on school leadership (Dimmock & Walker, 2000; Hallinger & Kantamara, 2000).

As Hallinger and Kantamara (2000) argued, culturally-grounded research is needed. Leading organizational change is fundamentally a cultural process, as many scholars believe (Bolman & Deal, 1992; Evans, 1996; Fullan, 1993; Schein, 1996), but these writers employ organizational culture as the conceptual framework for understanding change. Hallinger and Kantamara employ national culture as the conceptual lens. Their work shows that understanding leadership processes across cultures is complex but that "We can only understand the nature of leadership by exposing the hidden assumptions of the cultural context. This will open new windows through which to view educational leadership" (Hallinger & Kantamara, 2000, p. 202).

Separate country studies may no longer be sufficient to deal with the global forces at work in education:

> The argument is simply that as a field of study, educational management and leadership needs to reflect the globalising and internationalising of policy and practice. To do that, we need a comparative branch to the field that is rigorous and reflects a cross-cultural dimension. The reasons and benefits are manifold. First, the transfer of policy across boundaries that continue to ignore societal culture is likely to heap up many future problems. Second, while scholars and practitioners remain largely ignorant about societal, economic, political, demographic and cultural differences between systems, they are likely to draw fallacious conclusions regarding the appropriateness of importing policy and practice. Third, by understanding the contexts and education systems of other countries, we may come to a better understanding of our own. (Dimmock & Walker, 2000, p. 145)

While agreeing with these points I would also like to add another. Watson (1997) noted that what is happening at the grass roots in educational systems is often overlooked because many comparative and international studies really only deal with macro level issues. Watson believes one should undertake contextualized research at the lowest possible level by observing schools and individuals within those schools in relationship to the local community. In this way scholars can then compare micro-level activity with the macro-level *within* nation states, or whatever is the unit of analysis, as well as comparing *between* countries. Comparative studies must not develop on the basis of unwarranted generalizations. We should simultaneously sustain grounded and empirical studies with wider perspectives. Only by ensuring contextualized knowledge of systems will we reap the benefits of cross-cultural studies of educational leadership.

Fifth, given the interpretation of headship in England that I have set out here, other countries that may be interested in learning about school leadership and improvement should proceed with caution. Any country or educational system that adopts the same concept of leadership as applied in England may find that they have also borrowed a concomitant set of power relations, which create the circumstances for their schools to reflect, at best, a circumscribed view of democracy.

While staff in schools may *talk* about democratic ideals, what pupils *see* is that their school is not a democratic organization. Like Jackson (1989), I believe schools and classrooms have "greater moral potency than is commonly understood" (p. 4). It is unacceptable that schools are led by leaders who dominate their institutions, because this negates participative democracy (Southworth, 1995a). Thus other nations looking to England for examples of school leadership must be very careful lest they inadvertently injure their own civic and communitarian ideals and goals.

References

Ball, S. J. (1987). *The micropolitics of the school.* London: Routledge.
Ball, S. (1997). Policy sociology and critical social research: A personal review of recent education policy and policy research. *British Journal of Sociology of Education, 15*(1), 79–91.
Bates, R. (1989). Leadership and the rationalisation of society. In W. J. Smyth (Ed.), *Critical perspectives on educational leadership* (pp. 131–156). London: Falmer Press
Bolman, L., & Deal, T. (1992). *Reframing organizations.* San Francisco: Jossey-Bass.
Bredeson, P. (2000). *Global perspectives on school leadership: An examination of the work of school principals in three countries.* Paper presented at the annual meeting of the American Educational Research Association, New Orleans, LA.
Coulson, A. A. (1976). The role of the primary head. In T. Bush, R. Glatter, J. Goodey, & C. Riches, *Approaches to school management* (pp. 274–292). London: Harper & Row.
Coulson, A. A. (1978). Power and decision-making in the primary school. In C. Richards (Ed.), *The study of primary education: A source book* (Vol. 3, pp. 77–82). Lewes East Sussex, UK: Falmer Press.
Deal, T., & Kennedy, A. (1982). *Corporate cultures.* Reading, MA: Addison-Wisley.
Department for Education and Employment. (1997). *Excellence in education.* London: Author.
Dimmock, C., & Walker, A. (2000). Developing comparative and international leadership and management: A cross-cultural model. *School Leadership and Management, 20*(2), 143–160.
Evans, R. (1996). *The human side of change.* San Francisco: Jossey-Bass.
Fiedler, F. E. (1977). *Improving leadership effectiveness: The leader match concept.* Chichester, England: Wiley
Foster, W. (1986). *Paradigms and promises: New approaches to educational administration.* New York: Prometheus Books.
Fullan, M. (1993). *Change forces.* London: Falmer Press.
Giddens, A. (1979). *Central problems in social theory.* London: MacMillan.
Grace, G. (1995). *School leadership: Beyond educational management.* London: Falmer Press.
Hall, V., & Southworth, G. (1997). Headship: A review of the literature. *School Leadership and Management, 17*(2), 151–170.
Hallinger, P., & Kantamara, P. (2000). Educational change in Thailand: Opening a window onto leadership as a cultural process. *School Leadership and Management, 20*(2), 189- 206.
Hargreaves, D. (1995). School culture. *School Effectiveness and School Improvement, 6*(1), 23–46.

Hersey, P., & Blanchard, K. (1983). *Management of organizational behavior: Utilising human resources.* Englewood Cliffs, NJ: Prentice Hall.

Hood, C. (1991). A public management for all seasons. *Public Administration, 49*(5), 9–32.

Jackson, P. (1989 April). *Report on the moral life of classrooms.* Paper presented at the annual meeting of the American Educational Research Association, San Francisco CA.

Leithwood, K., Jantzi, D., & Steinbach, R. (1999). *Changing leadership for changing times.* Buckingham, England: Open University Press.

Mahony, P., & Moos, L. (1998). Democracy and school leadership in England and Denmark. *British Journal of Educational Studies, 46*(3), 302–317.

Moller, J. (2001 April). *Norwegian head-teachers' leadership identity: Making sense of mission and mandates.* Paper presented at the annual meeting of the American Educational Research Association, Seattle, WA.

Nias, J., Southworth, G., & Campbell, P. (1992). *Whole school curriculum development in the primary school.* London: Falmer Press.

Nias, J., Southworth, G., & Yeomans, P. (1989). *Staff relationships in the primary school: A study of school cultures.* London: Cassell.

Schein, E. (1985). *Organizational culture and leadership.* San Francisco: Jossey-Bass.

Schein, E. (1996). Culture: The missing concept in organizational studies. *Administrative Science Quarterly, 41*, 229–240.

Smyth, W. J. (Ed.). (1989). *Critical perspectives on educational leadership.* London: Falmer Press.

Southworth, G. (1987). Primary school headteachers and collegiality. In G. Southworth (Ed.), *Readings in primary school management* (pp. 61–75). London: Falmer Press.

Southworth, G. (1994). School leadership and school development: Reflections from research. In G. Southworth (Ed.), *Readings in primary school management* (pp. 13–28). London: Falmer Press.

Southworth, G. (1995a). *Looking into primary headship: A research-based interpretation.* London: Falmer Press

Southworth, G. (1995b). *Talking heads: Voices of experience; an investigation into primary headship in the 1990s.* Cambridge, England: University of Cambridge School of Education.

Southworth, G. (1998). *Leading improving primary schools: The work of heads and deputy headteachers.* London: Falmer Press.

Southworth, G. (1999a). Continuities and changes in primary headship. In T. Bush, L. Bell, R. Bolam, R. Glatter, & P. Ribbins (Eds.), *Educational management: Redefining theory, policy and practice* (pp. 43–58). London: Paul Chapman.

Southworth, G. (1999b). Headship, leadership and school improvement. In G. Southworth & P. Lincoln (Eds.), *Supporting improving schools: The role of heads and LEAs in raising standards* (pp. 69–86). London: Falmer Press.

Southworth, G. (1999c). Primary school leadership in England: Policy, practice and theory. *School Leadership and Management, 19*(1), 49–65.

Southworth, G. (2000). How primary schools learn. *Research Papers in Education, 15*(3), 275–291.

Southworth, G., Pocklington, K., & Weindling, D. (1998). *A qualitative study of primary, secondary and special school headteachers.* London: School Improvement and Leadership Center, University of Reading.

Waller, W. (1932). *The sociology of teaching.* New York: Rusell and Rusell.

Watson, K. (1997). Memories, models and mapping: The impact of geopolitical changes on comparative studies in education. *Compare, 28*(1), 5–31.

Webb, R., & Vulliamy, G. (1996). *Roles and responsibilities in the primary school: Changing demands, changing practices.* Buckingham; Philadephia, PA: Open University Press.

White, P. (1983). *Beyond domination: An essay in the political philosophy of education.* London: Routledge & Kegan Paul.

12.

Hong Kong Principals' Dilemmas

Basic Management and Consequence

ALLAN WALKER

Recent research designed to advance understanding of educational leadership has described principals' lives as beset by dilemmas. Drawing on studies of teachers' dilemmas, researchers in the United States, Australia, and the United Kingdom have investigated the dilemmas faced by principals in an educational reform environment fraught with uncertainty and contradiction. By contrast, little research has been conducted on dilemmas faced by Hong Kong principals. The shortage of empirical work in this area is indicative of a more widespread neglect of investigation into principals' lives in non-Western English-speaking contexts. Dilemma research conducted purely in such contexts disenfranchises large groups of principals, denies the identities of important racial, ethnic, and national groups, and risks restricting understanding to narrowly, even arrogantly, defined parameters. While the area of organizational culture has been researched extensively (e.g., Bolman & Deal, 1991), little work has been conducted into the influence of societal culture and context on leadership, organization, and management. This chapter purports to partly address this situation by investigating the role dilemmas play, or do not play, in the lives of a small group of Hong Kong principals.

This study is part of a larger project exploring the dilemmas faced by a group of Hong Kong principals. Our concentration on dilemmas is itself framed within a cross-cultural understanding of educational leadership in East and Southeast Asia (Dimmock & Walker, 1998a; Hallinger & Leithwood, 1996). In the first sections of the chapter we summarize a case for studying dilemmas, discuss the absence of studies into leadership in non-Western contexts, and provide a snapshot of the education reform environment in Hong Kong. This is followed by a brief description of the methodology employed. Next, the types of dilemmas experienced by a group of Hong Kong principals are discussed in terms of the basis of the dilemmas, how the principals managed the dilemmas, and the consequences of this management. Another section is devoted to explanation of why some principals did not conceive their lives in terms of dilemmas. Our analysis and discussion suggest that although the dilemmas faced by principals may be generic across cultures, the way in which they are formed and managed appear related to culture. Similarly, reasons for why some principals did not identify dilemma situations in their work appear grounded in cultural explanation.

The Importance of Studying Principals' Dilemmas

Studies focusing on the concept of principalship dilemmas have emerged as a valuable sub-set of the Western leadership and restructuring literature (e.g., Cuban, 1992; Dimmock, 1996; Grace, 1994). Such research is part of a broader quest for more accurate understandings of school leadership within the realities of school life. This includes understandings of the social and political aspects that provide a framework within which principals work and construct their leadership.

Studying the realities of principals' lives necessitates recognition of the place and influence of values and values conflicts (Busher & Saran, 1994; Cuban, 1994). Values provide principals with guidelines for selecting certain courses of actions from among alternatives. Yet the multiple values extant in the school community often conflict with leaders' values (Campbell-Evans, 1993). As a result of values conflicts, school leaders increasingly face situations where there is no solution that can readily satisfy all parties (Begley, 1996). Such values conflict situations can be classified as dilemmas.

Dilemmas are defined as conflictual situations that demand irreconcilable choices because of the existence of competing, deeply rooted values. While dilemmas are grounded in values, they often emerge from structures, resources, and relationships, and the interactions between these. Dilemma situations contain elements of contradiction, conflict, paradox, and inconsistency in the ways they are perceived, and in how they may be solved, since the selection of a course of action, or inaction, to deal with one aspect automatically leaves other aspects unsatisfied or more problematic.

Policy initiatives aimed at restructuring education have occurred across the world. Reforms have been designed to influence all areas of education—at first, school organization, structure and decision making, participation, and involvement in schools and associated power relationships, then latterly, quality of teaching and learning and equity issues. Dimmock (1996) proposed identification and analysis of dilemmas as a tool for increasing awareness of school leaders' conceptions of their professional lives within this context of continual restructuring. Cuban (1994) supported these sentiments and held that unless we can gain a practical understanding of values conflicts "deeply rooted" in the work of principals, as well as the ways in which they have learned to manage these, schools are unlikely to engage in sustainable reform.

While the concept of dilemmas is not new and has targeted extensively the moral and ethical aspects of educators' work, more is needed that specifically targets principals' work lives. Cuban (1992, 1994) suggested that we need to learn firsthand the practical dilemmas faced by principals, how they cope with these, and the variation in outcomes brought about by certain actions or inactions. Glatter (1994) supported Cuban's call for a practical grounding of dilemmas, thus: "Writers on moral aspects rarely examine real situations of conflict and tension in which there are genuine dilemmas to confront, for example, decisions about the allocation of scarce resources or about the exclusion of disruptive pupils from school" (p. 2). Fortunately, this situation is beginning to be addressed by researchers such as, for example, Dimmock (1996) in Australia, Grace (1994) in Great Britain, and Murphy (1994) in the United States.

Although many dilemmas are perennial (Glatter, 1994), they are, by nature, individual contestations between important values. Holmes (1965) suggested that the origin of educational problems lies in asynchronous changes taking place in society and education. Dimmock (1996) applied this idea to principalship dilemmas related to restructuring in Australia stating, " a dilemma in restructuring may be conceptualized in terms of asynchronous change *within* and *between* ... norms and values, institutional practices and structures, and resources" (p. 144, emphasis in original).

The Influence of Culture on Educational Administration

Until recently, research into the principalship has largely ignored the influence of national culture and context. Although a small body of literature on cross-cultural aspects of educational leadership (Hallinger & Leithwood, 1996), school effectiveness (Cheng & Wong, 1996), principalship preparation (Walker, Bridges, & Chan, 1996), and comparative Educational Administration (Dimmock & Walker, 1998a; 1998b) has begun to emerge, such studies are still in the early stages. The relative absence of cross-cultural analyses of educational leadership and management is not paralleled to the same extent in the fields of comparative pedagogy, teaching and learning, or in national and international studies that have adopted a macro-sociological-policy orientation. Important cultural differences, for example, have been noted recently between Western and Asian learners in regard to effective teaching and learning (Watkins & Biggs, 1996).

The scarcity of cross-cultural studies in educational administration also stands in stark contrast to work in business management and psychology (for example, see Bond, 1996; Hofstede, 1991). Researchers in these areas have long recognized the influence of culture on management and leadership practices and acknowledged the naivety of applying Western theories unthinkingly in foreign settings (Hofstede, 1991).

A number of consequences follow from the absence of research on principals' dilemmas in different cultural contexts. First, unless research is conducted to identify the dilemmas of principals in non-Western countries, there is a likelihood that the all-too-prevalent assumptions that Western-generated research findings are applicable to all settings will be made. Second, if one considers the very different cultural and social contexts of communities, such as in Asian societies, the prospect of universally shared values becomes untenable, implying that the shape of leaders' lives and the meanings attached to leadership will expectedly vary. Thus, the form of values conflict that underpins dilemmas in various contexts cannot be purposefully investigated if research exclusively reflects an ethnocentric bias toward Western traditions and Judeao-Christian thinking and logic (Begley & Johansson, 1997).

Accordingly, this study addresses the lack of attention given in the literature to educational administration in non-Western contexts through specifically targeting school leaders' perceptions of their dilemmas in an East Asian setting, namely Hong Kong. I acknowledge that dilemmas are but one part of principals' lives and that their study can give at best a partial understanding of principals in differing contexts. However, I believe that deeper exploration of dilemmas in principals' work lives is a worthwhile starting point for increasing cross-cultural understanding of school leadership.

The Hong Kong Policy Reform Context

A brief synopsis of the Hong Kong education system and selected policy initiatives dominant at the time that the research was conducted is sufficient to set the scene. A more comprehensive and up-to-date description can be found in Cheng (2000). There are approximately 884 elementary schools in total. Of these, 800 are government and government-aided, and 84 are private. There are 455 secondary schools of which 38 are government schools, 333 are aided, and 84 are private. Secondary schools range from highly academic schools to pre-vocational schools. At the time when this research was conducted, secondary school students were classified according to academic ability, and schools are "banded" in line with this—Band 1 being for the top academic students and Band 5 for the least academic. Elementary school students gain entrance to secondary schools based on their academic ability as measured in public, normed examinations. The majority of elementary schools were organized on a morning and afternoon shift basis, where two schools share the same building and meet at different times of the day. Secondary schools were predominantly whole-day schools.

By far the largest proportion of schools in Hong Kong are government "aided"—that is, they are regarded as being in the public sector but are run by "sponsoring bodies," such as church groups, who established the schools and employ the teachers. They are in effect, "public schools with private deliverers" (Cheng, 1994, p. 805). Aided schools operate under letters of agreement between the Education Department (ED) and the sponsoring body, and under a code of aid setting out the procedures to be followed in return for public funds. Each aided school is managed by its own School Management Committee (SMC), which is responsible for hiring principals and teachers and is responsible to the Director of Education for the proper functioning of the school. One manager is registered as the supervisor, whose main role is as the point of contact between the SMC and the ED. It has traditionally been the case that the administrative and authority structure in schools is hierarchical, with principals enjoying considerable power. In addition, the principal–supervisor relationship is often significant in the management direction of the school (Walker & Dimmock, 1998).

Recent policy reforms are exemplified by reference to the curriculum and school governance and management. Two of the most noteworthy policy initiatives in curriculum concern language and the introduction of a target-oriented curriculum (TOC) in primary schools after 1995 (Education Department, 1994).

In regard to language policy, in an effort to eliminate what policy makers considered to be an undesirable practice of language-mixing for different components of the curriculum, each secondary school was encouraged to adopt a firm policy on its medium of instruction. More information is expected on each child's ability in English and Chinese to enable a decision on the most appropriate language medium for each child. Special language learning courses are being developed to help students bridge from Chinese-medium primary schooling to English-medium secondary schooling. Courses are also being developed to help school-leavers prepare for using English in the workplace. Attempts to promote either English or Cantonese to prominence in all schools have recently failed, and as a result an edict put out in 1997 mandates a move to Chinese as a medium of instruction in about 75 percent of secondary schools.

The second curriculum innovation, the TOC framework of learning targets and related support materials, is being developed for the three core subjects of Chinese, English, and mathematics (for a fuller description see Morris & Lo, this volume). Despite some teething problems, it was decided that the TOC should be introduced to Primary 1 classes in 76 primary schools in 1995. TOC is an attempt to shift radically the way in which curricula are planned, delivered, and experienced. At the heart of the policy are notions of improved teaching and learning practices based around more learner-centered approaches; the division of the curriculum into progressive learning targets and objectives for four-key stages of learning; and the development of content, teaching methods, and assessment strategies geared to the learning targets. TOC derives from outcomes-based education reform in Western countries.

The third example of reform concerns school governance and management under the guise of the School Management Initiative (SMI) introduced in 1991 (Education and Manpower Branch and Education Department, 1991), and the closely related "Quality School Education" (ECR7 report) (Education Commission, 1997). Like TOC, SMI reflects similar educational trends in the West. The initiative aims to define more clearly the roles of those responsible for administering schools, particularly sponsors, managers, and principals; to provide for greater participation by teachers, parents, and former students in school decision making and management; to encourage more systematic planning and evaluation of school activities; and finally, to give schools more flexibility in the use of their resources. Membership of the scheme is voluntary—the government preferring to increase membership by persuasion rather than legislative coercion. However, in 1997 the government announced its expectation that all schools will adopt a more devolved system of school-based management by the year 2000.

Method

Data were collected from 15 Hong Kong principals of aided schools. The principals interviewed ranged in their experience of principalship from 3 to 17 years and had worked in their present schools for varying periods of from 1 to 17 years. The 15 principals included 12 males and 3 females. Four were principals of secondary schools, and 11 were principals of elementary schools. The fifteen principals were selected for interview using first, *criterion* and then *snowball* or *chain* sampling over a period of approximately six months (Miles & Huberman, 1994, p. 28). At the first stage, four principals who were active in the educational community and willing to discuss the difficulties they faced in their school were interviewed. The principals were also highly proficient in spoken English. At the conclusion of the interview, principals were asked to recommend principal colleagues who they believed had the potential to enrich the research. The aim of the study was not to generalize to broader populations but rather to identify relationships between constructs in order to better understand the case situations (Miles & Huberman, 1994).

Interviews were conducted in three phases: open-ended, semi-structured, and structured. In the first phase principals talked generally about their lives in schools and the major difficulties they faced. Questions used in this stage were purposefully open, for example: "Tell me about some difficulties you presently face in your school?" In the second phase we used more structured questions, based on the earlier discussion, to uncover more details of the dilemmas and, indeed, whether the principals saw their work lives as beset by dilemmas. For example, when a principal expressed difficulty in introducing a new instructional approach in a school with experienced and competent teachers, we asked questions, such as: "How did this situation make you feel"; "What choices did you believe you had in this situation?"; or "Did the situation cause you to feel trapped?" During this discussion, we introduced directly the concept of dilemmas using principals' own stories, and asked which, if any, of the situations they faced felt like dilemmas. An interesting finding was that some of the principals did not perceive their work lives in terms of dilemmas. When this occurred, the principals were invited to elaborate on their position. For the majority of principals who did see their work in terms of dilemmas, we moved forward to the third phase of the interview.

The third phase explored in a more structured fashion the nature of the principals' dilemmas. Using the principals' own situations as contexts, we engaged them in conversation about where they believed the dilemmas had stemmed, how the dilemmas were managed and with what consequences (see Walker & Dimmock, 2000). Questions at this stage were contextualized by the principals' own stories and included: "Why do you think the situation arose?'; "What actions did you take in relation to the situation?"; "What happened as a result of your actions?"; "Were you satisfied with the outcome of your action?"; "Why or why not?" Data were processed using methods of inductive analysis (Bogdan & Biklen, 1992). This process of interview followed by analysis meant that formal analysis was almost complete by the end of data collection and allowed interpretations to emerge and to be crosschecked on an on-going basis.

Hong Kong Principals' Dilemmas

The following section provides a description of a number of major themes that were formed from the data. Dilemmas were first fractured and then discussed on the basis of their sources, how principals managed them and the consequences or outcomes of this dilemma management. Perceptions of the Hong Kong principals who did not see their work lives in terms of dilemmas were also discussed.

Dilemma Themes

Five themes were identified that were individually, or in various combinations, present in the dilemmas experienced by the group of Hong Kong principals. The five themes—cultural values, teaching and learning beliefs, structures, personal conundrums, and internal/external to the school—are each defined below with an example.

Cultural values. Underpinning many dilemmas were cultural expectations related mainly to hierarchy, harmony, seniority, and relationships. Example: A principal was pressured by a supervisor to promote a teacher who was related to the supervisor but whom the principal and staff believed was unsuitable for a higher post. To reject the supervisor's advice would be to risk the good relationships with the supervisor and School Management Committee, but to accept the recommendation would damage the harmony which existed between principal and staff.

Teaching and learning beliefs. Many dilemmas are anchored in beliefs about the form teaching and learning should take. Example: A principal wanted to introduce more active, student-centered approaches to teaching in the school, even though exam results were already high, but staff preferred more traditional teacher-centered approaches. To impose her beliefs might place the present high achievement at risk and might alienate staff, but not to try would be to deny her strong personal beliefs about teaching, learning, and the purpose of schools.

Structures. Underpinning many dilemmas are the structural arrangements of the school, school governing body, or Department of Education. It is still relatively commonplace in Hong Kong to find that two separate elementary schools—a morning and an afternoon—share the same buildings. Example: A morning session (AM) principal wanted to impose his will on how an afternoon (PM) principal implemented a new policy, even though the PM principal had control over his own school. If the PM principal were to move ahead with his and his staff's ideas then the harmony between the two principals would be upset; but not to take action would be to deny his own and his staff's ideals.

Personal conundrums. Many dilemmas are anchored in personal choices involving career, study, or survival. Example: A principal was offered a position at a new school during times of crisis at his present school. The move would spare him the present turmoil, but would leave him feeling defeated and removed from a school that he had spent many years developing.

Internal/External. Underpinning many dilemmas is the tension between the principals' role inside and outside the school, especially concerning its image. Example: A principal had to decide whether to concentrate more on the internal development of her school or to remain actively involved in the broader education community. She estimated the school's development to be somewhat lagging, but saw it as important, for the sake of the school, to maintain a high public profile.

The dilemmas faced by Hong Kong principals are similar to those recounted in other settings (for example see Dimmock, 1996; Grace, 1994). Confining the analysis to this surface level, however, does little to expand knowledge of the dilemmas faced specifically in the Hong Kong context. While placing the dilemmas within the themes was useful for purposes of initial analysis, it failed to capture the true complexity of the dilemmas, and particularly the influence of cultural values. Leaving analysis at the level of simple categorization is also largely unhelpful because, without exception, the dilemmas grew from a number of interactive sources, making placement in a single category unrealistic. The origins, management, and consequences of dilemmas are multifaceted and difficult to disentangle. Nevertheless, a number of commonalties may be recognized and these are now discussed.

The Basis of Dilemmas

The dilemmas uncovered were without exception grounded in a complex web of factors. These included the governance structure of the school, beliefs about teaching and learning, and external demands on the principals. Values conflicts, either between the principal and others, or within the principal's own set of values, were preeminent in all dilemmas. Perhaps more noteworthy, all dilemmas appeared, in varying degrees, to be based in values conflicts linked to a number of Chinese values commonly identified in the literature (see Bond, 1996). The most conspicuous of these were dilemmas underpinned by the values of harmony and respect for hierarchy.

The need for harmony was woven into most dilemma situations in Hong Kong, reflecting a primary desire across Chinese societies for harmonious relationships (Bond, 1991). As one principal commented: "I think harmony is culture. Harmony is central to Chinese culture, I honestly believe that in our Chinese society, harmony comes first." The principal's belief is supported by Cheng and Wong's proposition that Chinese societies consider group harmony as more important than individualism, and that the maintenance of harmony is ultimately in the best interests of the individual. They suggest that, "This is quite different from the Western notion of the individual–group relationship where the group cannot thrive unless and only after individuals in it thrive" (Cheng & Wong, 1996, p. 38).

Many of the dilemmas stemming from a desire, or need, for harmonious relationships left the principals torn between maintaining smooth relations with either their superiors or their teachers. For example, in one recounted dilemma, a principal was asked by his supervisor to promote a teacher whom both he and his staff believed was an inappropriate choice. In attempting to think through the situation, he was torn between his desire for harmony with his superiors and with his staff, a perceived no-win situation. He was also concerned that the teacher was not upholding satisfactory standards of performance in the school. He expressed his feelings of frustration:

> The need for harmony makes me feel lonely as a principal. I was annoyed that I was pushed to promote one teacher ... this made me very upset. I tried to put forward my point that we want equity, we want performance. I put these to my supervisor—to gain harmony.

As reflected in the dilemma described above, many of the dilemmas discussed by the principals were rooted in their respect for hierarchy and seniority. This again appears in line with Cheng's (1995) assertion that groups and organizations in Chinese societies tend to be more often ordered around hierarchical sets of relationships and their accompanying behavioral rules than their Western counterparts. The values of harmony and hierarchy in Chinese societies relate to the maintenance of relationships and power structures. In the case of the Hong Kong principals' dilemmas we investigated, relationships appeared paramount and played a major role in how principals conceived the existence, shape, source, and management of the dilemmas. This supports Redding's (1977) assertion that organizational behavior in East Asian organizations is relationship-centered, while in Western organizations, behavior tends to be ego-centered.

Despite the prominence of cultural values in underpinning dilemmas, they were not the only variables present. In fact, all situations discussed with the principals suggested a tangled amalgam of sources that interacted with each other to form the dilemmas. These included conditions such as structural arrangements, personal considerations, educational beliefs, and external systemic pressures. Although these separate sources were difficult to distinguish, in almost all cases the cultural values appeared to be the conduit through which other conditions became confused, leading to the formation of dilemmas in the principals' minds.

An example of the above was presented by one principal. The Afternoon Session (PM) elementary principal, with the support of the teachers, wanted to introduce a more active approach to teaching in line with the thrust of the TOC. The Morning Session (AM) principal, however, did not agree with the approach and moved to discourage the innovation. In Hong Kong elementary schools, AM principals are often regarded, unofficially, as the senior principal. The PM principal was then torn between her commitment to active teaching, her relationships with her teachers, the expectation that she respect the seniority of her principal colleague (the structural arrangement of the school), and the need for harmony with all parties. To the PM principal this was perceived as a very confusing dilemma, one in which she could not win whichever way she chose.

A further element of the place of culture in principalship dilemmas was that some situations were confused by elements of what may be termed "culture clash." That is, a number of dilemmas were caused or intensified by some principals attempting to import Western beliefs and values about education into a traditional Chinese cultural setting. When these different values clashed, new dilemmas resulted or existing ones worsened. We aim to explore the phenomenon of culture clash in the formation and heightening of dilemmas in subsequent studies.

The Management of Dilemmas

The ways in which principals managed their dilemmas were multifaceted, but most were tracked back to the cultural values that formed the basis of the dilemma. Hong Kong principals' management of dilemmas assumed a number of different forms, frequently deriving from cultural characteristics and usually resulting in the status quo being maintained. Dilemma management strategies used by the principals included the following: acquiescing with superiors' wishes, creative insubordination, resorting to logic, emotive argument, delaying decisions, transferring the "problem" to another site, attempting compromise, withdrawing from direct involvement (or "hoping it will sort itself out"), adopting a fatalistic attitude of inaction, or appealing to school mission and tradition.

Managing dilemmas is often a very messy affair and involves unwinnable choices based on competing values (Dimmock, 1996). We have already shown that the principals' dilemmas were complex in terms of their form and basis and were often rooted in cultural values. Dilemma management, likewise, appeared firmly associated with the predominant cultural values of harmony, hierarchy, seniority, and age, rather than with professional considerations, such as teaching and learning beliefs. For example, one principal faced the dilemma of whether to lay-off an older teacher who had been performing poorly for a number of years. The principal and staff knew the teacher was seriously disadvantaging students, but would not dismiss the teacher because of respect for her age and limited employment prospects. The principal's strategy in managing the dilemma was to arrange for the teacher to be transferred to another school, even though he was aware other students could be disadvantaged. The principal was troubled over how he had managed the dilemma but felt that he had to help the teacher "keep face."

Maintaining harmony appeared an important consideration in how principals managed dilemmas. The problem was how to strike a balance of harmony between and with teachers in the school, with their superiors and the system, and within themselves. While maintaining harmonious relationships between so many constituents was at the center of most management strategies, it demanded a delicate balancing act by principals, which was rarely satisfactorily achieved. Dilemma management strategies forced choices about who were the most important constituents with whom harmony needed to be maintained. In addressing this aspect, most principals adhered to the formal system of seniority in their environments.

The pervasiveness of the influence of cultural values, such as hierarchy and harmony, in how principals perceived and managed dilemmas raises a number of questions related to understanding leadership in East Asia and more specifically, Hong Kong. It should be noted that the following questions themselves are unavoidably framed by certain cultural lenses.

1. Is the way Hong Kong principals manage dilemma situations detrimental to improving teaching and learning in the school? If the pursuit of harmonious relationships and respect for hierarchy dominate how principals manage dilemmas, how does this affect the core functions of school and the improvement of student learning?

2. Does the way principals manage dilemmas inhibit teacher commitment to school improvement? If principals manage dilemmas mainly through allegiance to hierarchy and seniority, can they secure the commitment of teachers toward school improvement and promote teacher empowerment and involvement?

3. Can principals develop other dilemma management strategies given the practical influence and forceful cognitive influence of values, such as harmony and seniority?

4. Does allegiance to powerful cultural factors influence principals' feelings about their jobs and work lives? Do principals feel a sense of helplessness in their schools?

5. Do principals expect the same adherence to cultural norms they show to superiors and staff alike, to be displayed by teachers in their schools?

6. Will principals' dilemmas and management strategies change with the introduction of restructuring policies which are designed to redefine their roles and relationships within schools?

The Consequences of Managing Dilemmas

Principals' dilemma management strategies resulted in a number of consequences, none of which appeared entirely satisfactory to them, or proved a resolution of the dilemma. In fact, managing a dilemma in one way often led to further dilemmas or accentuated the complexity of the existing dilemmas. The multidimensionality and growth of dilemmas support recent suggestions that many principals' lives are unpredictable and constantly beset by tension (Patterson, 1992). We found that the consequences of managing dilemmas, as described above, could be organized into four groups.

The first group of consequences showed that in a number of cases the way principals managed one dilemma often presented them with a new dilemma. The second group revealed that managing a dilemma in a certain way resulted in a return to the existing dilemma situation. The third group involved an amplification of the complexity of the existing dilemma. For example, in one dilemma situation, a principal committed to improving learning in the school was torn between keeping a teacher who was an outstanding practitioner, but who was also an agent for conflictual working relationships in the school. The principal managed the situation by avoiding direct involvement as a way of supporting his senior staff and eventually, the teacher resigned. Although this solved the relationship issue, the principal lost a good teacher who could not easily be replaced, thereby weakening the quality of teaching in the school. The fourth group showed that in certain cases, the way the principal managed the dilemma resulted in an alleviation of the dilemma, at least for the short term.

In summary, management strategies often proliferated dilemmas and although some dilemmas were lessened, they were rarely resolved, either in organizational or personal terms. For many, principals dilemmas were never completely resolved, and they were left with a feeling of frustration. The fact that the principals' attention was unendingly shifted by additional developments in dilemma situations suggests that further examination of the endurance, prolongation, and consequence of dilemmas would be worthwhile.

Whereas most of the principals involved in the study saw at least part of their lives in terms of dilemmas, some principals did not. Whether this difference in perception was an unconscious management strategy is unclear, but it might indicate that dilemmas are indeed internal constructs and are dependent on how principals view situations. An explanation of this phenomenon in the following section is worthwhile.

Principals with No Perceived Dilemmas

Despite considerable probing during the interview and our providing a number of concrete examples, a small number of principals could not conceptualize their work in terms of dilemmas. Their reasons can be grouped into three categories, each of which is not exclusive, listed below.

Expertise and respect. One principal believed that he did not experience dilemmas because his staff were largely untrained and therefore he thought he was the best person to make the decisions. He asserted:

> most of out teachers are untrained so they don't have much conflict within themselves to challenge me so they will follow what I ask them to do, (and) I have almost finished a degree, so teachers do not argue with me because I know more than them—so, dilemmas do not arise.

This principal seemed to assume that dilemmas only came from personal conflicts, which he did not face because of his position in the hierarchy. A number of other principals also did not experience dilemmas because their staff respected them and, in one case, the staff knew that the principal "always tried hard to solve any problems."

Harmony. A few principals did not see their jobs as dilemma-ridden because they believed they had good relationships with their staff and their supervisors. In the case of one PM principal, she thought she had the discretion to run her school as she saw fit. Another principal claimed, "We don't have dilemmas because we are all partners and learn together." She went on to say: "I share all the time and encourage others to share." Another principal supported this by stating that he consciously built open relationships, and since harmony had been achieved, "there are no longer any causes for dilemmas." Trust and respect between the principal and staff were seen as a sine qua non for a dilemma-free environment. Some principals believed they did not face dilemmas because they purposely encouraged staff to distinguish between personal and professional matters.

Non-negotiability. A further reason why a few principals did not experience dilemmas was a belief that schools really had no choice about what they could or could not do. On the few matters where the Education Department (ED) did leave the school some discretion, the principal/school simply made a decision not to proceed. As one principal explained:

> We have to do it, we have no choice. So we need not challenge the ED because it is the same for all schools, not just our school. Even if we do not agree, it does not pose a dilemma, since we must do it. Where we have a choice, we discuss it, and invariably decide not to do it, we just tell the ED "no"—so this is not a dilemma, we just don't do it.

This scenario is representative of the hierarchical beliefs of the principal. As indicated earlier in this paper, policy initiatives in the 1990s are designed to decentralize and devolve significant decision-making responsibilities to schools. One principal failed to see problems as dilemmas because, he believed, all schools needed to balance the things they do. He saw no contradiction, for example, between providing a strong academic education and a more "rounded" educational approach, believing that the one built on the other. This was at odds with other principals who saw balancing the two as a real dilemma. This perhaps reinforces the point that what is a dilemma for one principal is not necessarily for another.

Summary

The more complex dilemmas faced by Hong Kong principals were multifaceted in terms of both their basis and subsequent evolution. In most cases, the basis of the dilemmas comprised an almost indistinguishable combination of structural, professional, cultural, and relational elements. Particularly prominent in the context of Hong Kong were cultural values, which mainly related to harmonious relationships and hierarchy. This, in turn, interacted with other sources to complicate dilemmas, to create new dilemmas, and to drive management strategies. In no case could a dilemma situation be attributed to a single source.

The form and shape of the dilemmas appeared to change with management strategies, with one situation feeding another, thereby increasing overall complexity and making the management of the dilemma more difficult. In some cases, the consequences of managing dilemmas led directly back to the original dilemma. Principals' attempts to manage even the most multi-faceted of dilemmas were invariably grounded in one of the sources in partic-ular, namely, societal cultural values. For example, the tendency of principals to manage dilemmas through deferral to seniority or position are reflective of societal cultural values discussed in studies of Chinese culture (for example, see Bond, 1996). As Cheng (1998, p. 15) noted, "Chinese societies are orga-nized into a configuration of hierarchy [whereas] Western society [is a] config-uration of association." Hence, while the bases of the dilemmas were invariably multifaceted, principals adopted management strategies that related to dominant cultural values, especially the pressing need to maintain harmony in relationships with others in the school community (Bond, 1996; Hofstede, 1991). Some principals, however, did not see their lives as beset by dilemmas and attributed this to respect, expertise, established harmony, and non-negotiable policy impositions.

Conclusion

This chapter set out to identify and examine the dilemmas faced by a group of principals in Hong Kong. Research to date on principals' dilemmas, and indeed in most areas of educational administration, has been largely confined to Western settings. An investigation of the dilemmas faced by Hong Kong principals and how they perceive, manage, and "live with" them contributes to the construction of a more robust knowledge base in educational admin-istration. Whereas the dilemmas faced by the principals in this study appear, on the surface, similar to those faced by principals in Western contexts, the way the principals conceptualized their dilemmas in terms of origin, management, and consequences found some explanation in the Chinese cultural context. Both the dilemmas themselves and the way principals managed them seemed widely influenced by entrenched values identified as prevalent in Chinese societies (Bond, 1996). In this study, these values included harmony, hierarchy, and seniority. Whereas such values are certainly common in other cultures and societies, their influence and extent have been found to be more pronounced in contexts such as Hong Kong. For example, although all organizations are typified by unequal distributions of power, in many Chinese cultures, these inequities are seen, "as natural and proper, and there is a tendency to accept and not challenge authority" (Westwood, 1992, p. 126).

We recognize that this study makes only a limited contribution to increasing recognition and understanding of the lives of principals in non-Western contexts. More importantly, we hope it becomes part of a growing trend to explore educational administration and leadership from a much broader, societal, culturally-guided perspective in the future.

References

Begley, P. (1996). Cognitive perspectives on the nature and function of values in educational administration. In K. Leithwood, J. Chapman, D. Conson, P. Hallinger, & A. Hart, (Eds.), *International handbook of educational leadership and administration* (pp. 551–588). Netherlands: Kluwer Press.

Begley, P., & Johansson, O. (1997, March). *Values and school administration: Preferences, ethics and conflicts.* Paper presented at the Annual meeting of the American Educational Research Association, Chicago, IL.

Bogdan, R. C., & Biklen, S. K. (1992). *Qualitative research for education: An introduction to theory and methods* (2nd ed.). Needham Heights, MA: Allyn and Bacon.

Bolman, L., & Deal, T. (1991). *Reframing organizations.* San Francisco: Jossey-Bass.

Bond, M. (1991). *Beyond the Chinese face: Insights from psychology.* Oxford, England: Oxford University Press.

Bond, M. (ed.). (1996). *The handbook of Chinese psychology.* New York: Oxford University Press.

Busher, H., & Saran, R. (1994). Towards a model of school leadership. *Educational Management and Administration, 22*(1), 5–13.

Campbell-Evans, G. (1993). A values perspective on school-based management. In C. Dimmock (Ed.), *School-based management and school effectiveness* (pp. 92–113). London: Routledge.

Cheng, K. M. (1994). Issues in decentralizing education: what reform in China tells. *International Journal of Educational Research, 7,* 799–815.

Cheng, K. M. (1995). The neglected dimension: Cultural comparison in educational administration. In K. C. Wong & K. M. Cheng (Eds.), *Educational leadership and change: An international perspective* (pp. 87–104). Hong Kong: Hong Kong University Press.

Cheng, K. M. (1998). Can education values be borrowed: Looking into cultural differences. *Peabody Journal of Education, 73*(2), 11–30.

Cheng, K. M., & Wong, K. C. (1996). School effectiveness in East Asia: Concepts, origins and implications. *Journal of Educational Administration, 34*(5), 32–49.

Cheng, Y. C. (2000). Educational change and development in Hong Kong: Effectiveness, quality and relevance. In Y. C. Cheng & T. Townsend (Eds.), *Educational change and development in the Asia-Pacific region: Challenges for the future* (pp. 17–56). Lisse, Netherlands: Swets & Zeitinger.

Cuban, L. (1992 January). Managing dilemmas while building professional communities. *Educational Research,* 4–11.

Cuban, L. (1994). *Reforming the practice of educational administration through managing dilemmas.* Unpublished manuscript, Stanford University, California.

Dimmock, C. (1996). Dilemmas for school leaders and administrators in restructuring. In K. Leithwood, J. Chapman, D. Corson, P. Hallinger, & A. Hart (Eds.), *International handbook of educational leadership and administration* (pp. 135–170). Netherlands: Kluwer Press.

Dimmock, C., & Walker, A. (1998a). Towards comparative educational administration: the case for a cross-cultural, school based approach." *Journal of Educational Administration, 36* (4), 379–401.

Dimmock, C., & Walker, A. (1998b). Comparative educational administration: Developing a cross-cultural conceptual framework." *Educational Administration Quarterly, 34*(4), 558–595.

Education and Manpower Branch and Education Department. (1991). *The school management initiative: Setting the framework for quality in Hong Kong schools.* Hong Kong: Government Printer.

Education Commission Report No. 7. (ECR7). (1997). *Quality school education.* Hong Kong: Education Commission.

Education Department. (1994). *Report of the advisory committee on implementation of Target Oriented Curriculum.* Hong Kong: Government Printer.

Glatter, R. (1994, May). *Managing dilemmas in education: The tightrope walk of strategic choice in more autonomous institutions.* Paper presented at the 8th International Intervisitation Program in Educational Administration, Toronto, Canada, and Buffalo.

Grace, G. (1994). *School leadership, beyond educational management.* London: Falmer Press.

Hallinger, P., & Leithwood, K. (1996). Culture and educational administration: A case of finding out what you don't know you know. *Journal of Educational Administration, 34*(5), 98–116.

Hofstede, G. H. (1991). *Cultures and organizations: Software of the mind.* London: McGraw Hill.

Holmes, B. (1965). *Problems in education: A comparative approach.* London: Routledge and Kegan Paul.

Miles, M., & Huberman, A. (1994). *Qualitative data analysis* (2nd ed.). Thousand Oaks: CA: Sage.

Murphy, J. (1994). Transformational change and the evolving role of the principal: Early empirical evidence. In J. Murphy & K. Seashore Louis (Eds.), *Reshaping the principalship* (pp. 20–55). Thousand Oaks, CA: Sage.

Patterson, J. (1992). *Leadership for tomorrow's schools.* Alexandria, VA; Association of Supervision and Curriculom Development (ASCD).

Redding, G. (1977). Some perceptions of psychological needs among managers in Southeast Asia. In Y. Poortinga (Ed.), *Basic problems in cross-cultural psychology* (pp. 338–343). Amsterdam: Swets and Zeitlinger.

Walker, A., Bridges, E., & Chan, B. (1996). Wisdom gained, wisdom given: Instituting PBL in a Chinese culture. *Journal of Educational Administration, 34*(5), 12–31.

Walker, A., & Dimmock, C. (1998). Hong Kong's return to Mainland China: Education policy in times of uncertainty. *Journal of Education Policy, 13*(1), 3–25.

Walker, A., & Dimmock, C. (2000). Leadership dilemmas of Hong Kong principals: Sources, perception and outcomes. *Australian Journal of Education, 44*(1), 5–25.

Watkins, D., & Biggs, J. (Eds.). (1996). *The Chinese learner: Cultural, psychological, and contextual influences.* Melbourne: Australia Council for Educational Research.

Westwood, R. (1992). *Organizational behaviour: Southeast Asian perspectives.* Hong Kong: Longman.

13.

Conclusion

*Embedding Societal Culture in the Study
of Educational Leadership*

CLIVE DIMMOCK AND ALLAN WALKER

In a globalizing and internationalizing world, it is not only business and industry that are changing. Education, too, is caught up in a new world order. Growing numbers of school and university students are studying overseas. Universities are seeking international collaboration. International education agencies and consultants abound. Above all, the global transmission of policies and practices increasingly ignores national and cultural boundaries. The business of education is fast becoming just that—a business—operating on a globalized and internationalized scale. Multinational universities and schools are likely to be a significant development—in one form or another—in the twenty-first century.

While the terms "globalization" and "internationalization" are closely related (indeed, they could be seen as synonymous), some may recognize subtle distinctions between them. Globalization generally refers to the spread of ideas, policies, and practices across national boundaries, while internationalization relates to the adoption of outward-looking perspectives in stark contrast to ethnocentrism.

A scrutiny of the most recent journals in educational administration, management and leadership reveals an alarming ethnocentricity (Dimmock & Walker, 1998a, 1988b). Especially is this the case in the United Kingdom and United States, where researchers seem preoccupied with homespun issues. In the former, the research agenda seems largely dictated by government policy, with academics invariably in reactive mode. In the latter, the country's nature, size, complexity, and diversity explains a certain parochialism. In both countries, the pace of educational innovation in the last decade has been nothing short of breathtaking, thereby contributing to their ethnocentrism.

Meanwhile, the spread of policies and practices across national boundaries and cultures has continued with gathering pace. Efforts to restructure schools by emphasizing school-based management, devolution, and increased account-ability to the central bureaucracy have become the cornerstones of reform in many countries. Likewise, curriculum trends in different continents have targeted outcomes-based education and social-constructivist approaches to teaching and learning. These similarities are neither fortuitous nor coinci-dental. They are the result of many complex forces shaping the globalized world: they include the electronic and print media, jet transport, international conferences, international agencies, multinational corporations, and overseas education.

When measured against these contextual developments, the study of educa-tional leadership and management has generally failed to keep pace theoret-ically, conceptually, and empirically with practice. Even studies completed by agencies such as OECD and UNESCO generally fail to provide in-depth international comparisons, preferring instead separate country studies as their more usual format.

The argument is simply that as a field of study, educational management and leadership needs to reflect the globalizing and internationalizing of policy and practice. To do that, we need a comparative branch to the field that is rigorous and reflects a cross-cultural dimension. The reasons and benefits are manifold. First, the transfer of policy across boundaries that continues to ignore societal culture is likely to heap up many future problems. Second, while scholars and practitioners remain largely ignorant about societal, economic, political, demographic, and cultural differences between systems, they are likely to draw fallacious conclusions regarding the appropriateness of importing policy and practice. Third, by understanding education systems of other countries in context, we may come to a better understanding of our own.

The chapters in this book help navigate the way forward. They illustrate the theoretical, conceptual and empirical possibilities. From an array of issues discussed by the authors, we select the following five as being of special interest. They are presented as propositions for the field to consider embedding in future approaches.

Proposition 1

In order to make valid and informed judgements about the effectiveness and perfor-mance of other education systems and about the transfer of ideas, policies, and practices across national and cultural boundaries, there is need to develop a system-atic, robust comparative branch of educational leadership and management.

A relatively new phenomenon emerged in the 1990s, namely, the recip-rocal interest of Anglo-American and Confucian societies of East and Southeast Asia in each others' school systems. Asian educators and politicians, aware of the need for their economies to compete in the global marketplace, realized that their school curricula needed to emulate the West in its emphasis on creativity, technology, and problem solving. For their part, Western nations, intrigued by the apparently superior performance of students from Confucian-heritage societies on international tests, wondered whether they could learn from the East. Moreover, education policy as well as practice in both the curriculum and administration fields increasingly covers the globe as policy makers and practitioners improve their communication and global knowledge. Whether in Beijing, Bradford, or Baltimore, the pattern of responsibility and power for running schools is being reconfigured, often in similar directions. In addition, these developments have brought a new "internationalism"—a genuine willingness on the part of some scholars, policy makers, and practitioners to learn from the experiences of others, if for no other reason than they may come to understand their own situation better.

We should perhaps be optimistic about the above scenario. Such euphoria, however, would be misplaced. When comparisons between systems are made on superficial grounds with minimal understanding of the deep historical and cultural roots underpinning them, they are misleading and often dangerous. Both the formulation of policies and practices and their outcomes and consequences can only truly be understood when viewed in relation to culture and context. As Dimmock argues in Chapter 2, tension between forces of globalization and societal culture makes the recognition of, and respect for, cross-cultural differences (as well as similarities) more, not less, important. Consequently, the inclusion of societal culture in studies of the curriculum, teaching and learning, leadership, and school-based management is seen as an imperative for the future development of the field.

In our efforts to contextualize and to arrive at more valid and sophisticated judgments about the transferability of policy and practice, we need robust comparative models and empirical data. It is with these motives in mind that the present authors offer their framework in the first chapter of this book. To date, educational leadership and management as a field of study has failed to develop theoretical models and an empirical base for a comparative and international dimension in line with emerging practice. Indeed, as Heck points out in Chapter 5, while applauding the number of studies on school leadership conducted in different cultural and national settings over the past 15 years, few of them have been designed from a comparative perspective. The plea for a more rigorous methodological and conceptual orientation to comparative research on school leadership that promises to "expose a host of issues" hitherto under-explored is central to Heck's argument. In another way, MacBeath draws attention to one such issue in Chapter 6, namely, democratic learning and leadership. He sees globalization—in the form of political measures taken by governments for short-term gain—as placing "constraints on the latitude of schools to be creative, thinking, learning, democratic communities." Drawing on examples of school effectiveness and leadership studies from Hong Kong, the United Kingdom, and the United States, he demonstrates ways in which some schools have been able to retain democratic learning as their central focus.

Proposition 2

The concept of "culture" demands clarification, specification and measurement.

In championing the case for "culture" as a root concept in a comparative approach to educational leadership and management, there is a need to be mindful and cautious about its problematic nature. As Morris and Lo point out, culture is a "ubiquitous, overused and overdefined" concept. In addition, contemporary societies are often fragmented and pluralistic, characterized by sub-cultural and minority groups. As societies become increasingly multicultural, their traditional homogeneity may be threatened. There are dangers, too, as Morris and Lo acknowledge, in portraying complex societal differences in terms of oversimplified dichotomies, such as Western/Asian. As Walker and Dimmock affirm in Chapter 1, there is as much variation within Western and Asian societies as between them. These are all formidable challenges to a cross-cultural approach.

It is not the purpose here to address each of the above problems. Suffice to say that greater conceptual clarity is needed in respect of "culture," even though it may be difficult and unrealistic to expect universal agreement on what precisely the term means. Most scholars, for example, agree on values, norms, and beliefs lying at the heart of the concept, and that these are expressed in a myriad of ways through thoughts and behaviors. Some, however, prefer to reserve the term for those values and beliefs that are enduring and long established, while others are prepared to include modern or recent values, and to distinguish them from the traditional. There are also difficulties in distinguishing cultural from political values. Decentralization and devolution, for example, can be seen as politico-managerial phenomena or, if they are endemic throughout a society and strongly supported, even as part of the culture. Sharpe and Gopinathan pick up many of these issues in Chapter 9 when discussing the influence of societal culture on leadership in high achieving schools in Singapore. Their argument is that societal culture in Singapore can best be understood as an evolving mix of traditional and modernizing cultural forces, complexly related to dominant political and economic processes aligned to a wider national vision.

This view of culture as comprising a number of shifting, evolving dynamic cultures is supported by Bush and Qiang in Chapter 10. The authors conceptualize the evolution of mainland Chinese culture in a number of different sequential cultures, each of which has had profound repercussions for education and school leadership. For example, the traditional culture is reflected in the continued respect for authority, collectivism, and harmony in school; the socialist culture has reinforced traditional culture while further politicizing the principal's role; the enterprise culture has served to integrate market values into education and leadership; and finally, the patriarchal culture—partly linked to traditional values—determines the role of men and women in schools and school leadership. Thus, the present-day culture comprises an amalgam or an accumulation of different cultures that have developed over time, all of which have perpetuated to create a hybrid entity.

In similar fashion, Southworth—in Chapter 11—argues that traditional cultural norms and occupational traditions are perpetuated in the headship in England. Despite decades of reform threatening change in the role of headteachers, the ways in which these new roles are being played out has changed relatively little. While agreeing with Bush about the perpetuation of culture, Southworth's point is that it is principally one culture—the traditional—rather than a series of overlapping and evolving cultures, that has been perpetuated.

The above examples of Singapore, mainland China, and England well illustrate the diversity of experience with respect to cultural change and evolution among societies. Some have undergone more political and economic upheaval than others. Each is at a different stage of political, social and economic maturity, a fact that explains a different trajectory through cultural change and evolution. At the very least, there is an obligation on scholars in educational leadership to clarify such issues as those discussed above and to offer a position. We believe that in due course, with the development of models and frameworks based on universally identified cultural dimensions, greater clarity and agreement over the nature and meaning of "culture" in regard to school leadership will emerge.

Proposition 3

What is seen as "appropriate" school leadership and management in a particular society is partly a function of accepted ideas and practices of curricula, teaching, and learning. Since the latter is culture-dependent, it follows that what is assumed to be effective or suitable leadership and management in one system may not be in another.

If the main purpose of school is the delivery of curricula in ways that enable all students to realize their potential, then leadership and management need to be responsive and adaptive to the requirements and characteristics of teaching and learning. It became increasingly apparent during the 1990s that teaching and learning are culture-dependent. As Watkins says, different cultures may have different answers to the questions: "What do you mean by learning?" "What strategies do you use to study?" and "What is a good teacher?" If answers to these questions differ cross-culturally, then we should not expect the knowledge base on school leadership, let alone the leadership style of principals, to be universally applicable. The same point holds true, even more starkly, in societies such as mainland China, where the curriculum has an explicit political and ideological function to produce obedient loyal citizens to the socialist state. In short, the principal in mainland China has a different purpose from his/her counterpart in more liberal Taiwan, the United Kingdom, or Australia, and therefore a more specific contextualized knowledge base is required for the principalship in different societies. There are two points here, both of which are made by Dimmock in Chapter 2: first, the need to connect leadership with, and to see it in part derived from, the core activities of schools, namely, teaching and learning; second, the wisdom of grounding the study of leadership in culture and context.

The importance of contextualizing leadership is unravelled by Begley in Chapter 3 and Walker in Chapter 12. In the global lexicon of reform, terms such as "consensus," "shared objectives," and "collegiality" appear in many countries' educational policies. However, as Begley points out, they often assume very different meanings across those countries. In Russia, for instance, consensus is associated with a decision handed down from a centralized bureaucracy and thus reflective of a collective cultural norm. By contrast, in Canada it is associated with groups of principals or professionals working together locally, thereby reflecting cultural norms of personal and professional autonomy. The cultural specificity necessary in understanding the principalship is also underlined by Walker in his chapter on the dilemmas experienced by Hong Kong principals in decision making. On the one hand, many of the dilemmas were found to be common and thus generic to principals in other societies. But in two important respects, Walker found culturally explained differences. First, the ways in which dilemmas are perceived and managed are culturally related; and second, a small minority of principals recognized no dilemmas in their work at all—a perception that also seemed related to culture.

An important implication of Watkins' Chapter 4 is that educational administrators question their degree of cultural sensitivity. According to Watkins, societies differ in the relative emphasis they place on five learning phenomena—diligence (achievement); the development of understanding (deep approaches to learning); memorizing without understanding (surface approaches); dependency placed on the teacher; and the learning environment. In all societies, student self-esteem and low dependency on the teacher (internal locus of control) are associated with achievement and deep approaches to learning. It is the significant differences between societies, however, that we need to highlight. Policy makers, academics, and school leaders need to be culture-sensitive to differences in learning and teaching brought to our attention by Watkins and his colleagues. In contrasting the Chinese learning environment with the Anglo-American, for example, Watkins finds the latter's emphasis on getting the student on-task, improving classroom management techniques, and coping with behavioral problems is less relevant in the Chinese context. In general, students in Chinese societies are brought up to respect their teachers and hence they possess greater degrees of obedience, docility, and willingness to learn than is the case in UK or U.S. classrooms. Teachers can therefore devote more time and effort to teaching and learning. Indeed, even notions of "good teaching" differ, with Chinese students expecting teachers to be good moral models, warmhearted and friendly, while Western students expect their teachers to set interesting learning experiences. Watkins also points to other cultural differences in the role of questioning and student grouping.

Chinese societies attribute academic success more to hard work and diligence than to ability. Partly for this reason, Chinese educators see creativity and understanding as slow processes requiring effort, repetition, and attention. The contrast with Anglo-American notions of creativity associated with insight and spontaneity, is stark. For the Chinese, understanding and creativity are built up slowly; rote memorizing is a means of securing understanding rather than the antithesis of it. As Watkins also points out, Anglo-American students are typically motivated by intrinsic factors connected with ego and individualist assumptions, whereas Chinese students tend to be motivated by a more mixed range of extrinsic and intrinsic factors, significant among which are collectivist notions of duty and obligation to the family. Again, school leaders and teachers would need to understand these cultural differences in order to motivate their respective students and provide support and advice to their teachers. Academics also need to pay heed, recognizing that effective educational leadership, no less than teaching and learning, may not look the same in all countries.

Proposition 4

When globalized education policy is imported into a host system, the way in which it unfolds can be explained by its fusion with the local politico-cultural context, which may itself be comprised of different but interlocking arenas.

When policies and practices cross boundaries as part of globalization, they interact with host societal cultures. This phenomenon gives rise to many problems, some of which are taken up by authors in this book. Both MacBeath and Southworth emphasize two elements to the context of the principalship that aid its understanding. The first is the reform agenda captured in policy;

the second is the culture or the set of traditional values embodied in society and its institutions, such as schools. The principal's role and role change is a derivative of the interplay between the reform agenda and cultural norms. Both authors stress the reform context and its problematic nature even in the countries and societies of origin. However, as Dimmock points out in Chapter 2, this does not prevent the export of policies and practices to other host countries where new sets of problems are often encountered.

The way in which globalized education trends mix with local politics and culture to explain the unfolding of policy is a key theme of Morris and Lo's study in Chapter 8. Any notion that globalized policy, mostly emanating from the West, is imported into host systems and straightforwardly adopted before being implemented at school level is a gross oversimplification—at least in the case of Hong Kong. As Morris and Lo illustrate, a "Western" curriculum reform with origins in outcome-based education—the Target-Oriented Curriculum—created fierce political activity leading to fragmentation and competition among local groups in three arenas. Interestingly, their recognition of three local arenas—a policy-making arena consisting of a state bureaucracy conducting its business largely in private; a national political arena consisting of a number of interest groups, including teachers, the media, and politicians conducting its debates very publicly; and a schools' arena directly involved in implementation—may hold true for many other systems.

Morris and Lo show how each arena fulfills different functions. The policy arena, for example, is "global, private, and rhetorical." The policy-making arena symbolizes the government's vision for education and is hotly contested, consultative, and public. Processes and events in the schools' arena are influenced by events in the other two arenas. Thus fierce political activity in the national arena may affect how teachers respond in school. Morris and Lo's analysis destroys the myth that globalized policy is simply adopted by policy makers and smoothly transitioned down to school level where problems are suddenly confronted. Importation of globalized policy may ignite fierce contestation among protagonists and former partners at each of the three levels, especially at national and school levels. The case study shows in particular how globalized policy, when conflicting with traditional cultural values, can metamorphose a formerly passive teaching staff into a politically charged group of professionals.

By contrast, Sharpe and Gopinathan describe in Chapter 9 how school improvement initiatives emanating largely from overseas were introduced into Singapore from the mid-1980s. These initiatives gave principals more autonomy. Referring to two case principals and their schools, the authors describe how the principals achieved success by combining aspects of their traditional and modern culture on the one hand with imported policy and practice espousing autonomy on the other. This is a heartening example of how successful fusion of cultures is possible, though it often seems to depend on the individual attributes of the principal, a point recognized in the final proposition.

Proposition 5

With the importation of policy and practice into different cultural contexts, tensions may arise between the local indigenous culture and the tenets and practicalities of the reform policy, depending on the leadership and management capabilities of the principal.

That the principal is a key agent of mediation between reform policy and practice and the traditions and norms of the host culture is a theme addressed in a number of chapters. In cases of successful management of innovation, the principal is credited with the achievement because of astute mediation between apparently countervailing forces. In less successful cases, however, blame is attributed to the principal for failing to mediate between global forces and local culture.

As previously stated, Sharpe and Gopinathan (Chapter 9) refer to two successful Singaporean principals who managed to combine both traditional and modern cultural values as well as imported and local policy norms. By contrast, Walker in his Chapter on principals' dilemmas (Chapter 12), draws attention to the cultural origin of serious and deep-rooted problems faced by a group of Hong Kong principals. When presented with difficult decisions and change management, the ways in which problems were perceived and managed were filtered through the "lens" of the Chinese Hong Kong culture. Indeed, in some cases, the cultural norms exacerbated and even created the problems, turning them into intractable dilemmas.

Two other chapters—those by Morris and Lo and by Hallinger and Kantamara—present case studies of Asian schools and their principals attempting to implement curriculum and pedagogic reforms, the origins of which lie in Anglo-American contexts. Each of these cases tells a different story, but both attest to the same conclusion, namely, the crucial role of the principal in transplanting new pedagogy and curricula into traditional indigenous cultures. In the Morris and Lo study, the implementation was generally unsuccessful, for reasons largely to do with the principal; while Hallinger and Kantamara's three cases point to the directors (principals) as primarily responsible for success.

It was the principal of the Hong Kong primary school who engineered his school's adoption of the Target-Oriented Curriculum (TOC), a major curriculum reform introducing fundamental changes based on student-centered teaching and learning and new forms of assessment. The new curriculum contradicted traditional Chinese beliefs of student passivity, obedience, and exam orientation. Teachers therefore struggled to make the transition. Above all, they had little say in how the scheme was implemented, because the principal maintained his traditional Chinese autocratic style of leadership. It was the demands placed on teachers by the new reforms in concert with the principal's unrelenting traditional leadership style that brought matters to a head. The staff was transformed from a state of apolitical acquiescence to high political activity, where conflict, bargaining, and negotiating became the new established order. In consequence, the school culture dramatically changed. It must also be acknowledged that prior to its implementation in the school, the TOC had already been subjected to much political and professional debate in the national arena, a point not lost on the teachers. The moral is clear: when challenging reforms are imported from other cultures, they demand strong but sympathetic leadership and management from principals to mediate their introduction to the local cultural setting.

This negative Hong Kong experience of implementing a major curriculum reform can be contrasted with the three successful Thai schools reported by Hallinger and Kantamara. These authors report that the introduction of school-based management, parental involvement, and new teaching-learning technologies into selected Thai schools was an attempt by the Government to lessen the "compliance" culture. As Hallinger and Kantamara point out, these reforms present stiff challenges in their countries of origin, let alone in the strongly hierarchical cultures of Asia. Successful reform in the three schools is attributed to the three directors who adopted participatory leadership styles, to group orientation and teamwork, and to a combination of pressure and support for change as well as the fusion of spirit and celebration in traditional Thai style. The moral for success here is the subtle combination of traditional Thai leadership with new "Western" approaches demanded by the nature of the reforms. In other words, the school directors used their hierarchical position to win support for more participatory decision making. Achieving the "right" balance between traditional mores and new demands seems to be what matters.

A more adept leadership is required in the globalized world of the new millennium, as Hallinger and Kantamara acknowledge. School leadership in many parts of the world, including Asia, lacks an "indigenous knowledge base." By the same token, the field demonstrates an overreliance on "Western" ideas, policies, and practices. Attempts to reform education by importing ideas from one society to another must consider the overall contexts of the societies involved and display greater cultural sensitivity. In support of this claim, Heck argues persuasively in Chapter 5 for the advancement of school leadership study across different settings, including urban–rural, elementary–secondary, and cross-cultural. He goes on to discuss several important conceptual and methodological issues that deserve the attention of researchers in the field.

A possible research agenda might focus on the interactions between traditional cultures and new global change forces. Such an agenda might be profitably built around a number of key research questions (Walker & Dimmock, in press), such as those below.

- To what extent is it appropriate to transpose policies and practices of school improvement from one society to another without consideration of cultural context?
- How do sets of dominant values and practices associated with cultures and sub-cultures affect the meanings attributed to the implementation of change in schools and school systems? What meanings do key concepts such as "collaboration," "micropolitics," "school-based management," and "accountability" have in different cultural settings?
- In what ways do societal cultures and sub-cultures influence the practice of school leadership? For example, in what ways does culture influence relationships between the school and its environment, and influence processes within the school, such as appraisal, teamwork, and shared leadership?
- How can the development of cross-cultural research and understanding in educational administration and leadership inform the issues associated with multicultural schools within societies? For example, in what ways might an improved knowledge base on cross-cultural education have application for how multicultural schools can better understand and serve their diverse communities?
- To what extent can the development of cross-cultural research contribute to a better understanding of globalization and its relationship to policy formation, adoption, implementation, and evaluation?

A comparative, cross-cultural approach promises a rewarding way forward. Hopefully, this book has made a significant contribution toward that goal.

References

Dimmock, C., & Walker, A. (1998a). Towards comparative educational administration: The case for a cross-cultural, school-based approach. *Journal of Educational Administration, 36*(4), 379–401.

Dimmock, C., & Walker, A. (1998b). Comparative educational administration: Developing a cross-cultural conceptual framework. *Educational Administration Quarterly, 34*(4), 558–595.

Walker, A., & Dimmock, C. (in press). Moving school leadership beyond its narrow boundaries: Developing a cross-cultural approach. In K. Leithwood & P. Hallinger (Eds.), *Second international handbook of educational leadership and administration.* Netherlands: Kluwer.

Index